ROCKS
DON'T MOVE

Surprising Discoveries from Our Life Together
– An Autobiography

Jim and Anne Edgson

ROCKS DON'T MOVE
Copyright © 2018 by Jim and Anne Edgson

Unless otherwise indicated, all scripture quotations are taken from the Holy Bible, King James Version, which is in the public domain. • Scripture quotations marked (NIV) are taken from the Holy Bible, NEW INTERNATIONAL VERSION®, NIV® Copyright © 1973, 1978, 1984, 2011 by Biblica, Inc.® Used by permission. All rights reserved worldwide.

The content of this publication is based on actual events. Names may have been changed to protect individual privacy.

Printed in Canada

ISBN: 978-1-4866-1722-7

Word Alive Press
119 De Baets Street Winnipeg, MB R2J 3R9
www.wordalivepress.ca

WORD ALIVE
—P R E S S—

MIX
Paper from
responsible sources
FSC
www.fsc.org   FSC® C016245

Cataloguing in Publication information can be obtained from Library and Archives Canada.

Dedication

This book and all the life experiences in it would not have been possible without the fortuitous meeting I had with my future wife, Anne, on March 15, 1963. From that point forward began the many life-changing events in both of our lives. I wish to thank the Lord for bringing us together, causing us to grow together in Him, and keeping us together.

—Jim Edgson

Contents

Part 3: The Retirement and Political Years Thoughts and Events   157

Prologue

The writing of this book has been in both Anne's and my mind for many years. The whole idea started when we were a young married couple out visiting Anne's grandfather in the Vernon, British Columbia area. We were curious about his life, so I asked him to tell us about it. He began talking at 9:00 a.m. We sat transfixed as he talked almost nonstop until around 4:00 p.m. No one took notes; we just listened. We found out later that no one had ever taken notes. Anne had her albeit limited memories, but precious little was written.

The idea for the book gained momentum when Anne's mom died. Again, there were lots of memories. Anne's brother, Jim, her sister, Joan, Anne, and I had our own memories of Mom Ramsay, but not written down. Some of the stuff Anne told me was absolutely hilarious! The Ramsay siblings had taken possession of many "things" when we moved Mom into her final home. When Mom Ramsay died, Anne and I came into possession of several two-cubic-foot boxes full of random notes and many, many photographs taken by her father—the person who not only gave me one of his daughters but also taught me to fish and enjoy photography.

Anne sat down in front of those papers and boxes after her mom died. Feeling distressed, one of her comments to me was that all that was left of her mom and dad's lives was in those boxes. I was blessed with an answer for her: "Well, let's see what those boxes tell us. You tell me about the pictures and other material, and I'll write the memorial."

We did just that. We worked together. Mom Ramsay came from the Vernon area, so we went into Vernon's library archives and found many missing clues. A memorial book was crafted that gave all living relatives a nice clue about her parents' lives. While we did save many memories, we would recommend to not wait until someone dies before writing things down.

Later in the book we explain how we chose our weird title. No one in our family would remember it or why we used it if we were dead and gone and hadn't written it down. A lot of material in this book would be forgotten were it not written down before we died. One pastor we met noted that dying before your life is put down in writing is like a library burning down. You lose everything. How true! Now we are writing this book.

We are blending a lot of memories in our book. To be frank, we aren't arguing that everything in this book is totally factual. It's as factual as we remember it happening, and Anne and I vetted this book with that understanding. One of our close friends was concerned about us naming people, to which we replied, "Don't worry—we are changing some names to protect the guilty." Or we actually do not even mention names!

One of the factors we note is how events tend to repeat themselves. If any of you think the story you're reading is describing you, be careful—the story written may have occurred with someone else at a different time in our lives, in a different place, with different people, and under different circumstances. The purpose of our book is to help others who may have similar events happening in their lives, and we hope that you will learn from and be encouraged by our experiences.

We originally thought putting our history down in a strict chronological order would be best, but we discovered that some occurrences meant little until they influenced more important events later in our lives. We do make references to specific chapters in the book when applicable so that readers can look forward or back to gain a better understanding of how and why things happened.

The reader will note that there is a fair amount of Christianity in this book. We were going to write a secular book until we realized that much of what we did even before coming to know the Lord at forty-four years of age was influenced and driven by the Lord. To provide a fair and honest reflection of our lives, we had to share all the circumstances and what drove those circumstances, as well as how the results played out over the years. We aren't ashamed to do so, and we hope the reader will see this honesty as statements of facts as we remember them and as we have seen the results unfold.

—Jim Edgson

Introduction

While there have been many seasons in Anne's and my life, this book is mainly about the seasons we've shared together. When you're young or entering university, college, or trade school, or starting a job, you may not think much about what you're doing. At some point, though, you make a decision about what you're going to do. Some say they never made that decision, like those who just went out and "got a job." Well, folks, "getting a job" is a decision. Whatever you do or don't do in life regarding a career—or lack of career—is a decision. Sometimes those decisions are pushed on us, but even if you acted upon those decisions, you made a decision to do so. Even those who "got a job" probably received on the job training.

Anne and I met at the University of Alberta in Edmonton. Prior to meeting, we each had a life full of youthful experiences. Some of those experiences were fun, some were bad, and some were life changing, but that season occurred. As this is a book about our life together, we will focus on how those experiences influenced us after we met. We do not ignore our youthful memories. How you behave as an adult will be shaped by your youthful experiences.

Anne and I will briefly discuss experiences during periods in our lives together. It is hoped the readers of *Rocks Don't Move* may see some of the influences or repercussions of those experiences and occurrences as related to their lives and take them to heart. Some of our experiences and occurrences will be light and funny. Of course, some of those occurrences and experiences just might reveal a darker side.

University Days 1962–1966

I entered the University of Alberta in the fall of 1962. My decision was a little ambiguous and had been influenced by the many reminders from my parents that my mother's three brothers had PhDs. I did not progress in university education beyond a Bachelor of Science, although in the book I outline a time when I fleetingly considered doing so. This degree would lead me on many wonderful and varied paths throughout my working career, even though I stayed with one company after university and prior to retirement from the oil industry.

Anne wanted to go to university to receive a teaching degree and then teach elementary grades, but her parents couldn't afford it. Realizing this, Anne realigned her wishes, initially pursuing a path to nursing. In addition to this, we were products of an older age in which it was assumed that girls went to university to get a guy. Indeed, the joke amongst us university guys in the early to mid-1960s at the University of Alberta was that there were a lot of girls taking the Husband 101 course in their first year. It may sound crude and out of place today, but an analysis of the number of first-year girls versus second-year girls attests to this trend.

Anne was not one of these girls, and indeed to this day we both despise that attitude. While she did get a guy—me—it initially was not her plan. After we became a married unit, she was living proof that a wonderful, dedicated woman can work with and help her husband through thick and thin so that the marriage unit can truly become a team and be seen as such. I didn't achieve any successes in life apart from Anne being alongside me. This is illustrated as you read on. Indeed, in the writing of this book, I was the major storyteller. Anne was the editor—both for English and for the stories! We are and always have been a team.

We met on March 15, 1963, near the end of my first year. There is a story about that! I started out well, but my grades went downhill after my first year. Indeed, I took four years to earn a three-year degree. A combination of circumstances led to this, mainly the lack of personal direction I felt during my "first" degree. Anne had found nursing to be beyond her capabilities, so she received a Nursing Aid Certificate. She knew her limitations; I did not. Because of this, Anne worked at helping me understand my limitations while encouraging me to grow in our marriage and in our time as parents. I give her full credit for my very successful career after university.

Attending university went beyond book education for both of us. We could be considered loners prior to meeting each other, and not necessarily of our own choosing. During the last three years of university, we knew that we would get married after graduation. We were formally engaged during the last year, so we literally had to learn about each other and study at the same time! On top of this, I was gone five months each year to Grande Prairie, Alberta for the first three summers of our relationship to work for my tuition and books. This was not a wonder-filled season for us. We had to learn how to relate to each other under these circumstances.

We became dependent on each other—me especially. (Anne still says I was and still am "twitterpated!") As we approached the completion of our university days looking forward to the next season in our lives, we grew independent of our parents.

The Oil Patch Years

We were married July 15, 1966, after I received my BSc and after I joined one of the largest oilfield service companies in the oil industry. Throughout this book, we refer to this industry as either "oil patch" or "oil industry." We do this because while this industry was a well-run entity, the patch was ... shall we say ... interesting! It definitely could be fun—rough, but fun!

We worked together to be sure I had a successful career after university. "Successful" to us meant that we have had, and are still having, a wonderful, varied, and interesting life together. No, I did not become president of any company. That level of advancement does not define the types of success we've enjoyed.

We were already committed to each other during university, which carried over to our lives together in the oil industry. I spent thirty-two years in the industry with many high points, many low points, and some flat points. We were never fired. I came close a few times but was blessed with a very successful oil industry career. Anne had some interesting work experiences during this time, which certainly helped the Edgson family unit. She was a stalwart, working outside the home and at home, becoming the financial backbone and the financial manager of our marriage.

It was during this time, ten years before we decided to end our oil patch season, that we were close to breaking up. My oil patch career appeared to be flourishing, but Anne and I knew that our married life was not. We had hit a low— a very deep low—in our married life. Fortunately, we both had a life-changing experience and came to realize that a stronger influence already existed in our lives, of which we were ignorant. As noted in the Prologue, we came to know and trust in the Lord Jesus. We climbed out of our nearly-disastrous, life-destroying low. Both our career and marriage blossomed and grew all the more! (I say "our" career because Anne was right there encouraging me, so it was "our career.")

Retirement and Political Years, 1998 to the Present

Then came "retirement." I use quotation marks because once retired from the oil industry, we discovered there was no such thing as that term in our lives! We became much more active by volunteering, which Anne continued to do as I successfully entered local politics. Eventually I became an elected politician. My political job was essentially the same as my oil industry job—serving people. The only difference was I was paid 1/8 as much! I retired from politics to become somewhat of an advisor both in our Christian life and for those still in politics. Neither Anne nor I were financially remunerated for this later phase.

We had three main seasons in our life together. We met and liked each other, learned to love each other, and worked toward a very hopeful married future. We took what we learned from that time and grew during the employment years between 1966 and 1998. We then built on our early retirement experiences and are growing more now that we are truly retired ... and as some wag suggested ... "freely available!" We hope the experiences we had in our seasons will be a blessing to you and will help you no matter what season you are in.

And the naming of the title of this book will be explained—eventually!

—Jim and Anne Edgson

University Days
1962–1966

CHAPTER 1
Think You Are the Instigator?

There is an old story about a man who was driving around in circles trying to find a parking spot. He said, "Lord, please find me a parking spot; oh, never mind … there's one!" The man believed he was in control and that the parking spot just happened to be there—a coincidence!

People like to believe that the circumstances in their lives are the sole result of their efforts or are "coincidences," just like the parking spot popping up. Even after coming to know the Lord, we are tempted to take credit for something happening, rather than believing that some greater being could be in control of everything in our lives. Such was the case of how I met my wife in my first year in university.

During that first year I dated several girls, some of whom I had known in high school; however, most of the girls I was friends with from my high school days either had boyfriends or were already engaged. Those girls were friends, not "girlfriends," and we mutually knew and respected the boundaries. My dates with other girls didn't result in anything serious, but in 1963—the second half of my first year—life changed. The girls I'd dated for fun found more serious boyfriends, and I started dating girls whom I hadn't known previously.

Shortly into 1963, I began to examine where I was going with respect to members of the opposite sex. One girl I dated early in that year was a chronic complainer and smoker. I didn't smoke, and I didn't want to commit to someone who had developed a costly habit. As for the complaining, that turned me off completely. Another girl wore plenty of makeup and fancy clothes which, to be quite honest, made her appear attractive—until I saw her one day with sloppy makeup and plain clothes. She looked awful! I started thinking of the cost of all her high maintenance and then stopped dating her. Another girl I dated was a year older than I, which didn't bother me at first. As time went on, however, I felt that she came across as superior, which wasn't justified. That turned me off older girls. Another young lady wasted no time in throwing herself at me, which made me grossly uncomfortable. She didn't display one bit of decorum.

The more I analyzed the situation, the more disillusioned I became with my choice of dates. I began to realize I was no catch—especially when others saw who I dated! I examined myself and pondered where I wanted to go in life beyond a university education and a job. Just what did I want in life for a partner … a life partner?

The science courses I was taking required a lot of study, so I threw myself into them. Dates were still part of the picture, but I made my priorities clear to the girls I went out with. It was a very effective way of losing some of those dates, especially the husband hunters, the makeup artists, or the make-out types! One girl laid it out pretty clear—I looked like a curly, brown-haired geek with a high forehead! Frankly, this was true, and I admired her for being forthright. But we quit dating, mainly because I stopped asking!

March came around with mid-term exams. I wasn't all that good at math, and I knew it. By this time, I was fully committed to my studies. I had heard that praying helped sometimes, so I decided to go to a church on Sunday, March 10, 1963, to pray for my upcoming math exam. While praying that prayer, something inside of me urged me to pray for a desire I'd never thought of praying about before—what I wanted in a girl:

"Lord," I prayed, "if you're there, I would ask that you find me a girl younger than me, shorter than me, with a zest for life and fun to be with, who is just a plain girl who is naturally pretty and does not smoke, who looks good without makeup, and who will understand the necessity of me getting a degree. Amen."

I had no idea where all that came from! It just popped into my head. I wrote the math exam the next day and aced it. I was buoyed by this and phoned up one of my past dates, setting up a date for the coming Saturday. As I had discovered a new way to help get through my exams (note my "I had discovered" attitude), my ego soared, and I had a temporary case of "Joe Cool" going into Friday, March 15.

Noon hour on that day found me and a male engineering buddy waiting on a small hill looking down on the Ring 4 bus stop at the university, close to the administration building. It was cool and overcast. I was on my way to the bank to get some cash for my Saturday date, and my buddy was going somewhere else. We were yakking away about things guys in university talk about (girls) and failed to see a young lady walk up to the bus stop and stand with her back to us. Then the sight of her caught my eye. All I could see was her beehive hairdo, a long winter coat stopping just at her knees, and the nicest set of legs below that I had ever seen!

I stood up and said to my buddy, "I'm going down to make a move on that girl."

"What about me?" he replied.

We tossed a coin, and I won.

"Joe Cool" sauntered down, preparing his opening gambit as he went. I approached from the left side. The girl was short … under five feet tall. Perfect! She was slender. Perfect! I got beside her, and everything fell apart. Here was a girl who looked thirteen to fifteen years old, was carrying books, and had an absolutely gorgeous face! Way too young! Her books were high school text books. My pre-planned lines disappeared and I blurted out, "Oh, a high school student!"

"Want to fight about it?" she replied with a look of disdain on her face.

I backed off, plotting my next move … which was to allow her to get on the bus, with me standing back a little. I'd let her sit in a normal seat and then sit beside her and hem her in while I talked things over with her.

She was smarter than that. She got on the bus and sat alone in the seat right behind the bus driver and above the front left wheel, so no unwanted advances could be made toward her. I had to sit alone across from her above the other wheel, in full view of the bus driver. Smart girl—knew how to handle herself. She opened her coat, and I must admit there was this most beautiful little figure dressed in a blouse and pleated skirt, which was very flattering without being gaudy. She was so short, her feet didn't touch the floor. No makeup … not even lipstick. Just naturally beautiful. There was no odour of smoke or perfume coming from her.

I asked her if she came to the university often (she came daily), where she went (the library), what time frame (left the library around noon), and what high school she attended (Bonnie Doon High). I asked for her name and politely, yet not excitedly, got it … but not her phone number. In my hurry I forgot her name! I got off at my bank and said I hoped I could see her again. Then I realized I had no way of knowing if she would even show up!

Monday rolled around. I sauntered over to the library and walked up the inside stairs. She was at the top of the entrance stairs in a study hall, studying intently with a firm look on her face. Several things struck me. She was wearing the same clothes—the same beautiful, plain, flattering clothes. Still no makeup. Her feet weren't even close to hitting the ground as she sat in the high library chair. Her figure was perfectly wonderful. And she did not see me.

I walked in front of her and said "Hello."

Her reply? "Oh, you!"

Not hesitating, I said that I'd like to take her out for coffee to talk things over. "I need to study," was the curt reply. I obviously had to be bold if this was going to go anywhere.

"How long?" I quietly asked.

Her answer should have warned me about the future. She said five minutes. I stood aside and waited for ten minutes—double the time—then started to fidget. Taking the hint, she spoke in a tone that indicated she just wanted to get this incident over and done with: "Okay, let's go."

I helped her on with her coat, once again quietly noting how beautiful this very young girl looked, then I looked around to see how else I could help. She had put her books on another chair, so I asked, "May I carry your books?"

Her tone suddenly changed, and she blurted out in a very loud voice, "*What?*"

Realizing we were in a library, I hurriedly and quietly restated, "I was just wondering if I may carry your books."

Her more reserved reply was "Sure, sure."

That broke the ice. We proceeded to the nearby Tuck Shop on our first "coffee date." Anne's mood over the next week was more pleasant and enthusiastic toward me. She was finishing the high school math and physics courses she had failed; she definitely did not smoke; she was just shy of nine inches shorter than me; she didn't wear makeup, and she didn't want to spend the money on it. She was naturally just a very pretty young lady! And I got her phone number.

There was one problem, though—her age. I was eighteen and she looked around thirteen to fifteen—in my opinion, too young. I had to make up my mind to either ask her out on a "real" date rather than just a "coffee" date, or to keep up with the "coffee" dates until she was older. Honestly … this is how I felt back then!

On the third coffee date, which was the Wednesday of the first week after we'd met, I decided to get "cool" again.

"Anne, I was born July 6, 1944. May I ask when you were born?"

Her reply? "July 31." No year. Joe Cool had failed again.

As I walked Anne to the Ring 4 bus stop after that coffee date, I told her that I had a class that would last until noon the next day, so I'd probably miss her on the fourth potential coffee date. I said I'd try to make it, but I hoped I could see her again on Friday if I missed her. She agreed.

On Thursday, I sat at the back of my class, trigger-ready to leave once the class was dismissed. The prof finished ten minutes early! I literally ran over to the library, arriving right at noon. Anne was there with an expectant smile on her face! She later told me she knew I would be there. I offered to take her right away to the bus stop, but she said it was okay, and we had an abbreviated coffee date.

As with all nearly-perfect things, a day of reckoning had to come. Anne appeared too young. I made up my mind on Friday that I had to explain my misgivings about her age. With a heavy heart, I went up to the library. She was happily waiting for me, but she had one piece of jewellery on—a boy's high school class ring. That ring meant she was going "steady" with another guy. My heart sank, but I said nothing. I would ask for an explanation later; after all, I was dating other girls—I had no right to complain.

As we walked over to the Tuck Shop, I noted that Anne was perky with a confident upright posture that my other dates didn't have. They slouched. Anne later told me that since she was so short, she wanted to stand as tall as possible to not lose any height! As a result, the perky posture spilled over into the perky attitude. One more thing to like about this girl, even if she turned out to be too young. As per usual, I carried her books. There was no hand holding yet, as we weren't "dating," just "coffeeing." I opened the door to the coffee shop, politely saw her seated, got our coffees, and sat across from her, observing that beautiful, natural, enthusiastically smiling face, and started talking.

"Anne, I really have enjoyed this last week, and you're a very beautiful young lady. I must be upfront with you, however. I'm eighteen years old, and I firmly believe that it's improper for an eighteen-year-old man to date thirteen-to-fifteen-year-old girls. I'm greatly concerned that I may hurt you if we continue on the path we are going."

Anne frowned as she stated, "I told you my age!"

"Frankly, you said July 31 without giving a year," I noted.

"1944," she replied.

I was taken way back. "Really? You mean you're only three and a half weeks my junior?"

With a puzzled face, Anne replied, "Yes!"

I fell back in my booth seat and laughed, saying, "Well, that's really great! Anne, there's only one thing holding me back from asking you out on a date."

With an annoyed look on her face she asked, "What?"

"The ring on your finger."

She was getting more upset. "Well, he doesn't mean that much to me."

Thoughts flashed through my mind. I could ask her out, but there was a boundary there: the ring. "No, Anne," I answered immediately, "that's not the way it works. I'm looking for someone I can commit to and who will commit to me in return. You have to make up your mind—him or me."

She was stunned, so I went further and explained that we could keep going on coffee dates as friends if she chose her current guy, as I was doing this with several "friends" who happened to be girls and were committed to others. But we would just meet as friends.

Pause here, if you would. Anne had not worn that class ring since I'd met her ... until this one crucial day. She later told me that two days before this time, she knew she was "in love" with me. She also knew she would have to deal with her time of reckoning concerning the guy she was dating. As she puts it, she felt she was "walking erectly to the gallows!" But she would have to deal with it, so she wore that ring on this day to deal with part of her reckoning.

After all this, Anne asked me, "Will you guarantee that you will ask me out if I break up with the other guy?"

My answer was firm: "No guarantees. You have to make up your mind about what you want to do." I then said it would be best for me to take her to the bus and that I would hopefully meet her on Monday at the library. I picked up her books and escorted her to the bus stop, confirming I would be there on Monday. Anne was not happy, and she did not reply.

Monday came. I had gone out with my date on Saturday—my last date with that particular girl. As I walked to the library, I knew there was a high possibility that Anne wouldn't be there. It was something I was prepared to face. I had her phone number now, so I could call her—and I would, if needs be, even to be told to take a hike. But she was there!

Up the stairs I went toward a very angry looking young lady, Anne—simply but beautifully dressed as she was the week before. I didn't even get to the top of the stairs before she turned her head and gave me an extremely mad look, her eyes searing into mine. She just said, "Let's go" and jumped out of the library chair.

I hustled to help with her coat; she turned and started toward the door as I grabbed her books and ran to the door to hold it open for her. Anne went straight through the doorway, walking quickly without looking at me. I had to run to catch up to her. She was mad but still very erect in her gait. I ran ahead to open the coffee shop door; she roared past me and headed straight to the coffee booth we'd used the previous week. She sat down and looked at me with a very angry face. I sat down, put her books beside me, and was about to get up and go for the coffees when she slammed her ring hand down on the booth table. No Ring. Time to be truly cool, Jim!

"It's over?" I asked.

"Yes," she said with an angry face.

"Really over?" I replied firmly.

With a slightly less angry face, Anne replied, "Yes."

"Would you still like to go out with me on a date?"

Her face and body relaxed and, looking relieved, she gently replied, "Yes."

"Anne Ramsay, may I have the honour and privilege of taking you out to a movie and coffee this coming weekend?"

Anne's face perked right up, and she excitedly said, "Yes!"

Now we were both almost ecstatic! "What kind of movie would you like to see?" I asked.

She looked at me as if no other guy had ever asked that question before. "You decide," she answered.

My reply surprised me and her: "No, Anne, this relationship is going to be a partnership. We'll decide together. Tell you what … the newspaper with the movie listings comes out on Thursday. Before I meet you at the library, I'll buy one and we can both look at what's available and decide together."

She wore a look of pure joy on her face. What I had just said appeared to be the correct thing to say!

Tuesday came and again a coffee date—still no holding hands. That was my decision, so I didn't ask. I sat in the booth, elbows on the table, staring at her with a silly grin on my face. Anne looked at me and frowned and said, "What's wrong now?"

"Nothing. I just can't get over how naturally beautiful you look." Big smile from Anne!

Thursday came. We looked at the paper and chose a movie together. I was overwhelmed by an urgent sense to tell her something that might be out of place, but I had the feeling I had to say it, so I did.

"Anne, what I'm about to say might be out of place, but I feel it has to be said. You are the most naturally beautiful girl I've ever met. I really love the way you take care of yourself and don't use makeup. On our upcoming date, you don't have to wear any makeup to please me. In fact, I'd prefer if you didn't."

Anne looked shocked. "Oh," she said.

I thought I was in trouble. "But it's up to you; you do what you want."

"Oh, that's okay," she replied, still with a shocked look.

On Friday I went to pick her up. I was nervous, because I wasn't sure how my "no makeup" statement had gone over. Anne was upstairs getting ready when I arrived. When she came down, I saw that she wasn't wearing makeup—not even lipstick. She was wearing the same clothes she wore when we met on March 15, other than a set of high heels. My goodness, did she look gorgeous! The high heels set off her calves beautifully—there was no bunching, just smooth flowing lines from her ankles to her knees. Gorgeous!

We walked toward the bus stop (I didn't have a car in university), rounding a corner so that her house was not visible. Then I nervously asked if I could hold her hand. Her response was a shock to a guy who was trying to go out of his way to be a gentleman: "Took you long enough!"

I grabbed her hand and felt the most beautiful feeling I'd ever felt up to that point. Not only did this girl not wear makeup, but her skin was soft, silky, smooth, and tender. I excitedly shared this with her and asked if she used anything to keep her skin so smooth—no she did not! Naturally beautiful! I was so excited, I asked if I could put my arm around her waist, to which she giggled and said yes!

Here was this short, young, naturally beautiful young lady who was so petite I could put my arm around her and touch my hand to my body on the other side. She was just an absolute doll! Indeed, as time went on, I called her "my dolly."

We proceeded on our way, holding hands. Both of us were joyful! The date went very well, and as I took her home, I was in a battle with myself. I had been clearly told it was not proper to kiss a girl on the first date. Indeed, any of the other girls I'd kissed—after a couple of dates—weren't all that significant. I wanted to kiss Anne, but what should I do?

We got to her door, holding hands, and I hesitated. Man, she was so beautiful and delicate. I didn't want to lose her by being too forward. She smiled and suddenly grabbed my other hand with hers and pulled me toward her ... and we kissed. To say that bells rang, fire alarms went off, or any other description would not tell the full feeling in my brain. Her kiss literally blew my brains out! *Wow!* I gasped, really smiled, and said just that. Then I asked if we could go out the next weekend.

"Yes!"

"And go for coffees?"

Her answer was an enthusiastic "Yes!"

I then giddily stepped off the stairs and ran all the way back to the university, a distance of about five kilometres. I just about beat the bus home! I phoned her the next day and told her about my trek home.

From that point on, Anne and I were a number. We both had a lot of hidden baggage that we eventually shared with each other. The treatment she received from other guys before me was very poor, but I didn't care. She meant and means more to me than any problems. She saved herself for the marriage night, in spite of the attempts of those other guys. She had gone out with a much older guy when she was younger, which was nearly disastrous. No wonder she was puzzled about my attitude! I had girl and family troubles of my own, which were eventually brought out. The bottom line was that the love we had for each other transcended all this baggage.

After we came to know the Lord, and I had fully realized the meaning of *"rejoice in the wife of your youth"* (Proverbs 5:18), we came to an understanding of what happened back in March–April, 1963. The prayer and all those thoughts that popped into my mind were put there by the Lord. The "circumstance" of our meeting was of the Lord. Both of us were dissatisfied with our lot in life with respect to our relationships and our families. We were searching. Looking back, it's obvious the Lord put two people He loved on a collision course, knowing what would result. While "Joe Cool" tried, he was often a failure. When the Lord created the opportunities and caused us to respond in the fashion He had willed, our lives went very well!

Vital to all of this was the statement He made me say to Anne about *"commitment"* noted above. Anne and I are committed to each other in all ways. The Lord made me say it; the Lord made us commit and makes us commit to this day.

By the way … there are many times today, even as Anne and I age together, when she dresses up without makeup. She is still totally stunning! I am proud of her, and so happy the Lord put us together. She is still the perky, beautiful, enthusiastic, encouraging person the Lord caused me to meet on the Ides of

March, 1963—after He had put in my mouth what I thought was a silly prayer to Him on Sunday, March 10 of the same year. Think I was the instigator? Not in this case!

CHAPTER 2
Writing in Stone

There are times we put writing "in stone." It is there permanently. We can do this by having something in writing notarized, which is a deliberate, well thought out action. We can do this through emails, which can be forwarded, copied, and printed. That type of communication needs to be watched very carefully. We can do this through sites like Twitter and Facebook, but if we do we must realize that anyone can see what's there.

Anne and I learned through our political years not to "do" Facebook or Twitter. We saw too many people burnt by using them … some to the extent that they closed their accounts! We are also very careful what we write in emails, as we realize that what we put in writing there can be read later and possibly by those other than the intended audience. If there's something we must say or do in any form of confidence, we do it in as much a personal fashion as possible—like face to face conversations.

Now where do you think we gained that wisdom? Not from where you might think! It came from an instance of me putting some writing literally in stone! This story is about our university days but spans some time before that.

During the university days, it involved Anne. The time before did not. That was the problem!

During junior and senior high school in Grande Prairie, Alberta—way before I met Anne—I had an Australian pen-pal, a girl the same age as me. At first we were "just friends"—simple and fun. As we moved into high school, since we had occasionally taken each other into simple, confidential things, the long-distance relationship grew a bit. As I entered university, it got a little heavier. That changed when I met Anne, and my pen-pal and I broke off writing to each other.

The summer before I went to university, however, was a different story. I was getting a bit closer to my Australian friend … so much so that I decided to give her an unusual birthday present! Indeed, it became rather permanent, although I was pretty sure at the time it wouldn't be.

I liked driving out in the country and exploring by walking along rivers. One day while walking along a river bank west of Grande Prairie, I ended up across from a cut bank. I was on the side of the river where the water deposited all the sand and gravel—in short, where each spring flood would see sand, gravel, and rock dumped, covering things up. A large, flat slab of sandstone rested vertically against the bank, partially buried in the sand and gravel. I got a bright idea to come back with a hammer and chisel and carve a signed birthday greeting into that flat sandstone, with the date of the carving, to my Aussie friend! I did this, took a picture of it, and mailed it off to Australia!

Move ahead a couple of summers. I was in university, going pretty heavy with Anne. We were a committed couple, totally in love. Anne's dad was a relief railway station agent working all over Alberta north of Edmonton. He was also an avid photographer and loved to fish, so he mentioned that he was going up to Grande Prairie and asked if I knew of any place he could fish in a river around there. I did, and it was where "the stone" was located. I gave him directions, and he said he would try it out. The stone was not mentioned for rather obvious reasons. It never occurred to me that the sandstone slab wasn't buried. It *had* to be covered up, because there had been some serious flooding in the past two years. Bad assumption!

When Anne's dad got back to Edmonton, I went to pick Anne up for a date and met a very angry looking young lady at the door, with everybody laughing in the background. Anne produced a picture … one her dad had taken. I looked and knew I was in deep trouble!

Anne's dad had gone to a point on the river where he found the top of a big sandstone slab. The water level was quite high, covering a lot of the bottom of the stone, but he started fishing from that stone. Then he saw writing on it reflected in the water, so he went into the water and read it. And photographed it. And brought it back for Anne to see! Writing signed by Anne's boyfriend (fortunately dated)!

Anne wasn't mad because of the writing. She was mad because of the teasing she got. She was also mad that I was a little stupid to lead her dad to that place! What could I do? I could do nothing but agree with her and her family and then take my lumps. We still laugh about it to this day. The lesson in all this for the reader (and for the writer) is to be very, very careful what you write in stone—literally and figuratively!

We Married; Oil Patch Years
1966–1998

CHAPTER 3
Our First Christmas

This Christmas story is written with and from the perspective of my life-long partner, my wife Anne, who sometimes has a wonderfully different view of what happened in our lives! It actually begins in 1966 on July 15 when we finally got married after hanging out for over three years. Let's give Anne the opportunity to show how an incident in our lives occurred and how it benefitted us.

Mr. Newly-Graduated-Chemist in an engineering oil patch job found out he was going to be transferred from Edmonton, Alberta to Dawson Creek, British Columbia at the beginning of September. First we had a late honeymoon during his orientation week in Texas. Then we gathered up what personal belongings two broke university students could accumulate together and moved into a one-bedroom furnished apartment in beautiful northeast Dawson Creek. Jim promptly took off back to Edmonton for two weeks of classroom training, and I scrounged myself up employment as a Practical Nurse at the local hospital, which was a nice six or seven blocks walk down the hill from our apartment. Neither one of us owned a car. The company car Jim drove was a loaner they let him drive as part of his job because he had no wheels of his own.

We saw each other twice from the second week of September to December 21, when "the company" finally decided that maybe they wouldn't officially transfer him to Dawson Creek after all but base him out of Edmonton. We got together at Dawson Creek for a few days in late September when he was passing through between jobs. Later when it was colder but not too snowy I rode the Greyhound for a twelve-hour trip to see him in Edmonton one weekend. An oil patch "engineer" is married to his job, and a wife is the mistress—get used to it or run home to mother!

The company graciously loaned us a pickup truck and actually gave Jim time to drive up to Dawson Creek to help me pack. He found us a cool bachelor apartment seven floors up in a high rise on the south side of Edmonton, overlooking the North Saskatchewan River. There was five feet of snow already in Dawson Creek, and I was getting back and forth to work by cab or riding with two Registered Nurses who shared an apartment in our building. By the time we settled in Edmonton, the company informed us that the entire Whitecourt crew wanted Christmas Day off, so Mr. Junior Dogface was assigned to cover for them!

In three days we managed to get each other some gifts, and I was determined we would have home-cooked Christmas turkey dinner, even if I had to do it at a rig site! His folks were in Edmonton for a few days and managed to give us gifts and some money before they had to leave to drive back to Grande Prairie ahead of any bad weather. We bought Christmas tree decorations with some of the money they gave us as well as kitchenware and dishes and the world's cheapest three-room furniture set.

December 23 found us in a kitchenette motel unit in Whitecourt with all the fixings for a turkey dinner and Christmas tree decorations. On December 24, at around -24 F, we drove out in the country and cut ourselves a nice Christmas tree from a road allowance. We hauled the bottom half into our unit instead of the top half, and it happily took over all the space except for the bed and the kitchen. Between phone calls from the dispatcher about a rig that might or might not want services even on Christmas Day, we got the tree decorated and placed gifts under it. I checked my supplies for Christmas dinner and dug deep into my purse to buy a small container of pepper.

We actually rang in midnight, December 25, at the Whitecourt office, where the phone calls from the rig to their head office to our company head office to the Whitecourt office went on for over an hour before everybody decided the work could wait. Back home to our motel unit for some sleep. When we did awaken on Christmas morning, I got the turkey cooking right away, as there was no telling how much time we had together. We ate around 1:00 or 2:00 p.m. between some office phone calls. Just as we were cleaning up, Jim got the word that he would have to leave immediately to go out to the rig, which was about seventy or eighty miles out in the wilderness northwest of us. He wrote the rig directions down on the back of one of the cardboard packages in which a string of lights had come. We still have the side with the directions on it.

We called my dad in Edmonton, where he was having Christmas dinner with my sister and her family. My parents were living in Waterways, near Fort McMurray, at the time. He agreed to drive forty miles west of Edmonton to Carvel Corner and meet Jim to take me and all our stuff back home to Edmonton so that Jim could get up to the rig as soon as possible. We undecorated the tree as fast as we could and threw all our goods into the car for the sixty-mile trip south to the highway junction. Because life had been such a mad whirl for five days, and I'd already eaten, I didn't go over to my sister's.

I asked Dad to help me unload everything and stayed alone in our apartment for the next three days. After I sorted everything out, I was left with $1.64 in my pocket in an era when no banks were open for two days. Even if ATMs existed in 1966, there was no money in the account, and payday wasn't until January 2, as New Year's Day was a bank holiday. Jim got home some time on December 27. When the rig found out he was a green rookie, they called for more experienced crew as soon as possible. Jim had a $6.00 six-month safe driving bonus cheque in the mail December 27. That was what we had to live on until January 2. Welcome to Christmas in the oil patch!

Jim here—if anyone ever says Anne is not one tough lady, they're expressing an opinion, not a fact! And yes—we still have that cardboard package with the rig directions written on it. It is a precious possession we will leave for our kids and grandkids!

How did we benefit from all this? We got tough and learned to thrive together. Now that Anne's and my parents are gone, we're at the top of the family chain in our immediate family. Most importantly, neither of us would recommend the oil patch job we had unless you are a very tough person who is determined to go out and have the experience with or without a tough partner!

CHAPTER 4
Bad Husband Behaviour

There are times in our lives when we look back and remember things from the past. When Anne and I were a young married couple in the late 1960s, we quite often heard "old folks" say the words "I remember when …" To us at the time it seemed odd that these "old folks" would be sitting in their rocking chairs pontificating about their experiences, which were so obviously silly (to us, anyway) that we considered them ridiculous. I stated one day, "I will never say 'I remember when!'" Of course, that statement was *really* silly, and it showed what I thought of "old people" (they were probably in their sixties). It also showed how arrogant I was!

With that admission, "I remember when" we were first married—not only the romantic part, but the "getting started" part. We had no idea what marriage was all about. Oh, we loved each other and were very compatible … but knowledge of money management, cooking, and how to work toward being a marriage unit? We weren't just hopelessly in love—we were just plain hopeless sometimes! At the time we didn't think we were that way, but we were!

Elsewhere in the book we share stories about me and how I had a lot to learn. One of the skills I needed to learn was how to deeply care about Anne and about what she did. She really wanted our marriage to be self-sufficient in more ways than one! She wanted to be a good cook. To this end, she did quite well in retrospect, but as a husband I hadn't learned how to communicate this opinion to her. Indeed, the first part of this story shows my crudeness. In the second part, while better, the process leading up to what was eventually said needed some polishing!

Anne made every effort to learn how to cook from others and from good cookbooks. There were times she wanted to experiment, and she did. She could make good biscuits from recipes, but she used a box of ready-to-make biscuit mix for a time. This mix had the leavening ingredients included in it. One evening she went back to making the biscuits from scratch—and forgot to add the baking powder and soda! Things did not go well. The biscuits turned out hard as rocks! No matter, she offered them to me anyway. Neither of us liked wasting money or effort. Picking up one biscuit and taking a bite, I rudely shared my opinion.

I dropped it on the table and said, "Hockey pucks!"

It is certain that the reader of this book has more brains than I did at that time. Anne became very upset, and rightly so! She tried so hard yet got that horrible reaction from her husband! Of course I was sorry, but the damage was done. I suffered the eating equivalent of sleeping on the couch for a time! A couple of years passed until one day she put the most wonderful batch of tender and moist biscuits in front of me. They were really good ... and I said so, quite enthusiastically!

Being a better husband involves giving your wife some encouragement to try again while noting that you love her. I failed to do this at the time, but I categorically state that every effort was taken to thank her and appreciate her efforts going forward! Unfortunately, wives are very good at sensing phoniness as well ... thus, the second part of the story.

During university years, we'd go to a Greek restaurant that served killer spaghetti and meatballs. After we were married, we still went there for a dinner out. For a time, all spaghetti and meatballs in any restaurant we went to were compared to the dish offered by that Greek restaurant.

Anne soon decided to try it at home using cookbook recipes. They were good, and they were appreciated, but she could tell from me that what she offered didn't measure up to the Greeks, so she tried another recipe. I was thankful, but again she could read me well. She tried again. Same result. I was trying; she was trying, but Anne knew that what she presented was a little short in her husband's opinion.

One day in her frustration, as each recipe had something good about it, Anne just mixed up a whole bunch of recipes and presented the result to me. Prior to this she had been frustrated, and I had tried to keep my frustration hidden (unsuccessfully). This time I dutifully sat down and took my first mouthful.

My eyes shot full open! I had a full mouth but started to try to say something as I looked comically toward Anne, grunting with excitement. She couldn't understand what I was trying to say, so she asked if it was that bad! I finally emptied my mouth enough to loudly state "*This is great!* Do you have the recipe saved?"

Confused, she answered, "No, it's just a combination of several recipes."

"This was absolutely the best spaghetti and meatballs I've ever tasted! You have to write the recipe down," I blurted out.

Anne struggled to remember, and eventually she did. She did some more tweaking to make it even better, but her husband became a bit of a pest asking for more and more spaghetti dinners like that! Without a doubt, Anne now has a lock on the best spaghetti and meatball recipe I am aware of!

The truth is, her husband wasn't very considerate in either the biscuit case or the spaghetti case. While currently bragging about Anne's cooking as a whole, my way of "appreciating" her trying her best as a wife to serve wonderful meals in both cases was a little crass. True, in the second case she kept trying—which was and is a blessing. But she did so because she wanted to. She wasn't encouraged enough at the beginning. If this encouragement had been given, she probably would have been more grateful when I went nuts over the final results! As it stood, she initially thought I was putting her down.

As a result, I make a point of appreciating what she cooks today—and I let her know it. She accepts this graciously. At times hints are dropped regarding something I'd really like her to cook, which she eventually does. And it is truly enjoyed! Dropping positive hints is great for both of our feelings!

When Jim comments publicly about Anne's cooking, he likes teasing her by standing sideways, rubbing his current ample girth, and stating in a false Scottish brogue, "Anne is a great cook! The evidence is greatly before me!"

Anne's final word: I knew how to boil water and which end of a can to open but not much more when we got married. In our first year of marriage, Jim bought me the *Better Homes and Gardens* meat cookbook. This was greatly appreciated by both of us! I still use it to this day!

Partners in life, committed to each other!

CHAPTER 5
Knowing Your Limits

All of us have limitations. Those who think they don't may be playing God, knowingly or unknowingly. The challenge is recognizing your limitations before they reach up and harm you!

My post-secondary education led to a BSc with a major in Chemistry. Frankly, my marks were not that good. University education was a blessing, however, in two specific ways.

The first blessing was meeting my wife-to-be. If some higher Being hadn't directed the circumstances of our meeting and the subsequent events that led Anne and me to a wedded, lifetime partnership, I am thoroughly convinced that the further successes of my life wouldn't have happened. That first blessing was beyond normal belief!

My second blessing wasn't realized until a couple of years after joining the oilfield service company I was to be employed by for thirty-two years. The direction I took in university resulted from not knowing what I wanted in life. All my uncles were PhDs in something; my father didn't even have a high school education but managed to become a postmaster in Alberta. My mother was trained as a nurse. My parents knew they were dealing with a bit of a drifter as far as post-secondary education was concerned, but they pushed me hard to "get a degree." My mother went further—she wanted me to get a PhD. So I registered for the Bachelor of Science ... as a beginning. To add to the uncertainty of my future, often I was just plain not confident about a lot of things.

When I graduated with my BSc, I joined a company that hired engineers of all stripes, preferably electrical engineers. "Double Es" we called them. The company also hired geologists, geophysicists, and other Earth scientists. They hired one Canadian chemist—me. To my knowledge they didn't repeat the mistake during my tenure with them!

I planned to work for one year before going back to school and pursuing a PhD, but several things intervened. I actually performed terribly during my first year of employment. It was obvious to everybody, including me! I walked into my boss's office after one year with a letter of resignation, as I planned to go back to university, but my boss had a surprise for me.

I wasn't quitting because I was a terrible employee, but because my ego wanted me to go and get a PhD. I had no idea what was involved in this, or what I would study. I just wanted to get my parents off my back. Anne was pregnant with our first child, and we were financially ill-prepared for me to go back to school. My boss handed me a letter before I could say anything. The letter set me way back! Indeed, it made me very angry. He was giving me six months' notice, noting that unless I smartened up within those six months, I would be terminated. Furthermore, he informed me that my crew would consist of two driver-operators who had received the same letter. Additionally, he was giving us the worst—the oldest truck in the fleet to work with. We three duds were to take that piece of junk and become a worthy crew with a worthy truck or be gone in six months.

I pocketed my resignation letter and threw it away after leaving my boss's office. Going out to the shop, I brought the two operators together and we sat down over coffee. To compound things, my operators-to-be didn't like me. They knew they were dealing with a screw-up. At first nothing was said, but then the words came out of my mouth: "Well, guys, we have two choices. We can all quit right now, or we can go out and show these guys that they're wrong."

The look on their faces was priceless! It was one of sheer determination. They'd been told they were screw-ups, were getting a screw-up for a leader, and were getting the worst truck in the fleet. We all knew the company was trying to get us to quit so that we wouldn't get severance. We decided then and there to prove everybody wrong.

And we did. The worst truck became the "turnpike cruiser" after we got that piece of junk fixed up. Within three months customers were phoning in and requesting us because they liked how we worked as a team. Within four months our boss informed us that the notices of termination were being withdrawn. We worked as a team for a year and then each of us were put on different units to help others because we were so good. All of us stayed on with the company for ten years. Two of us stayed right up until I retired!

This was good news and bad news. My ego grew because "I" could be a leader and get people to work with me. My sense of my personal limits went out the window, but then I started thinking about my and Anne's fathers. It was a warning for me.

My father didn't finish high school but went to work to help support his mother and family after my grandfather died in the 1930s Depression. After being honorably discharged in World War II, he worked in the post office in Edmonton, married, and eventually became a postmaster in Edson, Alberta. From there he was promoted to Regional Postmaster in Grande Prairie. Life went well for quite some time, but there were some hidden troubles in Dad's background. He was a hard drinker until he met Mom, who wouldn't marry him until he gave up booze … which he did. He had an intense desire to serve people, which served him well in the post office for quite some time. Dad Edgson also had a big ego and a common misdirected sense of how to get ahead in the world. Early in my teen years he told me that all that mattered was who you knew. I learned as I went along that was not true at all.

In addition, his idea of working with people contained something of a military bent. He generally worked with people by telling them what to do and expecting them to do it—not always, but generally.

At the time Dad Edgson became a postmaster, the post office wasn't unionized. It became unionized while he was in Grande Prairie. Dad E. "knew" several higher-up people, and they supported him—to an extent. My father was now in a unionized situation where he had to work with people, listen to people, and understand the new-to-him situation of working with unions. He was used to "just doing the work to get things done" and expected others to do the same. Dealing with a union—a militant union—in that manner caused conflict.

Prior to the unionization of the post office, I'd never noticed that on Christmas mornings, after we'd opened up all our presents, Dad would quietly disappear for a while. By the time things had settled down in the early afternoon,

Dad was back to sometimes take us for a Christmas Day drive. As whatever he'd done had been done in a quiet manner, things seemed normal.

Something happened after unionization. A few months after Christmas, I learned that Dad had been hauled on the carpet and disciplined by the post office for something that had happened at Christmas. He had done some post office work that was deemed to be union work without getting the permission of the union before doing so. At this point, Mom Edgson explained what had been going on for years on Christmas morning.

After we'd open all our presents, Dad the postmaster would slip quietly away and go down to the post office, pick up undelivered parcels, and go around Grande Prairie delivering these parcels. He loved serving people and didn't expect his employees to go out on Christmas Day to do this. He just wanted to do this quietly without recognition to serve his post office clients. This worked very well until unionization occurred. The unionized employees would come back after Christmas break, see the pile of undelivered parcels gone, and believe someone had taken away part of their job. To them intentions didn't matter, so they complained to their union bosses, who took it to Dad's bosses, who then disciplined him. That was the beginning of Dad breaking. Other personal problems led him back to drink. From there, he eventually died an alcoholic.

Now let's discuss Anne's dad. He was the oldest of five boys. Dad was a very intelligent man—very quick to see things. He went to university at a very young age but didn't finish because he had to help his dad look after the younger boys after his mother died in childbirth. As the Depression was on, Dad Ramsay couldn't get a steady job. He did some work for the federal government, which eventually led to a job with the Canadian National Railway. He met and married Anne's mom and immediately began working as a telegrapher in Stewiacke, Nova Scotia. From there their lives consisted of constant transfers until they reached Wainwright, Alberta.

As alluded to in "Writing in Stone," Dad Ramsay was an accomplished amateur photographer. He even built one of his own cameras! He developed his own pictures and kept many purchased cameras. He was an excellent fisherman, and even built his own small boats. He loved canoeing and exploring the backwoods. In his day he would have been considered Bohemian.

Dad Ramsay knew he was a brilliant man, but he couldn't accept that some others knew more than he did. He was full of bravado; his method of working with people was to tell them what to do and expect it to be done the way he wanted.

At Wainwright alcoholism took possession of his life, and he lost his job just short of being eligible for a pension. Life was hard on the Ramsay family for a time, until Dad Ramsay took a job on the Northern Alberta Railway, which he kept until retiring. He developed cancer from smoking and eventually died from it.

Because of what happened to my dad, I admit that I absolutely hated unions for many years. After coming to know the Lord, my hate lessened. Because of some of my valued mentors, plus many years working as a marketer in the oil industry, I forced myself to learn to work with people, but not in the sense that I told these people to do tasks and expected them to follow directions. I could not do that and stay employed. My job required me to work with operations people within my own company to encourage them to do a good job, while at the same time working with potential clients to encourage them to hire our company. I literally had to facilitate the many procedures and processes to get everyone whom I served the best possible outcome, both in my company and in the oil industry. There was no "you shall." Indeed, I was blessed with a bunch of sayings. If I said "I recommend," that meant it was a good idea. If I said "I strongly recommend," it meant you would be silly/a fool/out of your mind not to do it! Because of this I grew as a skilled negotiator—not a hardnosed one, but one who worked for the best possible outcome for all concerned.

Retirement saw me working with a rural local government in British Columbia and their unionized employees. It was during this time that I discovered something at odds with what I'd thought about unions after my dad died. The oil industry company I worked for wasn't unionized, which I liked. The rural local government was unionized. At first, the old post office incident threatened to well up anger in me; however, I had spent decades in the oil industry learning how to successfully work with people. Being a free enterpriser, it seemed weird to work "for" any government. Then something was "discovered" —government staff people generally are hard working people who genuinely have a heart for their job and really want to serve people as much as I do! They love being "worked with." I was now in my element—working with people to serve people.

The personal problems from the past and the problems of our fathers were all the same. They were essentially problems of being unable to accept limitations— both personal and external. Once recognized and once dealt with by working with people, those limitations could become benefits.

Both of our fathers were somewhat short on education … not that this was a problem in itself, as many people I know without advanced education have done very well in life. Just because they didn't have an advanced education didn't mean they couldn't think!

Our fathers' problem was not accepting this personal lack of education or the strengths and capabilities of others who had higher education. They had difficulty accepting the concept that other people could be worked with to better serve people. The key was working with those people for mutual benefit to themselves and to those they served.

Recognizing the limits of our abilities and working to pair our abilities with the different abilities of others could result in a better outcome for any task. The problem with some people is that they confuse their own limitations with what can and cannot be done. They have difficulty accepting that others can do a better job. Rather than accepting this, they fight it in their minds. Sometimes those fights spill over into undesirable reactions, leading to depression, or habits and diseases like alcoholism.

One can serve his company, his church, and his family much better if all concerned make a point of working together to accomplish common tasks and reach common goals—not as a dictatorship, but as a team with the goal to better each other. Realizing your limitations, proficiencies, and skill sets is important. Seeking out others who have different limitations, proficiencies, and skill sets and then working with them collectively to serve people will result in a much happier community of people.

CHAPTER 6
Five Minute Rule

As you go through life, you do observe. Sometimes you do this to figure out how to improve yourself, and sometimes you do it to take advantage of a situation to improve the way you do things and interact with people. This is fine as long as you don't walk over people and hurt others in the process. Hopefully as you grow older you'll learn to work with people to benefit those around you and in the world.

Some people are impatient and take shortcuts to fame and fortune. They're generally capable people who would have gotten ahead in this world at any rate, but they want their way now. They often don't pay attention to the fact they may be hurting others. Getting ahead any way possible is their credo—moral or otherwise.

Early in my oil patch career, I observed some people doing just that. Nothing seemed to bother them. Some of these individuals cheated on their spouses; some were party animals; some were clearly selfish and self-centred. They seemed to have everything going for them. I got frustrated and approached my boss of the day about this. In a way I was jealous, but I really wanted to understand my boss's principles for life and work, because he wasn't like them, and he was advancing in the company at a decent pace.

After I briefly explained what was bothering me, he asked me, "Have you ever heard of the Five Minute Rule?" Puzzled, I said I had not. He reached into his desk and got me a blank piece of letter paper and a pen, handed them to me, and said, "Take these and follow my instructions carefully."

I positioned myself at the front of his desk and prepared to do what he said. "You will have four columns: the first one for the person's name, the next for the brief circumstances, the third for the time, day, month, and year—it will be important to note the time in minutes—and the last for the time, day, month, and year. Again, it will be important to note the time in minutes. This is something you'll keep quietly to yourself for the rest of the time you're with the company." Then he sat back in his chair.

I was really puzzled at this point and said so. "Well," he replied, "it's true that the incidents you're concerned about do happen, but if you dwell on them, you won't take the time to do your job properly. In most cases, you can do absolutely nothing about the situations. You can only do what you know and believe is the right thing to do for yourself and your job. If you do this, you will do well and your career will last for a long time. You just started a sheet that should be titled 'Five Minute Rule.' You'll keep that sheet to yourself and write down incidents that bother you, noting the name, brief circumstances, date, and time they occur. Then you'll leave the sheet alone and let the sheet do the worrying. When the named perpetrator quits or is fired, you'll note the date and time of his leaving. I can personally guarantee that within five minutes, five hours, five days, five months, five years, or multiples of these times, the perpetrator will be gone if what is bothering you is legitimately wrong. In the meantime, you'll attend to your job efficiently."

I left his office quietly wondering if he had his head screwed on correctly! I did what he said, and in the next thirty years I put dozens and dozens of names on that list while observing what happened to them. Some were quite high up in the company. I kept that list confidential for the whole time I worked for my one company in the oil industry.

When I left that company thirty years later, I noted that all the names on the list had quit under apparent duress or been fired. Some took up to fifteen years, but they got what was personally thought to be deserved. In the meantime, I lasted a total of thirty-two years and retired of my own free will. I came close to being fired but that never happened, as my value to the company kept me working there. Some on the Five Minute Rule list seemingly did nothing observable to others to be removed, but they were on the list because I observed something that bothered me at the time. No one ever saw that list but me—not even Anne. In the end, that hand-written list contributed to heating our home via our wood burning boiler!

The most important lesson learned from this experience? To make sure you're doing what is correct and moral as well as conducive to the advancement of your company. You may not become president, but not only will your co-workers and clients respect you, but you'll be doing your job in a way that will be respected by all those who know you.

Leave your concerns on the Five Minute Rule sheet. Let it do the worrying! Those on that sheet will be dealt with in five minutes, five hours, five days, five months, five years, or multiples of those times, as long as there was a valid basis for them being on that sheet. Do your job and let the offenders be dealt with. Do your job well with integrity; be a team member, and don't take shortcuts that will get your name on that sheet.

CHAPTER 7
Bank Manager Tough Love

Throughout our lives, Anne and I have been blessed with many forms of financial advice. As we grew in our marriage partnership, we learned to bounce this financial advice off each other, and to discern and apply when justified. We both value this partnership. It can be trying at times because, like all males, I have an ego that can be difficult to overcome. Thankfully, we have learned to talk to each other and reason proposals through, which is a powerful antidote to that ego of mine.

It was not always that way. While we were dating, what money we earned or received was of necessity dedicated first to our education. We occasionally had some leftover money for concerts and other dates—usually in the first part of the academic year. Later in the year we had precious little money, so long walks holding hands was the norm. Once we graduated and got jobs, the financial pressures eased off. Some debts remained, but we could now start spending money on things we wanted to do.

During our post-secondary education years, we didn't really "save" money. We lived hand to mouth. Once married, this "tradition" lived on. Five addresses in five years didn't advance our financial stability! Eventually we had two kids, a sports car, and a house … with me as the sole wage earner receiving a good paycheque. We were paid once a month and had no idea how to budget other than to look at the paycheque and think it would last each month.

One day about a year after we had our second and last child, our bank account was running low. There was essentially nothing left in our chequing account for the remaining week in the month! Anne told me about our situation, and my thoughts were: *We own a home and a personal car. I have a good paying job with a steady paycheque and I'm doing very well at that job. Why not just borrow $50 for a week until the next cheque?* We headed off to do just that.

Let's pause for a minute. Notice the list of possessions that accompanied the money problems in the preceding paragraph. Perhaps the husband had an ego problem! As well, the house and sports car we "owned" were heavily mortgaged— the bank owned most of them. We were also still paying off my university loans. True, that was to finish within a year, but we were paying off both the mortgage and education loans. Anne had learned how to write cheques and handled our finances while I was away doing my oil patch work. She knew how to balance the chequebook, which was how she discovered how low we were on funds. I didn't take any of that into account. My ego said we were good risks, and I felt we were worth a loan. This was also forty-five plus years ago—$50 for a week could be worth upwards of $500 a week today. Consider this in yearly terms.

Confidently we went to our bank, which just happened to hold our mortgage and car loan as well. We met with the manager, who politely listened to my request and asked some questions. We answered them in a confident, straightforward manner. After hearing our story, he stood up with a slight frown on his face and said to Anne and me together: "You need to grow up and learn to manage your affairs and live within your means." He stuck out his hand, said "Good day," and escorted us out of the bank.

I was crushed. I felt I had failed in everything I'd ever done! My education, my good job meant nothing at that moment. I had failed my wife and children whom I dearly loved. As a husband and father, I felt like dirt. My ego had been crushed. I got angry and vented on Anne. We returned to our mortgaged home and realized how tenuous our lives were.

Then resolve hit. Anne noted she had some money in her purse, and I had some as well. We looked at our cupboards and saw that we could eke through. That was fine for a week, but what followed was a quantum attitudinal change in our lives. We would make sure we had the basics in life and would become a lot more discerning in our spending habits. We would not only look at the next day, week, and month, but at the years ahead. We would budget and learn how to stick to it! Sure, my ego was crushed—but I had a partner I loved far more than my ego! We began to treat our marriage and our family as a business—a loving business, but a business all the same.

What came of all this? That bank visit stayed welded in my head right up until we retired. I couldn't stand to go into any bank alone to do business. Anne would occasionally get me to drive her to the bank and ask me to sit there while she did the financial work, pointing out occasionally to the teller that I was her husband—just to prove she was married! This worked well. She became and still is the financial backstop in our family.

We sold the sports car and got a family vehicle. I was promoted several times. When transferred after the above-mentioned story, we sold our first house and rented for a time until we could afford a home. We became debt-free in the next twelve years, and we retired debt-free with a good pension and investments. We bought land in British Columbia and built the home we had dreamed about for thirty-two years, after living in the modest homes we'd purchased as we transferred around. We never lost money on any of those homes—we came close, but we never lost money. We're financially stable now in retirement, even as we contribute to the charities we support.

My ego? Well, it was not killed. It flared up quite a few times after that bank visit, but with help from Anne and the remembrance of the incident so long ago, my ego dropped away reasonably quickly.

There was only one problem left to fix—a nagging problem that would not leave my mind. You see, I used to be terribly angry with that bank manager of forty-five plus years ago. Once retired, I began going into the bank we use now, even though it is a different bank. All the staff and managers in our bank are treated with great respect. Anne and I are both thankful for our financial planner. We have great joy in the fact that those with whom we work to help manage our finances have steered us toward a very comfortable retirement and financial future. Over time, both of us began to realize how much our financial stability was due to that one foundational piece of advice we'd received so many years ago. Not only was it foundational from a financial point of view, but it formed the basis of our belief in personal responsibility in all we do. I just couldn't live in anger any longer. My ego had been crushed—which was a good thing. A nagging problem needed to be resolved.

In April of 2015, Anne and I returned to the bank branch we had used forty-five years earlier and asked for the bank manager. We realized it would be a different manager and that the original man may not even be alive anymore. Both Anne and I realized that sometimes even bank managers would like to know that the hard advice they hand out, which will probably often be received in anger, does have positive effects in the long term. I confess I had tears in my eyes as I told the young lady manager what had happened, and how thankful Anne and I were that the manager of forty-four years earlier had given us his advice. Both of us told her it was the best darn advice we ever got! She very graciously accepted our story.

To all you out there who feel a savings or "reserve" fund can be used for buying video games, big screen TVs, more house than you need, or more vehicles than you need, remember this: living for the immediate may hurt your life in the future. Should you receive an ego-busting bit of tough love, foundational advice from your bank manager, I strongly recommend you accept it not only for your finances, but for your personal attitude of responsibility as well.

CHAPTER 8
A Young Child's Example to All

Sometimes a young child can teach parents and older people a lesson by their simple act of joy that is not cluttered with outside influences or opinions. An example stands out in Anne's and my lives to this day—a day when our daughter was only four years old.

It occurred early in my oil patch career. Having less seniority than others, I sometimes had to take vacations later on in the fall, after others in my company had taken their vacation in a better season when the weather was hopefully nicer. We took a tent trailer vacation in later September down to Mount Rushmore in South Dakota. We were expecting to have a great time, especially considering the crowds would be gone and we'd have no trouble finding a camping spot!

This was mostly true. We did run into a problem in that no matter where we camped, all the firewood had been depleted. And we mean depleted! Every dead tree and branch had been utilized; there was little if any firewood to be found … and this at a time when we didn't have propane camping appliances. To be honest, I didn't like pumping the old camp fuel stoves and lamps. My mood was sour every time we needed to fire one of those things up. And I was not pleasant when I was sour!

To top things off, we were in our "cheap" phase of life. We were learning how to live within our means from the bank manager incident outlined earlier, and we had begun to purchase land. Note I said "cheap," not "inexpensive." We had swung from living beyond our means to cutting costs wherever we could. We hadn't learned how to responsibly purchase something major with an eye to keeping it for the future. This would come, but we had many more lessons to learn before that.

We had bought a tent trailer—and I do mean "tent!" We had good sleeping bags, but that tent trailer was meant to be slept in only. When we got out of bed, we were cold! Everything else was done outside the trailer. Our car, a small station wagon, was too small for all of us to sleep in at night.

So here we were in the Black Hills of South Dakota, close to Mount Rushmore. Mountains. Mid-to-late September. I'm sure the reader will justifiably jump ahead to the thought: *It could snow!* Here was I, the man of the family, with equipment I personally had mental trouble with (at least), and no firewood. In the cold. I was not happy, and that certainly did not help my wife's happiness!

We decided to visit the Mount Rushmore site and take it in. As we walked toward the viewpoints, it began snowing—vigorous but gently falling snow! Man, I was now in a worse mood! Then something blessed happened that changed the whole mood for both Anne and myself. It was something our four-year-old daughter did. She started dancing and prancing along ahead of us with her arms gracefully flapping away from her sides, singing "Jingle Bells, Jingle Bells" in a clear and grateful voice. She couldn't care less about the circumstances bothering her dad and mom—she just saw gently falling snow with big flakes. I began to see the beauty of the situation, and my heart filled with joy. I realized that all my sourness was inappropriate. A blessing was happening that would stick with Anne and me forever!

The rest of the vacation went very well. While the problems and the sourness leading up to the "Jingle Bells" occurrence are remembered, today it seems we had absolutely no problems after that song—just joy. My mind still sees those big flakes and that little girl flapping her arms, dancing along. As time went on, we got better vehicles and propane appliances. Camping later may have had challenges, but they soon drifted away with the memories of Mount Rushmore. We wouldn't trade that time for anything in the world.

When you get sour about anything today, it is the author's hope you will find a "Jingle Bells" moment to drive away your blues!

CHAPTER 9
The Positive Side of Demotion

"Demotion." The word can mean many things. It can mean the harsh realization that you aren't deemed capable of doing your job. It could mean that there are too many qualified people in your salary grade, and you just happen to be the least best, so you are put back. It can mean there is a downturn in your business, and people above you are being demoted and moving down, so you have to move down as well. Indeed, there are others below you who are being demoted as well. Some below you might be getting demoted right out of a job. It can seem to be a crushing defeat. It certainly can bruise—even destroy—your ego. In some cases, though, it can be a blessing.

Elsewhere in this book we address the importance of knowing your limitations. Should you be demoted, you must be realistic with yourself. Have you actually reached your limitations? If you have, you should view a demotion as a bit of a relief in that you weren't fired. If you believe you haven't reached your limitations, you might consider upgrading your skills or pursuing another career path. If you aren't sure, you should consider another choice—stay with the job you're given and work your way into a new career path within the same company. Deal with each new reality as it comes up.

I was demoted twice. I describe the first time in "Know Your Limits." I deserved to be demoted, as did the crew that came along with me. We chose to come out of our existing mental attitudes and greatly improve, and the result was both surprising and wonderful!

The second time was an ego destroyer. I went from being a manager to a salesman. I believe that some upper management wanted me to quit—and in hindsight they were justified. Being "soft" as a manager, I let my employees manage me. The oil industry is a tough place, and being nice for "feelings'" sake could mean "you are gone." While there's nothing wrong with being a firm manager who works for the benefit of both his employer and his employees, being too soft or too hard will probably result in an exit.

I should note that prior to being demoted the second time, I liked working with people, but I lost sight of those I worked for. I only concentrated on those physically close to me. I was what could be called "a nice guy." In the position to which I was demoted, that desire to work with people rose a few notches. My former customers became potential clients in my new marketing job, and I also now worked with those above me in marketing and in operations. My "working with people" attitude was pushed to what most would consider "the limits." This was done in a moral manner while learning the business from both my company's and all my clients' perspectives.

Many people think this cannot be done. It can and was done. The objectives were the same with my clients and my company—maximize profits in a manner that was effective, efficient, and beneficial to all concerned. Once that mindset kicked in, my love of working with people flourished. This even resulted in a promotion to the equivalent grade of my previous managerial job.

While there was some talk about putting me back into management after my mindset had "improved," that idea was quickly quashed by me. I had found my niche. When that talk reached an almost insistent tone from upper management, it was successfully argued that I was most beneficial to my company where I was at. In an effort to get me to change my mind, the company offered to promote me to a position that was permanently set at a certain level. If I insisted on letting my company promote me to that position, no further promotions would occur.

Now that was a challenge to a guy with an ego who had suddenly brought himself out of a demotion funk and made a good name for himself! The challenge appealed to me! I could concentrate on improving myself, knowing there was an excellent job with good salary prospects ahead of me without having to "strive" to get out of that job to another position (from which I may get demoted).

I accepted the position and stayed in the job until retirement—voluntary retirement at a time that things were going well for me and the company. I grew in that position. Many papers were either authored by me or co-authored with me. A Distinguished Lecturer award resulted. My clients not only respected me—the industry admired me.

What happened? The demotion occurred before I knew the Lord, but I believe it was of the Lord. In hindsight, it was a blessing. My salary grew to the top of the bracket, which was often higher than some of our managers'. My vacation time increased each year, and it was given by seniority. My vacation allotment could be embarrassing, as I got priority on timing even over my bosses—and often got more vacation time than my boss and his boss! Add that to a fairly significant six figure salary in the 1990s and it would be suggested that Anne and I were very blessed!

Yes, getting demoted can be positive. Some would say it depends on one's attitude. While that is partially true, I now see that Someone had a plan for me throughout life—a plan that is ongoing. That hurt and that crushed ego? Temporary, folks—especially if you can turn it into a positive outcome.

CHAPTER 10
The Smartest Farmer

I was blessed many a time while travelling around Western Canada doing my job. It was constantly amazing what you could learn away from "the big city." One such instance helped me understand what financial and living priorities should be. It occurred in Kindersley, Saskatchewan.

It was summer time—slow in the oil industry around Edmonton where I was based and extremely busy in south-central Saskatchewan. I was a field "engineer" and was needed in Kindersley. (Note: I wasn't a professional engineer, so I couldn't call myself an engineer. I was a chemist.) The Edgson team decided to take our young kids with us and live out of a motel for a few days while I did my job in the field. This was particularly interesting for Anne, as she had spent some time in early grade school in Flaxcombe, a short distance west of Kindersley.

Coming from Edmonton to Kindersley proved to be very interesting. Unlike the area around Edmonton, there were very few trees around Kindersley at the time. It was flat farmland where they grew grain crops. Also, the farms were big—you could travel for quite some distance before leaving any one farm. It was also hotter outside than in Edmonton.

Kindersley was a good place for us to visit, and we were getting some time off for Anne and the kids. Mind you, she couldn't drive yet, so she was stuck in and around the motel for some time. We did get to see her childhood home in Flaxcombe, —an abandoned railway station—and a little brick school house that, according to Anne's memory, was blocks away from the station where they lived and reached by walking uphill both ways! In actuality it was about a long block away up a hill. That's what a little child in Grade One saw versus what an adult sees. Perceptions depend on what you believe in relative to what you see and know at the time of the observation. There was another perception I personally held that was about to get blown apart—a life lesson in priorities and how to handle finances, and one that influences our lives to this day.

One day my crew and I were called on to go to a job nearby. We had plenty of time, so we met at a local restaurant for breakfast and to discuss the job to be certain we were ready. This restaurant was popular with the local farmers. When I and my crew arrived at the restaurant, we happened to get a table close to the front window. There were many newer, high end cars parked out front—all belonging to the wealthy looking farmers inside. Those farmers were all well dressed, even for city folks. Their clothes were not what one would think a hard-working farmer would be wearing.

My crew knew that country and what life was like. I first confirmed that the other guys were actually farmers, and they were. I then commented that they must be very well off because of the vehicles they drove and the clothes they wore. This got a bit of snicker from one of my guys, who then said, "They're not the richest guys around here." I was a little incredulous and stated that to them!

"Just listen to them for a while," one of my guys commented.

I listened and heard a lot of crabbing about the cost of their new combines and tractors. There was also a lot of bragging about the air-conditioning and accessories in those vehicles. Here were these men/farmers comparing all their brand new toys/equipment in order to show each other they had the newest and the best. I found the conversation a little egotistical and told my crew so.

The other man on my crew said, "We have time; just wait for a bit and we'll show you the richest farmer around, by far." We indeed had at least an hour to spare, so I agreed to wait.

A few minutes later, I saw something I really took an interest in—some fellow drove up in a beautifully maintained 1956 pickup. At that stage in life, I actually wanted such a truck! Most of the 1956 pickups I'd seen previously were pretty rough, and the rest were either hot- rodded or restored to a point where they were too expensive to buy. This pickup was used but very well maintained. I was thinking about approaching the owner and offering to buy it, and I told my crew this. Their answer surprised me.

"Not much of a chance there. He's the richest farmer around here."

My jaw dropped as the farmer exited the truck—not only because he drove a 1956 pickup, but because he wore clean and very neat bib coveralls and looked like a hard-working farmer. He wore nothing that indicated he was the richest farmer. I whispered to my crew as the farmer came in, "Why do you say that?"

My guys noted that this guy owned one of the bigger spreads around. He waited until some of his neighbours had put themselves into financial difficulties with all their purchases and then bought them out—with cash. He had no need or desire to buy brand new equipment. He just waited until all the complainers got tired of their fancy rigs and wanted to get the latest equipment. He then bought those nearly new, scarcely-used rigs for pennies on the dollar. He made sure all his equipment was well maintained, doing a lot of the maintenance himself. He kept the equipment—which didn't cost too much to maintain or gave him much trouble—for decades, unless he happened on a bankruptcy auction with newer equipment or could buy some barely used equipment from some of the complainers who might be in the restaurant at the time. He would then put up his well-maintained equipment for auction and probably get the same or more than he had paid for it originally.

His favourite means of transportation was that 1956 truck, which he had bought new and maintained to a standard most people would not. He likely didn't want to sell his good maintenance.

I stopped, looked around, and saw this simple-looking man sitting down for his breakfast, being politely acknowledged by the crabbers and complainers. It struck me that those rich looking guys were actually viewing this guy's lifestyle as something they didn't want, but they wanted him there to take the equipment they'd become dissatisfied with off their hands!

Motioning to my crew it was time to leave, I told them breakfast was on me. They were happy, but a little surprised. I noted they had given me a life lesson that would be cherished and acted on for the rest of my life. Anne and I do so to this day.

CHAPTER 11
Unexpected Circumstances

While this book relates stories and experiences which in large part involve Anne and me along with others who were in our lives, there are many second-hand stories that provide humour as well as life lessons that may not have directly involved us. Since second-hand stories may contain some embellishments in them—and seeing as embellishments tend to grow when the stories become third-hand, fourth-hand, and so on—we must realize that the truth, if any, cannot be definitively proven at the date of writing this book. To that end, names and places in the stories have either been omitted or altered to protect the guilty. While in some cases no direct connection with Anne and I exists, there is at the very least grains of truth present in these stories. So read on and enjoy!

I'm Hungry!
In the oil patch in the 1970s, a service company would often be sent out to do a job on a drilling rig at a remote well site. Sometimes those jobs took a long time and required the service company personnel to remain on site for hours before or during the job. Most well sites were well equipped to handle their own drilling

crews along with multiple service companies that came and went through well planned camps. These sites had well equipped sleeping and dining quarters at the very least, along with excellent communication facilities used to communicate with those outside the well site.

Most of them.

One job required the service company crew to travel just outside Alberta's northern boundary. As the service company crew was used to "normal, remote campsites," they took nothing to eat and expected to be able to sleep in a warm camp if needs be. When they arrived, they found only a small, slightly shabby looking drilling rig with no camp! No kitchen ... nothing! The good news was the job was to begin upon the arrival of the service crew.

Even though the drill hole was shallow, the service company's tools that were sent down the well bridged, meaning that they ran into an obstruction as they entered. The drilling rig had to trip in with the drill pipe and send the drill pipe and bit into the hole to circulate the drilling fluid and clean out the obstruction. The rig was a very slow operating rig, so the service company went to sleep in their big truck and the engineer's car. On top of that, it was extremely cold. Fortunately, the big truck had an electrical generator, so the engineer's car could use its electrical heater. The service crew went to sleep hungry.

Finally the rig was ready for the service crew, and they went to work. By now they were really hungry! The nearest restaurant was four hours away, so it wasn't practical to send out for food. The best plan was to get the job done and get back south. Still, one of the required surveys had to proceed very slowly.

One of the truck drivers commented to the engineer that he was hungry. "I know, but there's not much we can do about it," replied the engineer.

A few minutes went by, and the same truck driver again said, "I'm hungry," but this time with more emphasis.

The engineer replied, "I know," also with more emphasis.

A few moments passed and this whole scene was repeated—with growing emphasis.

Finally the truck driver said, "I have to go!"

Relieved to hear that, the engineer gave permission. After doing his business out in the extremely cold -40-degree weather (the same in Celsius or Fahrenheit), the truck driver came back in and said, "Now I know I am *extremely* hungry!"

Annoyed, the engineer replied, *"And just how do you know that?"*

"Well, as I pulled my pants down and squatted to do my business, I heard 'crunch, crunch' coming from behind me. I looked around and saw that I was so hungry, my rear end was eating snow!"

Fortunately, the job was soon over and they returned south for a meal.

American Winter Relief

In the late 1960s and early 1970s, one Canadian service company would call on its American sister company to send up engineers to help them out during the cold winter season. You see, the southern USA had a slow time during the Canadian winter. One should also realize that the best time for drilling on sloppy swamp land in northern Alberta, Saskatchewan, and British Columbia was when the temperature was far below freezing, so the swamps were frozen solid and could hold all the heavy equipment. We're talking real cold—in today's terms, anywhere from -20 C to -50 C. Now picture an American engineer from the warm southern USA coming into this scenario.

One engineer, whom we'll call Billy Bob (to protect the actual "guilty" engineer), was flown into Edmonton in January to be staged up to northern Alberta—where it was much colder than Edmonton. He arrived in Edmonton and got off the plane in shorts and a T-shirt! As the engineer proceeded through customs, the customs agent noted his name (altered to protect the guilty) and said "Billy Bob ... that must mean William Robert."

Billy Bob replied, "No, suh, I was christened Billy Bob."

Things went downhill from there.

Working in northern Alberta ends when "break-up" occurs—the time when all that frozen swampy ground thaws and breaks up. This normally occurred around March 15. The service company also had a rule about their units—first in, first out. When you went back to the shop in northern Alberta, you went in line with all the other trucks that had come before you. As the jobs came in, the truck at the front of the queue went out. Billy Bob's truck was to go out next when break-up hit ... and break-up hit hard. No truck could go out for a month until the land dried out, and at the very least until the roads had solidified. That month was important.

During the time in the shop, the crew—including the engineer—was to make sure everything was ready to go for the next job. During that month of break-up, the crews rotated out and back. Part of getting ready to go out was to fuel the vehicles up. No excuses here—they had a month to do it!

That particular service company had its own communication system between trucks in the field and the field base. Break-up finished, and a job was called in.

Billy Bob and his crew went out on the job. A short distance from the base, the truck ran out of fuel! Billy Bob phoned back to base.

"Billy Bob to base! Billy Bob to base! Come in, Harry!" (The manager's name has been changed to protect the guilty.)

"Harry here, Billy Bob. What's up?"

"Well, suh, we done run out of gas."

To which Harry replied, "Is that right?" He was obviously annoyed.

Billy Bob replied, correctly as it turned out, "Tain't right, but it's so!"

To this day, when appropriate circumstances arise, Anne and I always say, "Tain't right, but it's so!"

They Did Not Think!

One of the reasons oil industry drilling occurs in swampy areas in the cold of winter is because the swamps are frozen solid until the ground thaws during spring break-up. After that time until the next serious freeze, the name "swamp" pretty well describes what to expect. Once a good hydrocarbon well and/or field is found in a swampy area, an access road needs to be built so that the well or wells can be serviced.

Swampy areas generally aren't flat and smooth. These areas undulate from water saturated depressions to less saturated higher areas. These undulations can be very small or very large. Roads built in the frozen winter time usually just followed these undulations until circumstances came about to build a better road. These undulating roads pretty well determine the speed at which they could be traversed—slowly. Occasionally an area with a bigger pond or small, shallow lake would emerge. In that case, the "road" going straight across this frozen water area would be smooth in the frozen winter. If that type of road was long enough, one could speed up for a time.

Quite often, these ponds or small lakes could end up at a bank of earth, at least on one side of the lake or pond. If that was the case, rather than dig out the frozen ground at the bank so the road could continue straight out of the pond or small lake, the exiting road was built at a right angle to the pond or lake road, going up the bank at a slope to minimize the amount of earth needed to be dug out of the bank. As these original rough roads were laid out, the builders may have run into an obstruction of some kind frozen in the ground. When that happened, prior to a more permanent road being built, the road builders would just go around the obstruction.

As for the flora in the swampy area, the trees tend to be rather scraggy. "Swamp spruce" or "swamp birch" describes sickly, thin trees that have grown in a water-logged part of the swamp. In really wet areas of the swamp, trees probably won't grow. Some areas in the swamp are considered to have "high ground." In those areas trees can grow thicker and stronger. Often that "high ground" isn't all that high—it just contains soil less saturated with water. It's important to keep this in mind as this story unfolds, for the circumstances of what happened will seem so silly as to not be plausible!

One time a big oil patch truck with two drivers was slowly going across one of these winter roads in north-eastern Alberta. Up and down. Up and down. While the road was straight ahead, the undulations dictated a very slow speed, and the truck drivers were getting a little impatient. Then the road turned to the right onto a relatively long, flat area. The winter road was built through an area with thin, sickly looking swamp birches on each side. But it was straight and flat! The driver sped up.

The truck was going at a relatively high clip when both the men in the front seats could see a larger birch tree coming up, smack in the middle of the road. The area around and behind the tree was still flat! They pondered on this as the tree got closer, expecting the road to just go around the tree. They didn't slow down much.

As they got closer, they discovered that the road turned sharply left! They were going way too fast, but they figured that the birch tree was just a sickly swamp birch, so if they hit it, it would just break.

The road builder made that sharp left turn for a reason.

The truck skidded into the tree head on. The birch did snap off at the base, but it wasn't a sickly tree—quite the opposite. The truck was a cab-over, and it hit the tree right in the middle of the front of the truck. That birch came partway into the cab between the two men before it snapped off.

There are a couple of points to this story. First, the persons in the truck weren't familiar with the road. They were fed up with driving slowly across an undulating road, so when they hit a smooth area, they sped up. They assumed a tree in the road wasn't a strong tree due to the frozen wet area, forgetting the road builder who would be using a big bulldozer didn't move that tree out of the way! Due to excessive speed, slow reaction time, some false assumptions, and *not thinking*, they ended up with a problem.

Is it not amazing that when someone says "I didn't think ..." they generally had not?

Assumptions Can Be Deadly

Along the lines of not thinking, there is a story out there in north-western Alberta that doesn't involve a tree but does involve a large lake. And a river. Together and at the same time, believe it or not!

In this part of Alberta exists a very large, shallow lake called Zama Lake. To see what actually existed in the middle to late 1900s in the area, one would need to look at a map of the area showing the lake as well as the Zama River. To tell the reader what that map would show concerning the relationship of the lake to the river would spoil the story, so the narrative will be shared first.

In the early years of oil exploration in the Zama Lake area, a winter road was built right across the frozen lake. It was a nice, long, straight road and only needed to be kept free of snow. Since it was a frozen lake, rookie drivers were often tempted to speed up, and they did. This was before winter tires. And the road was ice.

One day a rookie field engineer of a major service company was approaching Zama Lake and driving across undulating winter road built over the swampy area next to it. Suddenly he drove onto the lake. It was smooth and straight! Time to put the pedal to the metal!

In those days, mobile radio handsets were attached to the transmission hump in the car, with the main communication unit in the trunk. The handsets with a telephone-type receiver were big clunky things with three lights and screw-in holders for the lights. The "screw-in" part will play a part in this story.

As the rookie sped across the lake, enjoying the absolute smoothness of the road, he was oblivious to the weird fact that Zama River didn't flow into and out of Zama Lake—it flowed *through* the lake. But I digress ... more on this later!

Suddenly the road disappeared from under the car, and the car was sailing. Down it crashed and then skidded onto another smooth, frozen area. The impact was so great, the skidding car came to a stop within ten feet of the initial impact. The three screw-in bulbs in the radio handset popped out, but without stripping the threads! Obviously shaken, the rookie got out and saw that the drop was about five feet down, and there were banks on each side of the river. The car, while out of alignment, was driveable, so he continued on. Slowly.

The rookie then went back to his base office and looked at the map of Zama Lake. He had not noticed that the river was shown as going right *through* the middle of the lake! In any case, the rookie didn't even contemplate that the river would be lower than the lake, because he assumed the lake water would be at the same level as the river. Obviously wrong.

The truth is, in the spring, the river would swell over its banks and fill up the lake. As the summer progressed and the river water subsided, it would drop below its banks. But the banks stayed intact, acting as levees so the lake water wouldn't spill back into the river. By fall, the river was significantly below the lake level while continuing to flow through and past the lake! This could be seen on detailed topographical maps.

Once again, be familiar with your road and where you're travelling. Even if you see a river flowing through a lake, don't assume the water levels are identical. Consult with your fellow workers if you're a rookie, as they'll know facts you may have trouble believing. If you don't believe them, accept what they say as a warning and proceed carefully. Assumptions can be deadly!

That's Water over Dry Pavement, Correct?

While we're on water stories coupled with driving experiences, a lesson from a story needs to be learned about driving on paved roads in the spring, especially those covered by water from melting snow … with a temperature above freezing.

One male driver was proceeding along a freeway in an Alberta city. The freeway was below the level of surrounding subdivisions, with the road covered in water, but not so deep that he couldn't travel at a good clip. The water had come from melting snow along the sides of the road and from the subdivisions.

Prior to getting on that freeway, the driver noticed that there was no snow on the ground anywhere, and the roads were bone dry. There was no darkness on the road associated with either melting water or ice. It was also decently warm outside. The temperature a few days earlier was below freezing and there was snow on the edges of the sunken roadway.

Ahead sat a car stopped right in the middle of the freeway. The driver put on his brakes, but the brakes locked! The car sped up, even though the speedometer showed the wheel speed was zero. This couldn't be … surely the water on the road was on top of dry pavement, or at least pavement without ice! The car was out of control and slid straight into the car in the middle of the road, coming to a stop with damage to both cars.

Getting out of his car, the driver soon learned that the water on the road was actually over ice, because he slipped and fell into it! While he was not charged by the police, and the other driver was because he had stopped in the middle of the road, the damage was done. Was the collision avoidable? Definitely! A false assumption had been made about what was underneath that water. To this day, I never assume the water on the road is shallow, or that it's on top of something that will not cause my car to go out of control. The water could just be hiding ice in the winter, and in spring or fall it could hide a deep pothole which at best damages your car's suspension or tires, and at worst throws your car out of control.

Handling Tornadoes

Sometimes people can seemingly make silly demands on God—and He listens! This story involves Anne and me.

In 1987 (coincidental to Anne's birthday) a tornado touched down in Edmonton, which caused a lot of destruction. I wasn't at our company district shop in East Edmonton at the time because I was visiting a client in West Edmonton. Anne was at home, which was close to where the tornado hit but far enough away to avoid damage. While it was obvious something horrendous was going on east of where I was, I didn't get back to the shop until after the tornado had hit and done its damage. Upon my return, I certainly heard a lot about what happened. This story will be in two parts—the first part before someone made a demand on God, and the rest after.

The tornado started south of Edmonton. It was on a course to hit our shop on the eastern outskirts of the city as it moved north. One of our competitors was located a few blocks east of us. Our people and crews were able to see something approaching. From the radio news they all knew it was a tornado, but all they could see was a huge, black, debris-laden, swirling cloud. All could see pieces of plywood and other relatively big chunks of debris as the cloud approached. The roar of the approaching tornado was very clear!

We had a very crusty, very efficient, and certainly obeyed-by-us dispatcher in our shop whose office was located on the second floor above the office area. As all those in the shop area were running around and considering what to do, this character came running down the stairs into the shop area and stomped out the door. He stood outside, angrily pointed up to the sky, and with his angry face pointed to the heavens yelled, "We were here first!" He then angrily stomped back in and up to his office! The tornado promptly turned east a few blocks and hit our competitor! It then continued north, doing far more damage before it finally petered out.

There was no damage to our shop but we were surrounded by plenty of debris! All of us were amazed later on when we saw the trajectory plotted and the relatively sharp turn right and then left as the tornado did its destruction as it continued north. None of us were really surprised, for if any of us didn't follow our dispatcher's instructions, we were absolutely sure we'd get chewed out! Our district manager was a pussy cat compared to our very efficient and listened-to dispatcher! Listened to by God at the time as well, it would appear!

"Secure" Communications

In north-western Alberta in the 1960s, a communications system was put in place to supplement the existing government communications system. Various service companies subscribed to this system, installing it in their pickups, cars, and bigger units. As with normal mobile radios, a person could hear himself talk as well as the returning communication. Other units of the same service company couldn't hear the sender, except for a "beep, beep, beep" going on while the sender was speaking. When the receiving individual talked back, you could hear everything the receiver said. Service companies weren't supposed to hear the other service company's conversations at all. Supposedly.

Some personnel of one particular service company discovered a relay switch in their sending unit that, when switched, allowed them to hear and transmit to another service company. Today this would be called "hacking." Rather than report this, the individuals decided just to "listen in," because the other service company wasn't a business competitor. I'm not saying this was legitimate … I'm just stating what happened! The crew that discovered this method of circumventing security will be known as "Crew 1."

One day while working on a well site, Crew 1 uncovered the communications system and flipped the switch. There was silence for a time and then Crew 1 heard a phone ringing. A sleepy female voice came on saying, "Hello?"

Next they heard a "beep, beep, beep," and the female voice replied, "You're coming home? Oh, that's wonderful!"

"Beep, beep, beep."

"Oh, you devil," the female replied.

"Beep, beep, beep."

With more emphasis she said, "*Oh*, you devil!"

"Beep, beep, beep."

With fully expectant emphasis she exclaimed, "*Oh, you devil!*"

How the rest of the conversation went is hereby censored!

On another occasion, with the same Crew 1 listening, the conversation from the competitor went along a different path. First the phone rang, and then a rather angry female voice answered, "Hello!"

"Beep, beep, beep."

"Whadda ya mean you ain't coming home this weekend?" an angry female voice replied.

"Beep, beep, beep."

"I don't care! I've planned for you and me to go out on the town!"

"Beep, beep, beep."

"Listen … there's going to be some loving going on this weekend. If you want to be part of it, you better get your butt home." And then the angry female voice slammed down the receiver.

Ouch!

The point of all this is that when speaking on any mobile device, even today, do not assume others cannot hear you. The crew mentioned above was doing this for a poorly conceived idea of "having fun." The people on the other end never knew they were being listened to. What you say or write on any mobile device should never be considered ironclad safe. Keep your communication points safe by only using secure systems or methods with equipment that cannot be hacked. Sometimes it's best to make sure private messages are dealt with face to face.

Witnesses to an Accident

The company for which I worked hired qualified, university educated engineers and earth scientists to perform field jobs and manage unit field personnel. At the time of this story, they had hired a very qualified French Canadian engineer. English wasn't his first language, but he mastered it quickly, albeit with an accent. At the time of this incident, he was employed in the southern Canadian prairies.

Let's consider the landscape of the southern Canadian prairies. In the summer, it's hot and dry. Wild trees aren't that common, but grasslands certainly are. In these grasslands, antelope roam and graze. Antelope can be skittish—they jump, they are swift, and they can move unexpectedly. Now back to the story.

One Friday the manager of the area called his entire group of field engineers in for a safety talk at the end of office hours. It was a rousing safety talk. That manager left the meeting for the weekend fully satisfied that he had gotten the point of safety across.

On Monday morning he came into the office to find an accident report on his desk from the French Canadian engineer. He had hit an antelope and damaged his company car over the weekend. Under "Witnesses" he had written in pencil "two other antelope." After writing his report, the engineer had gone on scheduled days off.

The manager wasn't pleased, so he called the offending engineer in from his time off. The manager proceeded to not-too-gently admonish the engineer about not only the accident, but his attitude. "How could you be so flippant to write 'two other antelope' in the witness box? Don't you realize how serious this is?"

The engineer replied in broken English, "I know! Zat is why I put it in pen-sul!"

CHAPTER 12
Death Can Teach Us Lessons

The death of a person can be a difficult situation to handle, especially if the deceased is your parent. It can be even more difficult to handle without the reassurance of what death means and what happens after. It can create fear, confusion, anger, self-centredness, and even hate. It can also provide some valuable lessons.

Such was the case with the death of Jim's father. He was an intense, so-called Irishman—a self-made man who became an alcoholic later in life. He had little education, not even graduating from high school because he had to leave and get a job to help support his family prior to World War II. He was honorably discharged from the Canadian Signal Corp after a horrific, self-inflicted collision in which he broke both of his legs. Upon his return from overseas, he met his bride-to-be—Jim's mom. He courted her, but she was a member of the Women's Christian Temperance Union. She wouldn't marry him until he quit drinking, so he quit. Period. He worked his way up in the post office to become a postmaster who handled a defined area in addition to a home post office.

Jim's dad stayed away from drink for quite some time until one day he allowed himself to be pushed into taking "just one drink." Then his problems with alcohol reappeared. Combining this with work problems, in which he had difficulty working with union employees, resulted in full-blown alcoholism. One day in the deep of a cold, snowy winter, he drank a whole bottle of whisky, went into his garage, started his car, and tried to open the door so he could drive his car out. He didn't realize that there was a huge snowdrift holding the door shut. By now the whisky had taken full hold and he drunkenly staggered back, taking a run with his shoulder to push open the door, which wouldn't open. He reeled backwards inside the garage into some poorly constructed shelves filled with paint cans, causing them to collapse and bringing all the paint cans down on his head. He was knocked unconscious, totally drunk. The car was running; he never gained consciousness. He was asphyxiated.

At the funeral, Jim and Anne were present with all of Jim's dad's living relatives. Neither Jim nor Anne knew the Lord yet. Jim was grief-struck, confused, and angry. At the reception after the funeral, in the presence of all his dad's siblings, Jim blurted out, "Well, at least Dad volunteered for World War II!"

Jim was proud of his father, even though they didn't get along very well. These strained feelings were especially evident after Jim went to university, and especially after Jim met Anne and then married her. In the few years before Jim's dad's death, there was, at best, a relationship of tolerance, not love. Jim was still proud of his father for several reasons, including the fact that his father volunteered to fight in World War II. When Jim referred to this fact at the funeral, one of his aunts said, "Is that what he told you?"

"Yes," Jim replied.

"Would you like to hear the real story?"

Suddenly curious, Jim replied in the affirmative.

During the early part of World War II, Dad was employed by the Highways Department of the Alberta government. He was a hard drinker who liked to take his Friday paycheque and partially blow it with the boys at the local bar. He was a wild man whose job was to steer and control the road grader on a government highway building project around Legal, Alberta, north of Edmonton. The "grader" was not self-propelled but was towed behind a caterpillar tractor. Obviously Dad had to eat a lot of dust from the tractor! In the winter there was no heat, and Alberta winters could be brutally cold. Dad was always pleading with the foreman to let him drive the tractor. Wisely, since Dad had a reputation for being a wild man, the foreman would never allow him to.

There was a rule regarding damaging or losing equipment as well. You lose it, you pay for it. You damage it, you pay to fix it or fix it yourself. If you couldn't fix it or pay to fix it or replace it, you went to jail. Simple and straightforward.

It was December, 1941. Canada was at war; Dad had not volunteered. Pearl Harbor was attacked on December 7. After Pearl Harbor, Canada's war effort and war machine sped up.

The Saturday after December 7, 1941, Dad was in the local bar, drinking it up with his Highways Department buddies and getting plastered, as per usual. Once again, he pushed the foreman to allow him to drive the tractor. Dad was turned down flat. Angry, Dad got up from the bar table, went out the door, drove out to the construction site, jumped on the tractor, and started driving it around, up and down and all over the construction site, just to prove he could do it. The problem was, the grader was still attached to the tractor. The grader was totalled. Dad was arrested and thrown into the local drunk tank over the weekend.

On Monday, Dad was brought in front of the local judge. The judge noted that he had totalled the grader and there were two options for him—either pay to replace the grader or go to jail. "Can you pay for the grader?"

Dad's sober reply was "No, your honour"

The judge said that normally he would throw Dad in jail since he couldn't pay, but stated he was prepared to offer a third option to Dad, which he did.

That is how Dad "volunteered" for World War II.

Jim had received a very valuable lesson from this so called "volunteer" act. Often people will brag about something that is but a very small part of the total story, the total truth. From that point on through the rest of his oil patch career, carrying over into his volunteer and political career, Jim would analyze carefully the whys and wherefores of why people did things. If it was not immediately evident, Jim would carefully observe how the "volunteer" would behave after getting a job to determine if there was something hidden. Sometimes the hidden story would come out quickly; sometimes it would take years. Most of the time there was no hidden story, but when there was, it could radically affect the job someone was doing due to an attitude problem, which eventually would catch up with the individual.

Jim became so astute at this, he began to note he was an "AA." This was partly due to his dad's alcoholism and how he'd heard of the story behind his dad "volunteering," but mainly because Jim was a very **A**nal **A**nalytical type of person. Always be sure of the motives behind someone who is bragging about something. If you don't get the whole story, beware—don't fall into the trap of perpetuating a partial truth.

As an addendum to this story, in July 2016, Jim and Anne travelled to the bar in Legal, Alberta, where some of this story took place. Jim wanted to bring closure to this story while on the way to celebrate the 100th anniversary of Westlock, Alberta. Jim hoped the bar still existed. It did!

Inside it looked just like you'd expect of a hotel bar from the early 1900s, right down to the oiled floor, the bar, and the old piano. When Jim and Anne related the story to the bar manager, they were shown pictures of the bar in the 1940s. Closure had occurred in this part of Jim's life.

Death can and does teach us lessons. Things are not always what they seem.

CHAPTER 13
The Great Pumpkin

Anne is a great cook … there is no doubt about that! This doesn't mean she makes fancy foods, but she can cook up healthy, delicious meals, which her husband personally really enjoys! An earlier story describes how she learned to cook and how she was determined to make a super delicious recipe that caused her husband to "brag on her." This particular story is about how she wanted to do some good for others with her cooking skills, how she was temporarily thwarted, and how we ended up solving the problem. The side issue to this story is that some people make projects far more complicated than needs be, and how embarrassing that can be!

While we were in Estevan, Saskatchewan, where I worked as a station manager, Anne joined the local Oil Wives Club, which held monthly meetings. One year she was in charge of getting each month's themed door prize. Anne had the idea for October of getting a big pumpkin, writing out her recipe for making pumpkin mash and then using that mash to make all kinds of pumpkin desserts. Knowing how good she was at making pumpkin mash from fresh pumpkins, and further knowing how great her pumpkin pies were, the idea was enthusiastically embraced by me, her husband! She asked me if I could arrange to get a thirty-pound pumpkin in time for the October Halloween meeting. Agreed!

Estevan had a big market garden in the nearby Souris River Valley. They grew pumpkins. Thinking there was plenty of time, and as I was very busy with my job, I decided to go to a local grocery store we frequented and have them get a thirty-pound pumpkin to be picked up by me a few days ahead of time. It was assumed (without asking) they would just order the pumpkin from the noted local market garden. All this happened around the end of September. The local grocery store assured me they could fulfill this order in time.

Time went on. About a week before Halloween, Anne reminded me about the pumpkin. I dropped by the grocery store to see how things were going. They didn't have the pumpkin yet, but again assured me "it was ordered and on the way."

This seemed strange. If it "was on the way" from a place not far away, like the Souris Valley market garden, then it should be arriving in a matter of hours. "We'll call you when it's here." I reminded the grocery store that it had to be picked up by Halloween and that it was to be thirty pounds. "No problem," was their assuring answer.

Halloween arrived without a call from the grocery store. Going in after work, I said that the thirty-pound pumpkin was needed now. They looked kind of sheepish while saying they had the pumpkin, but it may not be what I wanted. My reply was a simple. "Let's see it." They led me through the plastic flap "door" leading to the warehouse in the back of the store. What I saw going through that "door" was startling—and hilarious!

Here was a three-hundred-plus-pound pumpkin on a gurney! A great big three-hundred-pound pumpkin!

Stunned, I said, "I ordered a thirty-pound pumpkin!"

They had ordered the pumpkin from California, which is why it "was on the way." The grocery store had just received it that afternoon. A rather obvious question was then asked: "Why didn't you just order it from the local market garden?" No answer. The next question from my lips was, "Why did you order a three-hundred-pound pumpkin?" Somebody had "slipped" a zero in somewhere.

There was no way I could take that pumpkin. They agreed to keep it. I hurried out of the store and headed to the market garden, arriving just in time before they closed. Of course, they had plenty of thirty-pound pumpkins, so the nicest one was immediately selected and taken home. I told Anne what had happened, and she replied with gales of laughter! The result? A bruised male ego but a laughing smile on my face.

What was learned from this?

To start with, I was just a tad lazy. I could have taken a quick trip to the market garden and ordered the pumpkin. I and the grocery store made the request far more complicated than needs be. We all were certainly very embarrassed! Next, I should have paid attention to my intuition when I wondered why it was taking so long. I should have asked where the pumpkin was coming from. Actually, I should have asked where they were going to get the pumpkin from when I ordered it! Thirdly, I sure learned that special orders require special attention— from both the person ordered from and the person doing the ordering.

To this day, Anne and I don't like to buy something unless we see it, if at all possible. I ordered from the grocery store because it was convenient in a very small way. That convenience was illusionary—silly, laughable, but illusionary. The extra time and bother resulting from ordering "online" in the old-fashioned way nearly burnt us. Point learned; point taken.

CHAPTER 14
I Was Outnumbered!

It was noted in "Bank Manager Tough Love" that we had a sports car. It was a Triumph TR250. It was actually our second sports car; the first was a Triumph TR4. Both of these cars are discussed and described later on in this book. From the "Bank Manager" chapter you will see that selling the TR250 was essentially an act of me (Jim) growing up a bit and becoming more fiscally responsible. Plus, it became part of the lesson that we had to learn to live within our means. It also meant giving up something I liked for our family, which included two children. It certainly made sense to do this for many obvious and good reasons at the time of sale. Those cars, while great looking and handling, were actually a maintenance nightmare.

I should have been happy to get rid of the TR250 in 1970, correct? Not really. Anne and I didn't know the Lord at the time and ... well ... the "boys with their toys" syndrome was still inside me. While it really didn't make sense to even have that TR250, it was fun for a male to drive, and it looked great!

I accepted my responsibilities and went on with life. Anne could see something had been given up that really meant a lot to me. She encouraged me to move forward, and by 1984 we had a pretty good life in many ways while still working toward a better one. She wasn't ignorant, though—she demonstrated that she could use my male ego and "toy wants" to her advantage!

In 1984 we were on one of my field trips for my oilfield service company. We had bought a used cabin cruiser boat and stored it on the Shuswap Lake in British Columbia. It was fun to use on the lake, but it was like the TR250—a bear to maintain. The boat was constantly in need of parts and maintenance. At the time of the field trip we were in North Battleford, Saskatchewan, which had a big outdoor recreational store. When we were done with my marketing duties, we went to the store so I could see if they had any boat parts, which would invariably be needed.

Yes, they did!

Without consulting Anne, I started to look around to see what else they had in the boating and camping line by going off on my own and browsing. At this point Anne was "lost" by me somewhere in the store. This was easy to do because the shelves were high and Anne was short! Finally realizing she was no longer with me, and further realizing I had neglected to pay attention to her, the search for her began. Never in my mind did it occur to me that she'd find something to buy, because this was a "guy store." It wasn't only a bad assumption, but it resulted in a turning point in our lives.

After looking around in places where it was assumed she would be, and never thinking she'd be thinking anything but what I would be thinking (talk about male ego), I consulted a clerk and asked if he knew where Anne was. The answer shocked me!

"Oh, she's over looking at our motorcycles."

Pause here. I had never been on any motorcycle, let alone driven one. My first thought was "Anne's got to be kidding!" I had parked the thought of actually ever having one, along with the memories of the TR4 and the TR250. Now that we were much older, the thought of buying a "bike" wasn't in my mind at all!

Speedily walking over to the motorcycle section revealed something troubling to me at the time. Here she was sitting on the back of a 1984 Honda Gold Wing on the passenger seat with a great big smile on her face! As I approached her, she blurted out, "I like this! I could sit back here and cuddle!"

Come on! She could hardly reach the passenger foot pegs with her feet! Humouring her, I helped her off. At that point she said, "Jim, I'm not kidding. We should get one of these bikes." I didn't humour her much at that point, but she got the salesman to come over and persuaded me to ask the cost of one of these big, heavy motorcycles. Frankly, I didn't even listen. I just grunted and hustled Anne out of that store as quickly as possible.

Anne didn't stop. The next time we went to North Battleford, she persuaded me to go back to the store and look at the Wings. This occurred each time we went to that town. The salesman kept "helping" her, but it was made pretty clear by me—no deal! This went on until late 1985. Then I got smart ... or so I thought. Some research on my part revealed the most popular colour scheme on the 1985 1200A Aspencade Gold Wing was beige and brown. I kept an eye on how many of these Gold Wings of that colour were left to be bought. It became very clear that bikes of that particular popular colour scheme in that model were completely sold out by September—in Alberta. Smirking to myself and agreeing to go one more time to the North Battleford store, I watched Anne and the salesman try one more time to sell me that motorcycle. It had been made very clear to Anne that this was the absolute final time we would do this or even consider it!

That final trip to the North Battleford store occurred in October, which was essentially beyond the motorcycling season. No matter, I wasn't trained to drive and ride these behemoths, and I had absolutely no intention of getting such training. After all, this silly exercise was going to come to an end—a very definite end.

With the two of us sitting down with the salesman, I prepared to say "No" for the final time. An offer was made that actually shocked me—it was really quite good! Still, I declined. Both Anne and the salesman looked very disappointed, but the salesman asked one question: "Just what do I have to do to get you to buy one of these bikes?"

Aha! My time to shine! "Just find me a beige and brown Aspencade!"

"That's easy," he replied. "I have one in a crate out back!"

Anne and the salesman really got on my case. I couldn't back down, because Anne made sure I was going to keep my promise! As she was so on side, I was outnumbered one to one with her. When that happens, any smart husband knows it's time to back down. As I had outsmarted myself with the colour scheme angle, it was time for me to finally be smart and realize I had lost the argument.

We bought the Wing. He asked what accessories I wanted on it, and I bought what they had in the store. Everything. If we were going to get into this, we might as well go full out! In addition, a small motorcycle was purchased to train on. Our training was done in the spring of 1986. We bought full clothing and communication and helmet gear for use on the big Wing. After passing the training course and getting my license, we went out to pick up the Wing later that spring.

Going from a 100cc small bike to a 1200cc touring motorcycle was a little scary at first, but now I wouldn't trade the touring experience with Anne sitting behind me for anything! Anne with her short legs is a happy professional passenger!

Later we were travelling north of Edmonton, Alberta, and Anne commented through the helmet communicators: "You really liked your TR250, didn't you?" Replying in the affirmative, it was also noted that was in the past. Anne's reply? "No, it matters. You see this Gold Wing we're on? This is your boy toy. You're to keep this until it craters or you crater."

Now you the reader can see I have one smart wife! Not only had she observed what was bothering me just a little bit, but now that we were getting "beyond kids," she'd made sure she had "outnumbered me one to one" in the purchase of something she knew would be good for me. She had shown she really cared for me, and we started a new part of our life.

Our 1985 Gold Wing? Anne is proud of me as I really care for our motorcycle. We love getting on our shiny, beige and brown bike and touring along the highways of British Columbia. It's over thirty-three years old and looks and drives like new! It's not a maintenance nightmare like the old Triumphs. It hasn't cratered yet—nor have I!

And for you sales and marketing types who are reading this—always ask the final question. And be sure the wife is enthusiastically on side!

CHAPTER 15
Looking Old, Looking Young

We've all seen how people's physical looks can lead an observer to believe they are old, middle aged, or young. Quite often we judge people's ages by the physical look of their faces. We're often surprised to discover that our judgement is way off course! This holds very true for Anne and me. What is interesting is the reaction from the two of us and others when the truth comes out!

As mentioned earlier, I wouldn't ask Anne out because she looked like she was in her mid or early teens, while I was eighteen. My upbringing taught me it was improper for an older male to date a mid-teen or younger girl. When I found out she was only three and a half weeks my junior, I was thrilled! As I got older, I liked noting that I married a trophy wife right off the bat! Anne's apparent age from her neck up never did jibe with her apparent age from her neck down. While now viewing this as a blessing, for many years after we were married it made me the butt of jokes.

Anne never has made it a habit to wear makeup. When she puts on a little makeup it does accentuate her youthful look, but she doesn't need to wear any makeup to look young or beautiful. Aside from her natural beauty, this absence of makeup made for great economies. What thrills me personally is what you see in Anne is what you get—there are no stories about people seeing her "beautifully made up" and then later viewing her as shockingly plain or less than lovely without makeup. Yes, the beauty you see in Anne is indeed the natural beauty you get.

I, on the other hand, have always looked at best "slightly" older. When Anne met me I already had a naturally high forehead. Even with youthful, brown, wavy hair, I looked slightly older prior to us being married. After marriage, my high forehead rapidly got worse, making me look all the older. About sixteen years into our marriage, my hair rapidly turned grey, becoming white in later years. Anne's hair stayed brown until into our retirement, and then only slowly showed signs of grey after that.

When we were courting, the apparent difference in ages caused great consternation for my mother and father. I almost had to produce Anne's birth certificate to prove her age! It didn't come to this, but I remember my mother checking the marriage papers for Anne's age! Anne did indeed look younger than she was.

Later in life when we had our new 1985 Gold Wing, two things happened that at first were extremely frustrating and embarrassing to me, while being extremely humorous to Anne. The first instance occurred when we took the Wing out to Vernon, British Columbia for a trip to see our land. We had no legitimate accommodation on our land at the time, so we decided to check into a motel for a base while we were there. We were both wearing black leathers and black full-face helmets at the time. These leathers, while being full thick motorcycling leathers, were not sloppy on our bodies. Anne and I got off the Wing, took our helmets off, and went into the motel lobby to see if they had a room. We went up to the front desk, and I asked if they had a room available.

"Yes, for how many nights?" asked the clerk as he looked us over.

"A couple, please," was my reply.

The clerk then looked me over again and asked: "Would you like the seniors' rate?"

We were in our early forties. Realizing that my grey hair and high forehead may have caused the misperception, I replied in an embarrassed tone, "No, I'm not even fifty yet."

I could feel embarrassment welling up in my face, but I held my composure. The clerk eyed me again, and then looked at Anne.

"And would you like a separate room for your daughter?" he asked.

Well, Anne started laughing! I, on the other hand, must have been turning red, because even my ears felt hot! I stammered out, "No, this is my wife, Anne, and she is only three and a half weeks my junior!" Anne helped (I think) by laughingly confirming this.

The look the clerk gave us was one of great skepticism, but he took our word for it. We checked in.

As we got to our room, Anne suggested we leave a big tip for that clerk, because he thought she was young. My answer then is not repeatable in polite company.

The second event started from a silly driving error on my part. Again, the 1985 Gold Wing was involved. Anne and I went camping with the Wing—real camping, with a small tent and the whole works stuffed into a small aluminum trailer towed behind the Wing. We were on our way to Meadow Lake in Saskatchewan when it started to rain. The rain didn't last long, but it did soak the ground. Up until the southern end of the park the road was paved. From there on the road was "compact" sand. This was a nice ride in dry weather because it was well maintained and very smooth. In damp weather, the sand road was relatively packed, but it was still sand. On one curve, I decided to "ride high" on the banked curve—almost at the edge of the road—in second gear. At the top of the curve, the road gave way! Down we went. I flipped the engine cut off switch; the sand was very soft, so nothing was damaged except one mirror, which was later easily fixed. The fall with the bike had crammed sand into the engine area and behind a lot of the plastic covers. Anne and I got the bike up and running and then proceeded slowly to the campsite.

At our campsite, we got out of our leathers and switched into lighter clothing. Anne changed into a blouse and short shorts. I unhitched the trailer and set up the tent then drove the Wing down to the water tap to clean the sand out from behind all the covers and the engine area. The water tap was about six wide campsites away.

It wasn't really a problem cleaning out the sand. Nothing was damaged, other than the one mirror. I was greatly relieved to see this as I flushed out the sand. My mood was changing from one of concern to one of looking forward to the next few days!

I looked back toward our campsite but couldn't see it because it was around a curve, and the area was well treed. I observed an older lady stomping down the road from the area of our campsite toward me. She had a look of anger or disgust or both on her face as she approached me. Initially thinking she was probably mad over my use of the water pump area to clean my bike, I prepared to answer accordingly. What she said stunned and shocked me as she began to take a strip off my hide!

A pause here. As noted above, Anne always looked younger than me. On top of that, she was a gorgeous woman in shorts and a blouse, which she was wearing now. Read on!

That woman could yell at someone for the longest time without taking a breath! At first I listened, because what she was saying wasn't making any sense. Then I realized she was tearing a strip off me because she was of the very firm opinion that I was some high-powered, grey- headed executive type on a fancy motorcycle who was shacked up with my very sexy-looking secretary on an illicit rendezvous up here in northern Saskatchewan!

When she finally took a brief pause for a breath before continuing on her rant, I stammered that the extremely sexy looking young lady was my wife, and she was only three and a half weeks my junior. The first word out of her mouth was "Liar!" I then offered to take her back to talk to Anne. She said that she didn't want to be involved in any way with our immoral undertakings. Blessedly, she then took off.

Finishing up my work saw my anger grow. When done, I got on the Wing and drove back to our campsite. I must have been some sight, because Anne asked what was wrong as I got off the Wing. I angrily explained the butt chewing that had happened, along with the reason behind it. Anne broke out laughing! All I stammered as I pouted was that she had to realize that I look old and she looked so young. She came up to me and gave me a big hug and said, "And this is a problem?" Then I got a big kiss and saw the humour of the situation.

Upon reflection, my embarrassment was due to my ego as I realized how old I look in comparison to Anne. I should have known then that Anne was also a "looker," especially in short shorts and a blouse or tight motorcycle leathers. Reflecting on the situations now, I am extremely grateful I have such a young looking, naturally beautiful woman for my wife and life partner. Granted, we are both older now. Well, I look older … Anne still looks much younger than me when we stand together. It's amusing to see older men giving sideways glances at her youthful looks and smiling face. I also am very grateful for her youthful enthusiasm, as it keeps me feeling young as well!

CHAPTER 16
Does a Degree Always Make You Superior?

This story is a bit tongue in cheek. As noted before, I have a BSc with a major in Chemistry. The service company I worked for hired engineers and earth scientists, like geologists and geophysicists. It has always appeared to me that I was the only chemist hired by that company in Canada during the time I worked for them. It was obvious to me that some engineers viewed me as something less than them. I also fully admit that I struggled to get my degree. Everything practically possible needed to be personally learned about what the engineers, geologists, and geophysicists knew in order to be able to understand my customers' needs and how to address them. Gaining technical knowledge intimate to those needs resulted in a better sales and service representative than I would have been based on my chemist education. True, there were "things chemical" that helped me with certain interpretation needs, but that was a bonus for me.

Working with people became a specialty to me, both to benefit the people worked for—clients and those in my company—and for me as well. One time an engineer in my service company complained about me to my boss. I was not told why; however, I was informed that my boss replied to the complainant by saying, "Yeah, but he can sure sell!" Interesting perspective!

Does a degree always make you superior? It's a very valuable beginning! Part of this type of education is to teach you how to think and problem solve. Learning how to problem solve and applying that knowledge enabled me to earn my degree. After getting my degree, the ability to think and apply thinking became critical to my success in my service company. What degree I had didn't dictate how I accomplished this. As long as I continued building on what was learned while getting my degree, plus what was learned doing my job, along with working with people, my employment continued and thrived.

So what about the superior point? And what about the bit about a chemist versus an engineer? Pause here a moment and consider that not all the people in the oil patch have degrees. Not all upper management in oil companies and service companies had degrees during my time in the industry. Yet those people did very well. Their rise to their positions may have been more difficult, but to be blunt, they knew their business far better than some of us with post-secondary education!

Let's examine a very humorous incident that occurred while I was working as a field sales and service representative in central Alberta. In the service company district I was in at the time, management took a bank of computers off a wrecked truck and put it in the shop to use to check downhole equipment. This freed up field units to do their job in the field. It was a neat setup and was used extensively.

One day I came back from my field sales calls and saw six engineers swarming around this shop computer. It became obvious very quickly that something was wrong. Operations manuals were all out. Switches were being thrown, buttons pushed, and everybody was consulting one another. Something wasn't working. The engineers hadn't called the instrument technician yet, as they wanted to solve the problem themselves. Good on them … to a point.

I walked by and casually asked if there was a problem and if there was something I could do to help. No, they were going to check everything out first. I asked what these six highly qualified young individuals thought was the problem. The reply was simple: "We're not getting power."

I just smiled and walked to the right, beside the computer bank, and saw something that led me to tell all six of these engineers to "come here, please." Keep in mind, I was in my forties while the engineers were in their twenties— "old dad" working with some "sons."

All of them came over and saw what I saw. An electrical cord not plugged into the wall for power. We all laughed. I then remarked that all six of those guys were indeed thinking, but from the top down rather than from the bottom up. Check the simple things first, folks!

The degree doesn't make you superior—it's how you use your degree. If what you learned is not of use to you, others, your company, or your institution, your degree could be no more than a nice piece of framed paper on the wall.

CHAPTER 17
Lincoln over the Cliff

It always "amused" me that so often when I was getting comfortable with what I was doing in my assigned job, I would be transferred! In hindsight, this was actually quite good, because the jobs I transferred to in my last twenty years with my company caused me to grow experientially. That being said, it was frustrating as well, because there was never an opportunity to vegetate in place and relax! I now believe this was the company's goal.

Life was going pretty smoothly when I was the salesman in Edmonton after transferring from Medicine Hat—not only in my job, but in the oil industry as well. I was therefore quite happy to hear that my boss from Calgary was coming up to see me. We were to meet at the airport in downtown Edmonton. My ego expected a big "thank you" and a raise, especially since a fairly flattering appraisal had just been received. It was assumed a sign off on that appraisal would take place, getting me back to work with more money in my pocket.

Well, a surprise occurred. Because I had done so well, my boss had glowingly recommended a transfer to Lloydminster, Alberta/Saskatchewan to either help grow it or get it shut down. With me getting a raise. While working with both the cased hole and open hole evaluation sides of that district, I would still be reporting to Calgary. My job was to evaluate the situation and do whatever would help get things back on track, or recommend the operation shut down.

My mind flashed back to the time I was manager in Medicine Hat. I hadn't done well there and had been demoted to a lower level salesman in Edmonton, reporting to Calgary. True, I had done very well marketing in Edmonton and had been promoted to a grade equivalent of a manager in operations. While this was my position at the time of the proposed move to Lloydminster, I was a bit scared when informed of where I was going and why. I was going out to Lloydminster under circumstances similar to what happened to me in Medicine Hat to ensure our business was turned around. To me hearing this in Edmonton at the downtown airport, failure was not an option.

The offer was accepted. Quickly in Lloydminster work was begun with a very competent manager who, like me, was not an engineer. Indeed, he had no degree at all. He did have one quality, though—he worked with people and wanted to work with me. I soon wanted to work with him! Between the two of us, we helped turn that district around and made it thrive. Both of us were lauded as the team that helped turn a dying entity into a thriving one. All the employees of our district were proud of being part of a winning team, including the shop employees.

One of those shop employees was an interesting individual. He liked big Lincoln Continentals and would go to auctions to buy them. As I recall, he had three of these big two-door monsters, each loaded with all the nice amenities. He loved driving a different one to the shop every time he could.

All this occurred in one of the centres of Canada's heavy oil industry, right on the border of Alberta and Saskatchewan. As we improved our performance for the industry, the price of heavy oil coincidentally rose steadily. Everything was going great, so we weren't only financially and operationally growing, we were flat out busy. They were good times!

But oil prices fluctuate, and when they get too high, they tend to crash. While history shows this type of price collapse is temporary, any responsible company will retrench when the business suddenly slows to the point where it cannot support its infrastructure in a certain area. This happened in Lloydminster within a two-month span, right after a peak time. We had to shut down the district. Everybody was either transferred, quit, or in (fortunately) a few cases, let go. I was in my office wrapping affairs up for my next transfer when into my office came the Lincoln owner all in a dither. I knew where he was going to be transferred but couldn't tell him because he wasn't my employee. I worked for Calgary; he worked for the manager in Lloydminster.

He excitedly started exclaiming, "Jim, Jim—what's going to happen to all of us? Where are we going to go? What are we going to do?"

I was pretty sure that where he was being transferred to would be a plum location, and he possibly might get generous moving expenses, so I was in a bit of a quandary. He actually had nothing to worry about, as it looked like he was going to a better location. I couldn't say anything about this, so I said the following: "Well, it's like riding around in one of your Continentals. You're going along, windows up, air conditioning on, smooth as it gets, stereo playing away. Suddenly, you drive off a cliff! *You can't back up, so you might as well enjoy the ride down!*"

We both stopped. He settled down and asked, "Do you think we will be okay?" I replied to the effect that since he'd been doing such a great job, as long as he continued doing so, he should be okay. A short time later he was in his new job. I have no idea if he kept his Lincolns.

The point is, as it will be in many cases in this book, do your job to the best of your abilities. Don't quit doing your best when circumstances seem to be going sideways. In all of the cases I was involved with in the oil industry, anyone who did this stayed employed and, in most cases, prospered. Even when you cannot do something about the company you work for, make sure you're performing your job well. Even when it appears you have driven off a cliff, stand back, look at the situation, and continue doing your job well.

CHAPTER 18
Humility Check

I experienced a very well-defined and appropriate humility check in the late 1980s when I was transferred to Calgary from Edmonton. Prior to this transfer I'd occasionally get four tickets to the Edmonton Oilers hockey games from my service company. Anne and I would then take customers to these professional hockey games. We were Edmonton Oilers fans when Wayne Gretzky played for them … rabid fans, especially for Wayne! So rabid that when transferred to Calgary, I still rooted for the Oilers and Gretzky!

One day Wayne Gretzky was traded to an opposing American team. Livid, I stomped around my company's Calgary office (which happened to be the Canadian headquarters), grousing bitterly. Finally, my boss came up to me and said something to the effect of "What the heck is bugging you, Edgson?"

To this I replied, "The Oilers sold Gretzky! There's no way Gretzky should have been sold or traded! Even for a million dollars!"

My boss took his index finger and gently and rapidly poked it in my chest as he said, "Listen, if someone came to me and offered us one million dollars for you, you'd be gone in a heartbeat!" He then walked away.

Whoa! What a comeuppance! I suddenly realized how silly and stupid this sounded from me, especially in the light of my behaviour in my company's office. What if this behaviour occurred in front of a customer, especially in Calgary, where their own hockey team was probably delighted their Edmonton rivals had done something so stupid? Obviously I settled down, not only because of how silly this sounded, but because I'd been reminded that I wasn't indispensable. Looking back now, my observation certainly made sense! My thoughts at the time sobered up with that revelation.

Soon after the Gretzky trade, when no longer an Oilers fan (like about ten minutes after my boss smartened me up), I had a sobering thought. This thought came to mind often whenever I got the occasional proud, indispensable feeling again—no one ever did offer a million dollars for me. Ever! To this day I'm not sure what was the greater humility check—the fact that I would be gone if someone offered a million dollars for me, or the fact that no one ever did!

CHAPTER 19
Joys of Looking, Listening, and Paying Attention

Sometimes we're too busy to just look, listen, and pay attention. Sometimes we make an attempt to slow down and take advantage of what nature might put in front of us, but we still get too "business like" to really absorb all the sights and memories of something that may be right in front of us. Other times we get upset at something and completely miss what is right around us. Both of the following stories originate from wild-berry-picking experiences Anne and I have had. While this may seem to make them less applicable to "normal" circumstances, read on! They may be of help.

The first is a short story of a little mousey in east central Alberta that gave Anne and me a cute and precious memory, causing us to reflect on the blessings we'll have if we just pay attention, even while looking for something else.

We were on one of my field trips southeast of Wainwright, Alberta and were passing by a small Saskatchewan park just east of the Alberta border. As we were ahead of time and only needed to get to a motel, we decided to stop and look around. There was a small lake with a beach, picnic tables, and a recreation area—nothing unusual. Then we spotted some ripe wild chokecherries! As noted elsewhere, we are berry pickers. There was no one around; we had a cooler and the means to pick the berries, so we got right after the task. Very quickly running out of berries where I was picking, I left Anne to finish off her area while I went looking in the nearby poplar forest. I found some, but only where sunlight got through. Going deeper in the forest I saw more open spots for me to pick.

There was no wind or highway noise, and I was too far away to hear Anne working. Picking a particularly great spot, I was distracted by a "crunch, crunch" sound. I stood bolt upright! Bear? Other wild animal? Looking around—nothing. The sound seemed to have stopped when I moved, so back I went to picking.

"Crunch, crunch." This time I only moved my head. Looking around, about fifteen metres away I saw an old, discarded potato chip bag with the opening face up. The bag was moving in place! I slowly got up and very quietly moved over to take a look inside. As I got closer, the crunching sound got louder. It was coming from the bag, which was moving gently.

I carefully looked inside. Here was a little mousey busy chomping away on the remaining chips in the bag. I gently left and ran over to Anne. We came back and approached the crunching bag, looked inside, and were overjoyed to see the little mousey look up at us and then go back to his meal. Never have we seen this again. Precious memory!

The other instance involved berry picking again. Anne was upset because we had moved from a house with lots of pin cherry bushes, which she had used to make delicious jelly. She was actually quite upset! We were on our way to see a historic site in northeastern Alberta and were passing through a long path arched by tall, branched bushes. Anne was pontificating about her loss of a wild berry source and not really taking in the immediate sites as we looked around. I was looking and saw something.

When Anne took a breath, I said, "Anne, did those pin cherry bushes have dark bark with marks that resembled those of a birch tree?" She replied to the affirmative and described the berries. "Like these surrounding us?" I asked.

Her head snapped *way* up and sideways, and the joy was palpable. We were surrounded by pin cherries! We ran back to the car, found bags to pick with, and got busy picking. We now had a wonderful berry picking spot for the future as well!

As noted, sometimes we're way too busy in our lives to just look, listen, and pay attention. Sometimes we should slow down and take advantage of what nature might put in front of us. Try not to get too "business like." Absorb sites and memories, some of which may be right in front of you. Never assume you cannot find something unique in your surroundings. You may be pleasantly surprised by what you actually find. Take some time and fulfill your life!

CHAPTER 20
Using "Graft" Constructively

Graft is an ugly word and one I don't like to use. It has a bad connotation, and it smacks of someone using an easy, lazy way out to reach a goal. In its basest form, it's immoral and quite likely illegal. This was evident to me as far back as pre-university days. I particularly dislike how some people viewed it as acceptable, because "it didn't hurt anyone." I felt this attitude was very self-centred—it may not hurt you, the one taking the easy way out in accomplishing your goals, but it did hurt me and others who strived to accomplish their goals legitimately. That's why I decided during my oil patch days to see if there was a way of using gifts legitimately and having some fun while accomplishing my goals in a manner that built up my company and my customers.

One of the first opportunities presented to me came when an oil company friend phoned me up about a golf tournament his company was putting on. He'd done this before when looking for small prizes from oilfield service companies. These small gifts were used to provide inexpensive advertising for those companies as the oil company employees were playing golf— things like logo-stamped golf balls, coasters, playing cards, coffee mugs, and the like. He wasn't looking for fishing trips or expensive items that could be used to influence peddle. I and my company had no problem providing these small types of advertising gifts. Many service companies were solicited for these items, so no one company could be viewed as a "favourite." At the same time, these minor items could be construed as "graft," so my company firmly instructed us that we wouldn't give these trifles on the condition of getting business. Under those noted circumstances, such things would be considered legitimate gifts.

This time my oil company friend phoned me up to have some fun. He had a young, very stuffy professional engineer working for him who was legalistic about everything, so much so that he refused to do business with someone in a service company who was not a professional engineer, geologist, or geophysicist. I was not such an individual; I was a chemist by education. I had a professional reputation with my friend because I made it a point to be legitimately knowledgeable about his business so I could be helpful to him. My friend told me all this in a prelude to his request of me, which was actually quite funny. He told me he was putting that young engineer in charge of getting gifts for his company's upcoming golf tournament, and that he'd be contacting me first. He and I both knew the young engineer would balk at that, because I wasn't a "professional" in his mind. I laughed, agreed, and we set the plot.

The next day the young engineer called and nervously asked for the gifts, obviously uncomfortable in the task with which he'd been charged. The reply agreed upon by me and my friend was, "Sure. How much graft do you want?" The young engineer immediately hung up. About two hours later my friend called, laughing his head off. The young engineer had come in to see him, almost in tears, and blurting out what he'd heard. Then my friend tore a strip off the young fellow and let him know he'd been set up! From what I heard, the young engineer was told to quit being so stuffy and learn the difference between a minor gift and genuine graft. Hopefully he learned a lesson. For that occasion, I provided logo-stamped golf balls and playing cards to my friend.

Another common sales approach was to take clients out for lunch. I say "out for lunch" rather than "out for lunch hour" deliberately. The so-called lunch hour generally started at 11:30 a.m. and lasted until at least 1:30 p.m. Hardly an hour. I confess I used this method quite a bit until I noted that quite often I was going out to lunch with the "influencers" who could recommend something but not actually approve a purchase. The approving people were called "the buyers." These buyers rarely went out for lunch unless they were with smaller oil companies. Often the lunch break was, at best, the first step in a two or three step process to getting the sale. Eventually the buyer had to get involved. One day I decided to see if the process could be shortened. I went over to a particular oil company at 11:30 a.m. and stuck around during lunch.

While my competitors were taking out the influencers, the buyers were staying behind, using the precious two-hour time frame to do their work. About noon they asked who I was there to see. When I told them I was looking at a more efficient way of serving them, the buyers invited me in and we had an uninterrupted session in which I learned about their legitimate concerns, and they learned how my company would either help them or would find out how we could help them. Then I would leave, taking up far less of their real lunch hour than if they'd gone out.

It wasn't too long before I'd receive a call after lunch, about 2:00 p.m., from an influencer, telling me that his boss-buyer had "requested him" to call me, have me come over, and explain to him something of interest to his company. This led quickly to a sale or two, because the buyer had already indicated it would be fine with him if the influencer agreed.

I had to customize my approach to each oil company. Some really liked the above approach, but some wanted to conclude business with my company and then go out to lunch to discuss details. Most importantly, I got far more business by treating this as a customized opportunity to work with others as opposed to "lunch graft."

The final personal tactic which on the surface could be considered constructive graft was the chocolate coated almonds approach. This idea began back when I had a client-buyer in rural Saskatchewan who would not personally see me. The influencers would see me, but no sales resulted. When mulling over this problem back home in Calgary, a youngster came knocking on our door asking if I'd support the local youth sports team by buying a small box of chocolate almonds. My mind clicked into gear, and I bought a whole carton of boxes! The youngster and his mother were thrilled!

I carried these small boxes on my next field trip, including to the rural Saskatchewan office. As per usual, the buyer was in his office but refused to see me. Indeed, he kept his door shut tight! The influencers, the production engineers, welcomed me in, but the buyer had to approve anything they recommended. My reply? "Not a problem! Just let me stick around a bit this time and watch what happens." The production engineers saw me smiling, got curious, and agreed to sit and talk with me and wait.

The buyer's office was at the front and had to be passed to get to the production engineers. On my way by I propped up one of the small boxes of chocolate almonds on the door knob. When—and if—he opened the door, it would come crashing down!

About ten minutes later we heard the loud "crash" of a box of chocolate almonds falling to the floor. I and the engineers were all holding back our laughter as the buyer—the boss—came down the hall to the offices we were in, munching chocolate almonds, and said "Alright, Edgson, you win!" From that point on I regularly saw the boss—the buyer! So began the chocolate almond sales approach.

Shortly after this episode my company had small, logo-stamped candy jars manufactured that were handed out full of candies as a one-time Christmas promotion. I took it a step further. Getting my hands on dozens of these jars, distribution proceeded to all my clients, both in Calgary and all over my contact route in southern Alberta and Saskatchewan. I would request the oil company office receptionist to keep the jars handy, which I then filled with chocolate coated almonds each time I came. I would buy cases full of bags of these almonds and carry them around with me. One bag would fill the little jars about two and a half times. Each time I visited, the logo-stamped jar would be filled and the partially emptied bag left with the receptionist. Believe me, every receptionist knew me by name, and for some reason it most often seemed I was received to see those who most needed to be seen. With some exceptions.

One exception in particular was another buyer in a different field in Saskatchewan who absolutely refused to see me, even if phoned weeks in advance. No matter—I would go out each time, fill the jar, leave the bag, and ask if the customer was available. Never. This went on for months. By this time, Anne was coming with me and would sit in the reception area and knit while I actually visited the client. The receptionists in the country were often interested in why she travelled around with me. They all got quite friendly with Anne. This story's one receptionist was no different.

One day after attempting to set up an appointment, Anne and I dropped by the office. I asked for the customer, and the receptionist gave the usual answer that he wasn't available. I filled the jar and was leaving the bag with the remaining almonds when the receptionist got a stern look on her face and said to me, "Wait here a minute." She got up and went down the hall. The customer came out looking very mad and said, "Come in." He took me into his office and gave me the line about how busy he was … too busy to see me. I asked him if there was anything he could think of that my company might possibly be able to help him with. Startled, he sat back in his chair and said, "Maybe." The ice was broken.

I listened, and two face-to-face meeting trips to his office later, we started to do business.

After a few months of doing some business, the customer was finally asked what had happened to get him to see me. He was surprised to hear that I didn't know. It turns out the receptionist told him I was there and asked if he would see me. He had said absolutely not! The receptionist said, "Well, Mrs. Edgson is here, and I'm going to talk with her a bit. What do you want me to do with Mr. Edgson?"

Talk about a brave receptionist! Bear in mind this was in a small prairie town, and good receptionists were hard to find. The point is, small, meaningful gifts consistently and thoughtfully given are a means to sometimes get you in the door. Giving as a sign you truly care about your clients and believe you can possibly help their business is not graft.

The final valuable lesson about the chocolate almonds was the income brought in versus the outlay for the effort. I did quite well; my sales expenses were generally lower than all the other salesmen (in my instance, mostly cases of chocolate almonds). My overall sales were quite high. It's true the nature of my responsibilities was such that very few gigantic sales resulted, but many small sales from many appreciative clients who would continue to use us as long as they were consistently and thoughtfully treated added up to very large overall income for my company.

CHAPTER 21
Antricot Wine

When Anne and I were full into our young oil patch days, we did occasionally behave the way many people who viewed people in the oil patch as behaving. Note I said we behaved this way occasionally. And our heads and bodies suffered accordingly! While later in our lives we viewed this behaviour with embarrassment, we do not overtly and judgementally condemn others who engage in similar behaviour out in public. Instead, knowing how harmful and silly our behaviour was, we quietly stand back until help is needed. As noted, we were guilty at one time!

Sometimes these "events" can be life lessons. This particular event was one of them and still influences us today. While we laugh and others laugh with us, it gives everybody pause to think about our conduct now and in the future.

Anne's dad—and my dad early and later in life for that matter—loved the "occasional" drink. We will refer to Anne's dad throughout this story as "Dad." And he was—to both of us. He was a merry old guy around us when his drinking went too far. He was skilled in many basic crafts, including the making of wine … from anything. Anne noted he could make wine from everything from avocadoes to zucchini (A to Z). Most of the wine he made that I sampled was best politely commented on and put aside. Most of the wine he made I sampled when I was sober.

One day Anne and I went up to visit Dad and Mom in Smith, Alberta, where Dad was stationed as a railway agent. In the evening we started to celebrate. All this began in the Smith bar, where we partook of many a beer. We went back to Dad and Mom's home (not too far away in Smith) and continued to deplete Dad's beer supply. We were quite pleasantly looped by this time. Then we decided to carry on with Dad's whisky supply until that depleted. None of us were under the table yet, so I asked Dad if he had anything else we could drink. He did. Antricot wine, which he had made.

Dad poured me a tall glass of this wine and I sampled it. It was absolutely the best wine I had ever tasted! I downed that glass and asked for more. At this point I should have noticed a twinkle in his eye, but his wine was so good I just had to have some more! After a couple more tall glasses of that homemade stuff, I got sleepy. We all decided to hit the sack.

As the reader can guess, I woke up in the morning with a roaring hangover. My head was throbbing so hard that if I'd put a hat on, the rim would have split from my head's movement! Two things mitigated that thought: the absolutely marvellous wine Dad had made, and the old theory that the best thing for a hangover was partaking of "a hair of the dog which bit you." Keep in mind I was unabashedly drunk when I drank his wine the night before.

"Dad, have you got any more of that great wine you gave me last night?" I asked as my head pounded away.

Again with a twinkle in his eye, he said, "Oh yes" and poured another tumbler of the wine for me. I took a *big* drink. Now I was sober. It tasted terrible! There was no way I could drink any more of that stuff! Everyone around me laughed with me at my reaction. Then I stopped and asked Dad why he called this stuff Antricot wine.

He explained that he made wine from lots of things. I knew that. He had received a whole bunch of over ripe and past due Apricots from the owner of the general store in Smith at no charge. Dad made up his batches of wine in a large, plastic garbage pail with a plastic lid and then let the mash stew. I nodded as he explained this.

Dad further explained: "One day I went to check the wine mash and noticed the lid was ajar. I checked inside and found that a very large number of ants had gotten in, probably because they smelled the sweetness. They had all drowned and completely covered the top of the stewing wine. Rather than waste the product, I just skimmed the ants off and called the finished wine "Antricot wine!"

I guess what blood I had in my head appeared to drain away at that point. Everyone else was laughing their heads off at my expense! But there were some lessons to be learned here that I use to this day.

First, don't get drunk. If you must have a drink, do so in moderation.

Second, if you don't obey number one, don't get so drunk you lose not only your senses but also your sense of taste.

Three, if you don't obey number one and two, then you'd better make sure you know what you're drinking before you even begin—and don't try anything new at that point!

Four, if you don't obey numbers one through three, and are suffering the head blowing consequences and decide to take "a hair of the dog which bit you," you'd better be sober enough to understand that the hair you drink may not taste like you thought it did when you were drunk!

That was the last time I ever allowed myself to get that drunk. In the end, I learned how to be moderate with alcohol because of Dad's Antricot wine. Perhaps that is the lesson that could be used to stop people from excessively drinking!

Thanks, Dad! (I think!)

CHAPTER 22
I'll Eat My Hat

Have you ever been so confident of what you were saying that you backed it up with the statement, "I'll eat my hat if I'm wrong"? If so, have you ever had to follow through on it? I did, and I ate the hat!

Sometimes confidence is nothing more than bravado—in other words, rampant ego. Or perhaps it's the result of misplaced confidence or desperation. This story concerns all of these. The end is a blessing and a very good lesson in life.

One of my clients wasn't really a client at all, as he used one of our major competitors exclusively. But I kept trying because I believed our company was a much better service provider. This in itself isn't a bad attitude, but one should always remember that you just might be relying on others within your organization to accomplish the task after you market it. Nothing on this earth is perfect, no matter how much confidence you have in it.

While I didn't spend much time with this client prior to getting some work from them, I made a point to contact them on a regular basis of one month or less between visits. To me this type of client was very important in that our company was the outsider looking in, unlike the norm for the rest of my clients.

They had simple needs most of the time, and the personal relationship between their upper management and the competitor they used was pretty solid. This client was a challenge.

My service company had a long spell of working without any issues whatsoever in the region in which the company in question was working. This was a big positive. As the oil company in question was what would be considered a medium sized entity, they often brought in partners to help with the costs—partners who happened to be good clients of my service company. The company of challenge was still the operator, but their partners sometimes paid the majority of the bill and would "request" certain services for that payment. Realizing this, and hoping this would be the case someday, I kept working on the operating company (the company of challenge) so they knew my service company was ready to help them when needed.

One day during my monthly visit, one of the oil company's geologists started asking questions about a set of our services—nothing unusual, but some other oil companies considered them superior, with good reason. After explaining what the service set was like, I asked if we could show them how it worked on their next well. They answered in the affirmative, noting that one of their partners wanted them to use our service set. They were hesitant to use us, though, because "way back when" our company had given them very poor service over several wells. They mentioned this and asked if we would give them good service. Noting we provided excellent service for other companies all around their area, I felt confident we could do a good job.

In the back of my mind I was thinking about how I would work with our field operations to get them to do their best. The crews and the manager of that area's field operations were hard working, careful people who did their best. Still, the client was nervous. "Will you do a great job?"

"*I'll eat my hat if we do not*," I replied.

This was mid-week; the job was slated for Friday. Excited, I went back to my office and discussed the situation with the field manager. Knowing his crews would do their best, I slept very well that night.

Friday morning dawned. I checked with the field operations of my company. The crew was on site getting ready to do the job. Everything looked great. Then 3:00 p.m. rolled around and I got a very angry phone call from the client. We had not performed well, and he was not happy. Furthermore, he said, "You told us you would eat your hat if you did not perform well. Be here early Monday morning with your hat and be prepared to eat it in front of us." I didn't argue.

How could I? I had no clue—yet—what had happened or why. I said I would be there Monday morning.

Immediately the field operations manager of my company received a phone call from one not-too-happy sales/service representative—me. While our problems resulted from a series of unfortunate instances, the only thing that really upset me was the lack of communication. I was caught blind; I wasn't prepared with anything I could say when the irate client called. I made that clear and went back to work.

I mulled over what I was going to do for about an hour, until a bright and very unusual idea came into my mind. It was as if someone or something put this crazy but interesting idea there! It was so silly it was worth a try, if for no other reason than no one else could have possibly thought of such a solution to my problem.

Occasionally I went to a bakery and got doughnuts or muffins for my clients as a gesture of good will; however, if we had given bad service, the last thing normally attempted was to try to placate a client by doing this. I would go in and take my lumps, knowing full well in the vast majority of cases the client was ticked at my company and not me personally. I wouldn't take the upbraiding personally. In most cases I could not, as there was no way I could solve the problem by myself. I needed to take ownership of the problem through my commitment to look at all the information and facts and, working with my service company, work out a mutually agreeable solution where all would win—especially the client.

This time when I went to the baker I explained my need and why, and through both of us laughing heartily, a "requirement" was worked out and committed to. The goods were to be picked up at 7:30 a.m. the following Monday.

Monday came. The goods were inspected at the bakery. Perfect! We again laughed, the baker wished me the best, the goods were put in a presentation box, and I took off for my 8:00 a.m. appointment with a client who had probably built up steam over the weekend.

Arriving at the client's office, I asked to see those involved in the job we'd done—the President, Vice President Geology, Vice President Engineering, the geologist, and the engineer. I took my coat off and waited with the baker's box in hand.

All the requested people arrived together. All had evil grins on their faces. They then saw the baker's box in my hand and one said, "Oh look! Little Jimmy is bringing us a bribe! Where's your hat, Jim?"

My reply as I opened the box? "Well, I knew I had to eat my hat, so I thought I'd make it palatable." Inside the box was a cake in the form of a perfectly shaped peaked cap in the colors of my company along with my company name!

The client personnel erupted into laughter! One ran down to the corner store to get paper plates and utensils while another looked for a camera. The mood turned joyful, and we sat down to look over our well information. The results of the information were very good; we had done a good job once we straightened out some well site issues. There was no retribution. The client realized we would go to any lengths to do a good job—even eat our hat if we had problems!

The client got what he needed, but not completely what he had asked for—a flawless job. All agreed this was asking too much, but a silly commitment had been made. As we ate "my hat," I was mercilessly teased about my absolutely silly guarantee. It was noted that my service company never made the guarantee—I did. I was supposed to represent my service company through my efforts. Instead, by me making a silly guarantee, I was representing myself. There was no way any sensible service company would make such a guarantee! I was humbled but jubilant. The client started using us a little at first and then a bit more as time went on. The only inquiry they kept making was if the job came with an edible hat!

That was the last time I made such a statement, and quite frankly, the last time my hat was eaten! Oh, and just to remind me—a picture of the "hat" still hangs on the wall close to my computer!

CHAPTER 23
Know What You Have and Trust It

Usually in life we do a good job of learning what the equipment we use is capable of doing and how to operate and maintain it to high safety and operating standards, while having faith that it will do what it's supposed to do. Still, there are times when it appears the equipment is operating safely and correctly yet is giving results that appear to be incorrect. It's wise at that moment to stand back, take a look at what's going on, and review and check everything to be sure things are safe and the equipment is operating correctly. If everything is operating correctly and safely, then you should trust the results your equipment is giving and move forward with the task at hand. It's still a good idea to proceed cautiously, but you should trust that the results are correct ... assuming you know what those results should be, and if trying to override the equipment would be foolish. A case in point concerns an incident that gave me very nice recognition for the faith I had in the results of a piece of oilfield equipment and its computer evaluation. First a bit of background.

Up in northern Alberta was an oilfield with reservoirs for oil and gas in the form of underground pinnacle reefs. These reefs were very tall and narrow, so generally only one well per reef could be found and produced. The crude oil was light, so assuming the reef had the same quality of porous rock throughout and was a hydrocarbon bearing reservoir, one would expect a reservoir with gas on the top, oil in the middle, and salt water on the bottom. The wells in this area were drilled, evaluated, and completed for production in the 1960s and early 1970s. The well in question was evaluated through coring during the drilling process, and open hole well log evaluation took place before casing was run and cemented in place. It began its producing life as a good oil producer.

As the rest of the story involves well logs run in the cased hole, a brief explanation of "logs" is in order. These instruments are something like electrocardiograms (ECGs). They were run into and out of a well on a steel wireline with insulated electrical conductors running down the middle. These tools were run to the bottom of the well and turned on to their running mode so they could observe and record (log) the natural and induced results of the formations as they were slowly run up the well as the cable was withdrawn from the well. Several instruments were run in combination and sequence in the day. These instruments looked at such things as responses of the formations to electrical, acoustic, and radioactive natural and induced impulses. From the information gathered from these responses, we could determine which reservoirs were capable of producing hopefully marketable hydrocarbons.

Once the core and open hole derived log data had been interpreted on what appeared to be a good producer, and the well was tested, casing was run and set in place with cement. The well was completed by perforating the casing across from the appropriate oil producing formation. Most of the time in this area prior to perforating the casing (punching holes in the casing with explosive-shaped charges), a cased hole acoustic cement evaluation log was run to make sure the cement sheath around the casing was sound enough to prevent unwanted fluids, like water from below or gas from above, being produced as well.

All proper procedures had been done on this well. For a time, the well did produce oil in commercial amounts. After a few years, the oil production tapered off along with a small amount of salt water being produced. The well was no longer a viable oil producer. While this is expected over time, this well "ran out" of oil in what seemed to be a short time frame. We decided to evaluate the reservoir to see if the gas cap observed at the time of open hole evaluation was viable to produce.

Very little salt water was being produced. The well originally had a very large water reservoir below the oil part, and a small gas cap. The well's production was just poor; it didn't appear like any significant gas or water had broken through.

The cement looked good, so there didn't appear to be any communication through that cement behind the casing from either the gas cap or the water zone below.

I recommended a cased-hole pulsed neutron log along with an attached natural gamma ray be run in the well to evaluate the entire reservoir behind the casing, primarily to see if the gas cap was still there. The well's bottom had been artificially cemented back inside the casing, so the water area would not be accessible for re-evaluation. Still, there was enough oil reservoir below the existing perforations to see if the water had seeped up into the oil reservoir.

The log was run, the results were delivered to our computer well log interpretation centre, and I headed off on a previously planned vacation. As this should have been a relatively straightforward evaluation, I gave instructions to the person overseeing the computer interpretation to just deliver the results to the oil company's production office in Edmonton so they could decide what to do next.

Three weeks later I came back and followed up with the oil company's Edmonton office to see what the re-completion results had been. They hadn't received any interpretation yet! Obviously, I had egg on my face because the interpretation should have been delivered and the well re-completed! I followed up with the computer interpreting person. What unfolded next was what could be labelled as plain foolish. The computer interpreting person had spent two weeks trying to force an interpretation on the results to say what "should have been," while the cased hole logs were saying something entirely different. The results showed that the perforated area was depleted of oil, the gas cap was intact, and there was still plenty of oil below the depleted area.

To be fair, "depleted" on the interpretation shows as "no oil." As there normally would be another fluid replacing the oil—like gas or water—the interpretation's "no oil" showed "water" across from the existing completed area. The person doing the computer interpreting thought that would mean the water had come up from the water zone way below the oil zone, so the oil zone below the existing completed zone could not exist.

I must admit I chewed out the interpreting person for imposing his will on the interpreted results and told him to deliver the original interpretation to me immediately, free of any of his suppositions. He did, and I delivered the results to the Edmonton producing office.

Let's pause here. My company gave an award to their employees who "discovered" unknown or unexpected producible hydrocarbons for their clients using interpretations from our well logs. Before that award could be given, the production had to be verified by the hydrocarbon company, and they had to verify the role of the recipient. No credit was to be given to any of the oil company's personnel! It was every person's dream within my section of the company to earn that award.

When the oil company's representatives sat down with me, I explained the interpreting person's dilemma and why the delay had occurred. They were perplexed as well—the results were not what any of them had expected. They asked me if I felt the log's interpretation was correct, and I said I did. Hard to believe, but valid. There was oil without water indicated below the zone that had been produced. There was a very minor indication on the interpreted results of a slightly dirty zone immediately below the "depleted" zone. "Dirty" could mean impermeable to fluids passing by it. Looking at the well records, I saw that the well had been completed above this very narrow "dirty" zone in the hopes of preventing water from below from seeping into it. I explained that this dirty zone had done its job so well, it prevented oil coming from below as well!

Everybody from the oil company got a wicked smile on their face and said, "We will re-complete just below that dirty streak, and your company is going to do the re-completion." They smiled because they normally used one of our competitors to do the completion work. This time they wanted me and my company to be without excuse should that re-completion give "the wrong results." Sticking to my guns, our unit was ordered out to do the completion.

The day of the completion came. I received a hurried phone call at my home early the next day, requesting me to get over to the oil company's Edmonton office. The mood of the caller was jubilant! When the trigger was pulled on our perforating equipment, oil chased the perforating gun out of the hole. The well tested at five hundred barrels of clean oil per day. Believe me, there were some very happy people in that oil company's office that day—especially the very relieved me!

The oil company wrote the letter that would lead to me being recommended for the award. The tone of the letter was jubilant. A few weeks later I received a letter from the president of my company noting that my particular award was the first in Canada resulting from a cased-hole interpretation, and that the oil company must have had great faith in me perforating below water in a pinnacle reef!

This was the first of six such awards personally received—a record at the time I retired. I trusted what we had for an interpretation the first time. If that computer centre interpreter had done so rather than trying to alter the results, he could have won the award. He eventually left my company's employ for a successful career in another company. Personal opinions should always be backed with all the facts and information available. In the end, one must know and trust what the equipment indicates.

One last bit of information: Long after the fact, I went to the Calgary office of the oil company and looked at the core results. That "slight dirty/tight streak" was a very impervious narrow band of rock. It could hold back anything if the well's casing was cemented properly— one more bit of information which could, and did, show the interpretation of the cased-hole log to be correct.

CHAPTER 24
Coming to Faith and Baptism

We have alluded to our Christianity, which came about later in our lives. From what the reader has seen so far, life looked pretty good before we knew Him. Anne and I were experiencing life's lessons together and seemed to have been doing well. But surface appearances do not always reflect total reality—*things are not always what they seem.* I could get very angry at times, so you need to understand what was actually going on in our lives to fully understand why we believe we need to write this book so others can benefit from our experiences. We want you to have a complete background on why we are doing this. What you do with this information is entirely up to you.

We didn't understand many things ... and didn't want to take the time to understand them... before December 1988. One thing that bothered us was the hypocrisy of those who said they were Christian because they had been baptized yet behaved in what appeared to be un-Christian ways. We had attended church but saw no real reason to do so. It was convenient at some points in our lives but seemed unrelated to the lives we were living—not that the lives we were living were something to always be looked up to! To top things off, I was a degree-holding scientist—not exactly a qualification for a Christian, or at least what I had been told by some supposed Christians. It was almost like I should renounce my degree or something similar!

So here we are at this point in the book *Rocks Don't Move*. Anne and I were a different kind of rock before December 1988. How come we moved? This is how we came to know the Lord, how we came to be baptized, and what baptism means to us today.

Anne and I were in what appeared to be the best time of our lives in the late 1980s. We owned retirement land purchased in British Columbia, we had a twenty-four-foot cabin cruiser, which we fished off in the Shuswap, I was thriving in my oil patch career, we were debt free, we owned and rode a big Gold Wing motorcycle, and we had our own personal car plus an assigned company car that I could use on personal business. Pretty nice at first glance. But situations in our personal lives were falling apart. My job was intense, and I didn't always come home happy. This showed in our life together. Oh, we loved each other—there was and is no doubt about that. But our conduct sometimes didn't reflect this. There was a big hole in our lives, and we had no idea what it was.

We had attended church nominally. Indeed, we began attending church while we were dating because Anne's parents had a strict rule about no boyfriends on Sunday. So we met at church, and I walked Anne home after the service before heading back to the university. Going to church was an excuse to be together and nothing else … at least in our minds at the time.

This continued for three years until we were married in that church. We don't remember much being said about the Bible or Jesus. Our hearts were focused on each other, not on the Lord. Still, the Lord had provided a way for us to grow in our love for each other before we were married. It also helped instill a sense of morality in us. After we were married, our church attendance was sporadic, if at all. We needed no more excuses to go to church, as we were then together.

In the fall of 1988 we were both forty-four. We had "everything" but were searching, and we didn't know what we were searching for. As noted elsewhere in this book many times, my ego was always at least a covert problem. One day the mail brought us an invitation to a new Presbyterian church plant. Anne strongly suggested that we go. The church wasn't too far away (you could walk to it), so we decided to scope things out. Little did we know we were being directed to go. This we would find out later.

We went to our first service. Oh my! They were talking about concepts we had hardly heard discussed in a church after our marriage—the Bible and Jesus. We were shocked and wanted to escape! When the benediction was finished, we made a beeline to the exit. Then one of the elders stopped us and asked if we'd like to attend a Bible study. I smiled and opened my mouth to say "no thank you," but what came out of my mouth surprised both Anne and me.

"Sure!"

On the way home Anne asked me why I'd said that.

"I have no idea," I replied honestly.

We began "going to" that church. It was common to hear the words "Bible" and "Jesus." This continued until the day a Bible study had been cancelled because the teacher had a splitting headache. It was the same day I'd had a big fight with my daughter on the phone. After I hung up, I told Anne there was no way I wanted to go to the Bible study anyway. But Anne disagreed. She believed that we needed to go. Neither one of us knew the Lord at that point.

Anne phoned and asked if the Bible study could go on. Reluctantly the teacher agreed. We went, and there were only four of us there besides the teacher, who had an icepack on his head. He went on about some part of the Bible, but I wasn't listening. I was feeling sorry for myself. Suddenly, I felt led to pick up the Bible, so I opened it near the beginning. What happened next shocked me.

The page in Genesis I had turned to darkened save for one verse, which I read. Shaken, I moved ahead and stopped. Again, the page darkened except for one verse, which I quickly read. Rapidly moving ahead, this occurred time and again! As I read these highlighted verses, I was convicted of my sins. Finally, in Luke, I burst into tears. Keep in mind that it had been many a year since I'd last cried. My usual reaction was anger when feeling upset. This time I was convicted and felt filthy, grimy, and dirty. I needed help and knew it.

The teacher saw what was going on and asked if I was okay. I opened my mouth and words came out—not from my brain but from my heart. I didn't form these words ... they just came out. "I know that I'm a sinner and I need the Lord Jesus to save me." I had been irresistibly led to the Lord Jesus by the Holy Spirit! A rush of relief came over me, and I joyfully stated that I believed in the Lord Jesus who had died for my sins. My tears dried up. Anne then came to that knowledge—both of us had been brought to the Lord at the same time!

As an aside, the Lord has a sense of humour. He knows I can be a skeptic ... a trained scientist kind of skeptic. He made absolutely sure I would remember the exact date of this blessing. It was Pearl Harbor Day, December 7, 1988.

Anne and I dove right in after this and fell in love with the Lord. We were clumsy children in the Lord for some time. I immediately started up a Bible study at 6:30 a.m. each Friday in my company office. We were blessed! Fellow

Christians came out of the woodwork to attend. One of those attending was a young Christian who attended a Baptist church but had not been baptized. This puzzled me. He hadn't been christened in a covenantal church, like a Presbyterian church, either. He objected to baptism because it was a requirement for membership in the Baptist church he attended.

I knew very little of the Bible yet, so I started reading and asking questions in the Presbyterian church Anne and I attended. I found out that since the young Baptist had never been baptized, he would need to be to become a member of our church. This also puzzled me. My question to the Lord and others was: If I'm saved, why do I need to be baptized? The answer from the Presbyterians puzzled me—I had been christened, so this was taken care of. Coming to know the Lord was of the Lord, as long as it was truly of the Lord.

While this is true, for a scientific, analytical mind of a new believer it was not nearly sufficient as an answer. Diving into the Word and other Christian literature, I was blessed by the Lord with the realization that baptism was a public sign and seal of personal belief in His grace that had brought me to a saving knowledge of Christ. I actually asked to be baptized in the Presbyterian church but was told that my christening as a baby was enough.

I asked the young Baptist to come early one Friday because I needed to talk to him. He arrived at 6:00 a.m. and I informed him that I'd been convicted of what baptism meant, and that he would have to be baptized before becoming a member of the Christian congregation to which I belonged. I explained that baptism was a public declaration of his belief in the Lord Jesus and the fact that He had been the one who led the young believer to that saving knowledge.

I was set back a bit because the young Baptist stood up and left! The next Friday he returned with a portly pastor—his pastor—who wanted to meet the Presbyterian who had convinced a Baptist to be baptized! Praise the Lord! The young Baptist had gone out and been baptized the Sunday right after the previous Friday! The Lord had used our little Bible study in a marvellous way!

Anne and I had been saved by the Lord Jesus. We had learned about baptism because He had used circumstances through that young Baptist to open our hearts to His Word. He had used me to help a young Christian. What came next was a continuation of this blessing, and hopefully will show the reader how the Lord works in mysterious ways, even in baptism.

Anne and I were now thinking strongly about our baptism. We knew and loved the Lord, but we'd been told that we didn't need to do more. Indeed, we may have been on the wrong path, as we were trying to work our own way to a solution. To that end, we prayed and left it in the Lord's hands. While we were confused, we went on vacation.

The church we had been attending while on Shuswap vacations after December 1988 was led by a retired Pentecostal pastor who had a heart for the Lord as well as for Anne and me. Our summer vacation of 1994 coincided with a baptismal session in the Shuswap Lake. We didn't know it until we got out to the Shuswap, but when we heard about it we immediately asked if we could be baptized. What we heard shocked us, but the advice and direction given was followed.

We were told, "No, you two need to go back and examine your hearts through prayer to be absolutely sure of what you believe in. If you still feel convicted in one year, then come back to me." We reluctantly agreed. That pastor knew we were members of a Presbyterian church. While some may disagree with what he told us, it turned out to be very good direction from the Lord.

We read the Word, prayed, gave our lives over to the Lord more and more, prayed, loved each other through the Lord, prayed, talked about it, prayed, and came to a conclusion ten months later. Then we phoned the Shuswap pastor and said we wanted to be baptized. Hallelujah! We also told the young Baptist from our Calgary group who had been led to be baptized through our little Bible study. He immediately changed his vacation so he could come out to the Shuswap and witness our baptism! Another hallelujah!

The day arrived. We went to the Shuswap church with a blue sky above. As we sat in the church, we had doubts—the evil one was at work. We prayed again. No calmness in our hearts resulted, so I opened my mouth and the words "Anne, let's just leave it in the Lord's hands" came out. Calmness came over us. We all finished the service, those being baptized changed into baptismal clothes, and we all walked down to the lake.

By now the sky had clouded over. The young Baptist brought his video camera to record the event. As we got to the lake, the sky became very dark. The first baptisms went forward. Then it came to Anne's and my turn. We were the last ones to be baptized that day.

As we entered the lake, it started to pour. Really pour! The pastor was full of "Praise the Lord" as he pointed out to all attending our baptism that Jim and Anne wanted to be baptized to show their love and faith in the Lord and not just for membership. "And the Lord has blessed them by ensuring that they get sprinkled and dunked at the same time!" Hallelujahs rang out. All this we have on VHS cassette from the young Christian Baptist to this day.

As we left the water, the rain quit and the day brightened. To this day it is Anne's and my firm belief the Lord did all this to show that those who truly love Him will be honoured by Him in ways He will use to show others the rewards He has for us through that saving knowledge, even on this earth.

We were not saved by baptism. We came to that saving grace from the Lord first. We were blessed tremendously by our baptism, by the Lord showing everyone that day how He truly blesses those who truly love Him and have taken Him to their hearts.

As noted at the beginning of this part of the book, there were some things that had bothered us. Anne and I firmly believe we must not leave this story without further comment now that we have come to understand what being a Christian is all about.

First, we aren't defined by being Presbyterian, Pentecostal, Baptist, or any other Christian denomination. We are Christian; we believe in our hearts in the Lord and all He stands for. We have been members of a Presbyterian church and are now members of a Baptist church. "Church" is not a building; it is the people therein.

Secondly, baptism is a simple word but often misunderstood. Anne and I believe very strongly that full immersion baptism is a public sign and seal of our faith in the Lord Jesus and our love for what He has been and is doing in our lives. It's a public declaration of this belief. As we have unfortunately found out, even before we knew the Lord, baptism does not mean that you actually know the Lord. To us it's a sign and seal of faith in the Lord Jesus, so Anne and I make sure we honour that sign and seal by the way we behave—with the aid of the Holy Spirit.

We know of several strong Christian believers who are covenantal and were christened when young. In no way do I want to detract from these believers. If one is directed by the Holy Spirit to not be fully immersed, then I say Praise the Lord! Faith in the Lord is in the heart of the believer, brought about solely by the Lord, and should be celebrated. Both Anne and I were christened when young. As such, we had no idea what was happening, and the Lord worked on us later in life after we came to a saving knowledge of Him to go further.

Anne and I know what is in our hearts and who put it there. One issue we must address concerns me being a degree carrying scientist. At the beginning of this story, I noted I was told by supposed Christians that I wasn't exactly qualified to be a Christian because of my scientific training and leanings. This used to tick me off and make me judge those people. This was wrong of me. Once I came to know the Lord, my scientific, analytical attitude drew me all the more to the Lord through His Holy Spirit and His Word in the Bible. *Nothing is impossible with the Lord I know and love.* More importantly, the Lord infused in my heart that He is the judge, and that I should pray for those people who judge others and let Him do His work. To those who judged me and Anne, you have been forgiven. We are thankful we can indeed pray for you, so hopefully you will be blessed the way we have been.

Praise the Lord!

CHAPTER 25
You Just Can't Win!

Sometimes you just can't win! We want to share two cases in our lives that were at least mildly frustrating … at first. The first case deals with planning based on what you think you know, or in our situation, planning where you will live without checking with those who should know. The second case illustrates how you sometimes cannot win with what you think are bratty teenagers, particularly concerning the music you listen to compared to the music they listen to.

These cases reach back to when we transferred to Lloydminster, Alberta/ Saskatchewan in February 1983. We say "Alberta/Saskatchewan" because this city straddles the Alberta/Saskatchewan border. We were moving from Edmonton, where our kids were being educated in the Alberta school system. All Lloydminster postal addresses were noted as being in Saskatchewan, but the physical addresses were based on which side of the border you were on. The high school was located on the Alberta side. Saskatchewan had a sales tax at the time; Alberta did not. Stores in Lloydminster on the Alberta side had no sales tax.

It seemed natural to buy our house on the Alberta side, both from the tax point of view and from—we thought—the schooling point of view. Note the "we thought." We didn't check about the schooling at first, so we bought just west of the provincial border, in Alberta.

After we purchased, we discovered that the school system in Lloydminster was run on the Saskatchewan system as per an agreement between the two provinces. While the two school systems were essentially the same, some courses were only offered in one semester. The Lloydminster/Saskatchewan system had already run courses starting in September of the year previous to our move, which Alberta didn't offer until January/February of that year.

This lesson benefitted us a little later in our lives—do not put pen to paper in a house purchase until you know all the facts. This paid many dividends later in our lives, as noted elsewhere in this book.

The second event involved our teenage daughter. She was and is a very beautiful lady—so much so that when she turned fifteen, my hair turned grey in one year! Anne wasn't impacted the same way, but one episode did affect Anne. It's one that I really laughed hard at and that taught us one lesson on how *not* to handle teenagers. The lesson? Don't be too quick to criticize the music your teens listen to!

As teenagers, Anne and I listened to everything from early rock and roll to symphonies, jazz, country, rockabilly, and the "interesting" music of the 1960s. Both of us were very opinionated about the music we liked and listened to. Our teenage daughter listened to the "music" of the 1970s and 1980s. She was in her teens and was developing a mind of her own—one which occasionally clashed with our opinions both in music and in life.

One day Anne and our daughter were in the kitchen listening to the radio as one of our daughter's "songs" came on. Anne promptly commented that this "music" was not what she considered to be appropriate (and to be honest, I later agreed). Anne went further, though—she asked our daughter why she couldn't listen to more appropriate music, like the music Dad and she listened to in our day.

Our daughter didn't need to answer. The next song came on the radio. It was a "golden oldie," a nonsense song from when Anne and I were younger called "The Purple People Eater" (Sheb Wooley, MGM, 1958). As the song played, Anne grew really embarrassed, and our daughter literally rolled on the floor laughing! When I came home from work, Anne related this to me. I did my best not to laugh at the circumstances, but I must admit that our daughter had a point!

Years later our daughter gave us a present—a little purple monster doll with a pull string. When you pulled it, it played "The Purple People Eater" song. We treasure that doll to this day, because it helped us when we came to know the Lord and began attending church on a regular basis.

We now go to a church that plays upbeat, joyful, and modern Christian music. We are in our seventies and really enjoy it! We also treasure Bible studies, events, lunches, and dinners where gospel hymns and older Christian music is played. At home we play modern country Christian and other modern forms of music that are uplifting to hear. We learned with the "Purple People Eater" incident not to be too judgemental too quickly. Anne and I love to go to church in the summer on our 1985 Gold Wing motorcycle. All the youth and most of the older folks think this is "really cool" and encourage us. Sadly, we do see some older folks who frown on us doing that. Anne and I believe that as long as we're setting a good example for those people growing in life and in their faith, we can inspire them to be less judgemental than we were many years ago in a Lloydminster residence.

CHAPTER 26
Grace through Discipline

I had some personal baggage that was difficult to get rid of in 1992, even as a recent convert to the Lord—mainly because I didn't recognize it as baggage at the time. Hey, I was a safe driver. I had plenty of driving experience, and I hadn't killed anyone. I'd taken motorcycle training and knew how to avoid accidents. I had no "at fault accidents." I did have an ego, but I didn't think about it.

In 1992 an event occurred in my life that had far-reaching consequences—one which taught me the true meaning of discipline by the Lord and helped me recognize His overarching grace. It humbled me beyond any other secular event in my life to date. It changed my attitude about driving.

Being one of the good salesmen in my large oilfield service company in 1992, I was flying high. They had entrusted me with a big, new company car with niceties to carry out my work duties. This car provided me with more comfort than the Chevrolet I'd been driving ... one which I purchased for my wife because it was in great shape. Part of my job was to help train our younger field engineers—a job I relished. The only problem with the new car was that it had several handling quirks, but I was confident I could manage them. I was used to the Chev; I was not used to the new car.

This event took place in mid-November of 1992 in Calgary, Alberta. I had an appointment to go to the company's training centre out of town in Airdrie, deliver a lesson, then proceed on a field sales trip. There was a lot on my mind, and I was in a hurry. This "hurry" bit had become normal. Then my day unfolded.

The morning dawned with a very wet snowfall—the first of the season in Calgary. The day's events had been prepared for, yet the weather annoyed me. There had been no indication of snow in the forecast the night before. All I thought about was those other crazy drivers, who didn't know how to drive, sliding around and creating accidents, perhaps involving me. Heaving a sigh, the thought of all the motorcycle training I had taken and given kicked in. My mind raced with thoughts of how to prepare to avoid all those inexperienced drivers as they careened at me. One thing consoling me was that the new car was a full-sized sedan and much heavier than my motorcycle. The thought of all that weight gave me comfort. I also noted that the snow was melting as it hit the ground. My busy mind rationalized that the road would be wet, which could be handled. Never did it occur to me that snow might mean frozen.

There was a fight going on in my mind as I headed toward the door of our home over the type of coat or jacket to be worn—either a medium heavy jacket, or my new full parka with a hood. A full parka took up space and would be inconvenient to take on and off compared to the lighter jacket. Anne saw me fidgeting and asked what was going on. I told her, and she didn't even hesitate when she said, "Take the parka." Grumbling, I put on the parka.

I went out to the car, put my laptop and briefcase loosely in the back seat—in too much of a hurry to put them in the trunk—fired up the car, and took off. Sure enough, cars were moving slowly because of the snow. I was getting frustrated because the sound of slushy, very wet snow under the Ford could clearly be heard. Nothing indicated that the snow would be a problem.

Finally, I approached the northern end of Calgary. Traffic was much lighter; the sound of wet slush was still there. Speeding up to over the 100 kph limit, I reached the northern border of the city. The slushy sound stopped. *Great! No more racket. I can speed along in peace and quiet.* The snow had intensified into a blizzard, but I passed slow-moving cars. *A blizzard! Man, this blizzard could impede my sales trip after delivering my lesson at the training centre!*

I pulled out to pass a vehicle ahead of me on the four-lane highway. Suddenly my car started speeding up, going sideways, and spinning. It then hit the car in front of me sideways on my driver's side—right at the driver's door. Where I was sitting! The collision was so violent, all the windows on both sides of my car were blown out. The driver's door collapsed inward, pushing me sideways; my glasses flew out the now-open driver's window. The car straightened up and slid rapidly sideways toward the ditch.

All I could think about was that the ditch was probably not frozen but soft with the melting snow. *My car has a loose laptop and briefcase in the back.* If the car hit that soft ditch sideways, it would roll and I'd be decapitated as the laptop and briefcase flew around inside! I couldn't move, and I didn't understand why. I wasn't in pain.

Just before hitting the ditch, the car turned enough to roll quietly straight into the ditch and come to a stop. I offered a prayer out loud to the Lord, thanking Him for keeping me safe and asking that He tell me why these events had occurred.

Then the pain hit. Trying to move, I could not. While buckled in, I couldn't move to release the buckle. I painfully looked around and saw that the force of the impact had pushed the driver's door in a couple of feet, causing the split front bench seat on the driver's side to ride over the seat on the passenger side. I realized how fortunate I was for that seat, as my former Chev didn't have a split bench. If this had happened in the Chev, I could have been more severely injured, if not killed.

The blizzard was raging a bit later as a policeman walked down into the ditch to see me and ask how I was. I was okay, but in great pain and could not move. Noting it was fortunate I had a parka, he pulled the hood up over my head from outside. He couldn't get the door to open, so he told me he'd dispatch an ambulance. He had to leave because there were fatalities further on to be taken care of. Then he put my glasses on my face. They had flown out through the driver's window of my car and through the rear window of the car I hit, just as his rear window shattered. The glasses landed in the passenger seat of the other car. *Not one scratch was on those glasses!*

Waiting for the ambulance, in great pain but warm because of my parka, and unable to move but at peace, the realization of what had happened sunk in. The slushy sound was heard in the city because the roads were salted and the snow was melting. The slushy sound stopped outside the city because the roads weren't salted. The melting snow had frozen on the road, creating black ice. I also praised the Lord for giving my wife the foresight to tell me to wear the parka. Without its hood, my head would have frozen. I then tearfully realized that discipline by the Lord had occurred.

Why? Well, I'd had fifteen "accidents" prior to this one. None of them were serious, and all were "not at fault." All were in company vehicles. As I'd never been at fault, my ego said I was "not at fault." However, all of those "accidents" could have been avoided. All of them occurred because I was in a rush, or distracted, or angry, or upset, or just plain thinking of myself over anything else. Selfish. Egotistical.

The Lord wasn't finished with me yet. I was due for some further disciplining, even if I didn't realize it at the time. The ambulance came, and they had to slit my new parka to get me on the body board. I was lying in the hospital, in pain, wearing my new-but-ruined parka, with my wife and pastor at my side. A nurse came in and hesitantly asked if I was the "Snake."

"Yes," I said. "That's my company nickname."

She said that someone from my company was worried about me and had called to ask if I was okay. When I asked who, she named the one person in my company I had trouble with. I burst into tears. No one else in the company called but him. In front of my wife and the pastor, my eyes welled with tears. I told them that he was the one individual I really had trouble with in the company. He was always teasing me, which I couldn't stand sometimes. I had judged him and judged him severely. The Lord had just made me realize that I had no business doing such judging—that was His job.

I had cracked my ribs and shoulder but was soon back home, healing. When I eventually returned to work, the first thing I did was approach that person and ask for his forgiveness. He didn't understand why, even when I explained. No matter … the Lord had shown me that I needed to be forgiving.

Now came the tough part. I was an "older" salesman and had been with the company twenty-six years. Fortunately, I was a good salesman; otherwise, my terrible driving record over the years would be just cause to terminate me. Instead, the Review Board decided that the best course of action was to examine my attitude. I was very humbled. My extremely stupid actions had cost me and my company greatly—not only the car, but in lost sales. I knew what was deserved. The board asked me what I thought should be done. Heaving a big breath, I stated that in addition to whatever they decided, I should be required to visit all the field offices of my clients and give a safety talk using this incident as an example. This was agreed to, along with me being required to take an internal course on driving safely.

While the safety talks I gave went over very, very well, the most important thing for me was the driver safety course—not the technical part, as I already know about that, even though I had trouble adhering to it. This wouldn't be allowed to happen again, and it has not. I haven't been in any collisions since that event. What was most important was the attitudinal lesson I received in that course. Note that I say "accident" in the first part of the story, but then "collision" in the above paragraph. This is the attitudinal change referred to.

At the beginning of the course, the instructor asked me in front of the class what had happened to me. I answered by saying, "My accident happened …" At this point the instructor bluntly and not too kindly stated, "You didn't have an accident. An accident occurs when a DC10 airplane drops on your car without you knowing it. You had a collision. You could have avoided it!"

Instantly all the previous incidents of "no fault accidents" flashed through my mind. I again realized that they all could have been avoided. They were all collisions. That single change in attitude changed my overall approach to driving. After that lesson, I was blessed with no collisions.

To this day, Anne and I watch the news and realize there are rarely, if any, "accidents." Those "accidents" are collisions. The media and others seem to be uncomfortable with the term "collision." They shouldn't be if they want to do the public some good. This change in attitude made a huge difference in my life, which is thankfully ongoing.

Discipline, while sometimes painful in many ways, can be very beneficial. Even to someone older than a child.

CHAPTER 27
A Hawk Story

After my collision in 1992, I no longer had a company car. I presumed this was due to my collision; after all, too many of them had occurred! Actually, the new company policy was that you provided the vehicle, and they paid your company mileage. This was no problem. As noted in the last story, my old Chevrolet company car had been purchased for Anne prior to the collision. It was in great shape, and we used it right into our retirement.

We used that Chev for both personal and company business up to the next spring and into the summer as this story unfolds. As noted elsewhere in this book, part of our trip was east from Calgary into southern Saskatchewan. Once you got across the Alberta/Saskatchewan border, there was a low microwave tower on the north-side hill of the Trans-Canada Highway, with a deep slope off the highway to the south, down to relatively flat land in a broad ditch. At the base of that slope stood a big, old poplar tree. In the crotch of the tree was a huge hawk's nest that year. As we travelled east toward our Saskatchewan destinations, we noted a clutch of eggs in the nest. We decided to monitor this on future trips, which we did. We watched when the eggs hatched, but never saw any adults. But the chicks started to grow.

One day I asked my boss if we could take any vehicle we owned on these trips and still claim the mileage. His said he couldn't care less if I took a Rolls Royce, as long as an acceptable image was presented to our clients! I didn't mention to him that my other vehicle was a motorcycle!

Anne and I took off one day on our Gold Wing, with its cargo trailer full of sales material, and headed east. We observed the chicks and decided to give them a few more days while we were doing our company duties in southern Saskatchewan. As we were returning to Calgary, we pulled over on the two lane highway and parked safely. We were wearing leathers and full-face helmets. We took our helmets off while retrieving my single lens reflex film camera from the trailer, and then I proceeded down the hill to the poplar tree. Anne stayed with the Wing.

The lens on the camera was sufficient to zoom in on the three big chicks … and I mean *big*! Why they hadn't fledged and flown off was beyond me. All three glowered at me … or at least it seemed that way! More likely they just looked at me with a normal, cranky, hawk-like face! I moved around the tree to the most advantageous point to get a good shot. In doing so, I positioned my head such that I couldn't see the Wing or Anne back up the hill. Steadying myself and positioning the camera in my hands, I focussed to be ready to take the picture. Suddenly Anne yelled out, "Incoming!"

My head snapped toward Anne, and all I saw was beak and claws! I immediately fell to the ground as Mama Hawk screamed by me. Anne was up the hill laughing her head off at the sight of her big husband collapsing to the ground. I gained my composure and got back up and repositioned myself.

Steadying myself, I advanced the film and readied the camera for a shot. Anne again screamed "Incoming!" I looked up the hill—nothing! I immediately snapped my head the other way—beak and claws! Much closer this time. I collapsed to the ground. I definitely felt the breeze going by my head this time. Mama Hawk flew over to a fence post close to her nest, landed, and proceeded to swear at me in loud screeches … at least I assumed she was swearing. Her footprint was so large on the post, the claw's diameter was greater than the post diameter!

Again Anne was laughing her head off. Quick shots of the chicks in the nest were taken, as well as one of Mama still "swearing" at me on the post. Then I left quickly while Mama sat on the post, "beaking off." I got up the hill, and Anne was really laughing by now. Just to show how much she loved me, she stated that I should be really thankful she had warned me, because she was torn between doing so and taking a prize-winning picture of the hawk raking my bald head. To this I meekly responded, "Well, I couldn't leave my helmet on and take the pictures."

To this day I have the "blessing" of the images I saw as Anne warned me, plus the pictures of the chicks. All that could be seen was a very angry looking hawk head with full open beak with two fully open sets of claws just below and to each side of her head. Make no mistake—it was terrifying! I was truly fortunate to have Anne spotting for me, or I could have lost an eye when I turned to see that hawk. One fact to remember ... Anne cannot drive a motorcycle, so I had to stay healthy, even if I looked hilarious!

CHAPTER 28
A Look at a Couple of Forms of Fear

Fear and its consequences can be interesting, terrifying, and amusing. Fear can stem from an awareness of something that could harm us. This "something" could be of a human, animal, or inanimate nature. Taken to the extreme, fear can paralyze a person's thoughts, leading to irrational and dangerous behaviour. Understanding what causes this fear can lead to a well-considered response and actions designed to overcome the fear, thus giving a person a way to either handle or avoid it … especially if such understanding can be gained before the fearful event! Sometimes fear can be a factor that leads someone to act to effect positive results. From the perspective of someone who has lived through what could have been many fearful situations and survived—indeed, eventually thriving in most cases—fear can lead to wisdom, as long as the outcome is morally positive! Two kinds of fear have a strong impact on our lives—secular fear and holy fear. The first fear we experienced mainly before coming to know the Lord.

Secular fear is just that—fear connected with this world. It can be very irrational. An event occurred in my oil patch life that put secular fear in perspective about two years after turning my life over to the Lord. A young up-and-coming salesman came into my office, racked with a whole bunch of worries that had obviously taken control of his thoughts and actions, even if temporarily. As he was going on, an extraordinary, blessed thought entered my mind. When the young salesman paused to take a breath, I asked him: "Do you know how to spell fear?"

Puzzled, he asked what I meant.

"How do you spell the word 'fear?' F E A R: **F**oundless **E**xpectations **A**ppearing **R**eal." Then I suggested rather strongly that he figure out possible solutions to his problems and get back to doing his job. This definition of fear often defines what Anne and I call secular fear.

Both Anne and I view the term "fear of the Lord" as something wonderful. It is the powerful awe and respect we have for the Lord that makes us realize He is in control not only of our lives, but everything on this earth and in the heavens. This fear is the realization that the Lord knows what we will be doing, even if our actions take away from His honour and glory. More importantly, He knows we will do things before we do them! Realizing this gives both Anne and me an awe-struck reason to try and temper our actions so that we give the Lord all the honour and glory in everything we do. As we believe He is in control, it's easy for us to trust that if we honestly seek His will, we will end up doing something related to His honour and glory in a meaningful way. We have come to treasure this holy fear as a wonderful influence on our lives, one which helps us grow in our knowledge of the Lord and, frankly, our role in this world.

Take a person's ego, for example. In the secular sense, one's ego can lead to exaggeration of their importance, or the importance of what they're doing or have done. This exaggeration can be mild and unobtrusive, or it can be very obtrusive, even crossing the border of truth and untruth. When this obtrusive form of ego is realized by the perpetrator because others are concerned or offended by it, then a fear of repercussions comes in—a secular form of fear of which the cause was self-generated. It could have been a downright lie that is harmful to others resulting in threats of legal action. Then secular fear—fear borne of an exaggerated ego—comes to play.

We all have egos, but they can be controlled. When one considers how to present themselves in a way to give honour and glory to God by sending a sky telegram to the Lord before opening their mouths, it's amazing how their thoughts seem to be guided. This whole process is a form of holy fear—realizing that there could be unsavoury results and that there is One who is in control, and that the Lord asks us to give Him honour and glory through our actions. Taking an action borne of your ego or pride to the Lord and asking Him to guide your tongue in order to give Him the honour and glory—even in silent prayer—can yield marvellous results.

As another example, often as a politician I was involved in worthwhile projects, some of which resulted in many millions of dollars granted to regional projects. Potential instant ego! Local media love these stories, but they often have a rather interesting way of interviewing you about them. One example of this concerned a major commitment by the provincial government to improve a local highway. A local TV station began their interview with me by noting (in their words) that I had been "pushing and pushing" for this for ten years. At first glance this may have appeared true, but it wasn't and I knew it. Quick sky telegram! My reply: "No, this is not true. I and my committee have learned to work with people. We are but part of the picture. While we have helped Highways understand what is needed, Highways have done all the planning and ancillary work to reach the point where the money can be spent wisely. I and the committee are very happy to be part of a total picture that will benefit the people using the road."

While stunned, the interviewer went on, and the story resulted in a quite nice TV spot that didn't highlight me but the efforts of all. Ego controlled ... fear of the Lord used for good.

A politician must realize that the part of the world he works for is like a giant pyramid. He may be close to the top, but he is not the boss—there is a board, or a council, or a cabinet of which he is a part. This board, council, or cabinet is the overall leader. Under that leader are literally tens, hundreds, and sometimes thousands of people working to accomplish goals that the leader has set. Ego has no place at the table. If there is ego at the table, then others at that table need to put it in place. If this doesn't occur, that ego will control decisions to the detriment of those whom the table serves.

Use the knowledge of what fear is—both secular and holy—to enable you to be an asset in literally all you do on this earth!

CHAPTER 29
Rocks Don't Move

Now is the time for the reader to hear how the title of this book came about by a very unusual life circumstance. It happened in a very interesting way. My sales and service job in the oil patch required me to travel throughout Alberta, Saskatchewan, and parts of Manitoba and British Columbia, resulting in many life-altering incidents that are discussed throughout the book. Anne and I learned many things by travelling the backcountry roads, especially in Saskatchewan and Alberta. At first glance, these trips were no more than travels and visits to do my job. Backcountry travelling, or "shunpiking," involved leaving the two main highways in these provinces—Highway #1 (Trans-Canada Highway; TCH) and #16 (the Yellowhead Route) and driving down less travelled paved and gravel roads in Alberta and Saskatchewan. Often it paid to just go a little bit off the main highways and seek local attractions. We found attractions the locals enjoyed that the traveller-in-a-hurry wouldn't even be aware of. Most of the time these local features could be enjoyed by simply walking out your motel door and looking for them. One of these hidden events resulted in the title of our book.

Part of my itinerary from Calgary was to visit local oil company offices in smaller cities and towns in Saskatchewan en route to or from Regina. Directly to Regina from our home in Calgary's northwest was about eight hundred kilometres. Normally we would stop at local oil company offices between Calgary and Regina, some of which were quite off Highway #1. I would rotate by going directly to Regina then visiting the other field offices on the way back to Calgary.

Occasionally, when the need to spend more time in Regina arose, or when the trip would continue from Regina to offices southeast of the capital of Saskatchewan, we travelled directly to Swift Current and stayed overnight before continuing on to Regina. This trip was particularly wonderful—that is, if you took the time to look beyond the ditches of the main drag! If you didn't, the trip between Medicine Hat, Alberta and Swift Current, Saskatchewan could be just plain boring. In the later years of working for my company, Anne came with me. We made a point of looking beyond the ditches, and what we saw was far beyond boring! More stories come from this as you go along in the book.

Arriving in Swift Current, we learned to do two things relatively quickly. First, there was a great Chinese restaurant on the highway. We became so familiar with the place that when we went in, they knew us, welcomed us, and asked if we wanted "the usual." Generally, we did! It was wonderful to be from out of town and feel like we were part of something local and appreciated by some of the locals.

Secondly, there was a shopping mall. I received a meal allowance ... a maximum dollar amount for three meals a day. Only I could claim it (not Anne), and receipts were required. The first day's lunch was made before we left Calgary. As we were on a health kick, we cooked our own breakfast of hot oatmeal made of milled wild oats. We had a little electric hot pot that looked like a plastic coffee pot in which Anne would prepare breakfast for both of us. The milk was purchased from the Swift Current shopping mall the evening before. No receipt. Supper was obtained as above. Receipted. Anne generally made lunch at the hotel before we left for Regina, using tins of salmon we'd purchased at the mall (receipted), up to the maximum dollar amount allowed. This was repeated at the many stops we made on the field trip, and any surplus "tinned groceries" we bought on the way were taken back to Calgary for the next round. For quite a few years we enjoyed salmon sandwiches on a very regular basis. Of course, it helped that fish was healthy, considering long hours sitting in the car!

One late afternoon in early summer we found we had extra time, so we asked the motel clerk in Swift Current if there were any walking trails close by. Right out the back door! There was a paved path that travelled along Swift Current Creek right up to the reservoir, park, and dam. We took it and found it delightfully pleasant. While the name of the creek would suggest there was "swift water," there wasn't. The creek was slow moving, but fast enough to not be overgrown with weeds. The insect population was negligible, so Anne and I could enjoy each other's company while discussing matters of importance, enjoying an exercise walk, and observing the waterfowl. Much more fulfilling than watching television! It was "hidden in plain view" and pleasantly surprising, considering the walkway began so close to the Trans-Canada Highway.

After several trips, we got used to a routine of arriving in Swift Current, going to the mall for milk and tinned salmon, checking in, going for Chinese supper, and then going for a walk along Swift Current Creek. The walkway crossed the creek in several places with steel bridging, so we could stop and look down into the creek for any wildlife—like the occasional duck paddling along. One evening we took our time and ended our stroll near sunset. The creek was in a very shallow valley that opened up as it entered the dammed reservoir area. At that point there was a foot bridge, which we crossed. With the sun on our backs and us looking in an easterly direction, everything appeared in various shades of grey fading essentially into black. The still reservoir water was a light blue-grey. Shoreline features like shrubs, trees, and the shoreline itself as well as shore rocks all looked black. It was beautiful! We couldn't get over how a small prairie city could have something so beautiful right in the middle of their urban area.

We walked over to the well-treed park and briefly looked around, lost in the magical beauty of the scenery. It was a treasured moment. Then we needed to get back to the hotel before dark, as the trail was not lit when we travelled it. We rapidly walked toward the bridge and began walking over it, our minds totally relaxed and grateful we could discover such beauty so close to a major highway. Something caught my attention out of the side of my eye, and I turned my head in an easterly direction. In the middle of the reservoir was a domed rock ... or what appeared to be a domed rock. As with every feature in or near the water at that time of the day, it was shaded black.

On our many walks I hadn't noticed this rock before. I realized the reservoir was shallow in places, so seeing a rock there was possible. I stopped, but Anne kept going, though not too far. Why was this rock not noticed before? Why was it not seen as we walked over the bridge a few minutes ago? Then I saw something. "Anne! Come here!" Anne turned around and walked briskly back. "Look over there," I said, pointing to the "rock."

"What?" she said.

"Look at that black object in the middle of the reservoir," I whispered.

Anne looked and said, "It's just a rock."

"Rocks don't move," I replied. She looked at me, very puzzled. With me whispering that the water was glassy smooth with no wind at the time, we both noticed rings of water waves emanating from the "rock." Then both our eyes opened wide. In the shadows we could discern no movement of the "rock." Suddenly, the "rock" dove under the water. It was a muskrat! We watched it come to the surface and swim away.

We had plenty to talk about as we went back to the motel. We had seen a beautiful prairie creek reservoir in the waning sunset, with gorgeous, many-hued greys to black shadows in a dead calm, warm summer evening close to an urban area adjacent to one of Canada's major highways, with hardly any person besides us on the paved trail. We surmised no one else had seen what we saw. When we got back to the room, we laughed and noted that *things are not always what they seem*. Shortly after, we made up our minds that the book we were going to write about our lives would have that fortuitous title *Rocks Don't Move*.

CHAPTER 30
Whirlpool Theory of Layoffs

Sometimes an incident that appears tragic can lead to further tragedy … or even humour. Take the example of layoffs in the oil industry. During the thirty-two years I spent employed in that industry, there were five downturns that resulted in layoffs in our company. The term "layoff" could be a bit of a misnomer. In the "professional" end of the business, "layoff" generally meant termination with a package. Keeping that interpretation in mind, consider the following story.

During one of the downturns, a young colleague of mine came into my office racked with fear. Several of our friends had been let go. He was so irrational, it was affecting his work, so I asked him to sit down. I sent a sky telegram, because I had no idea what to say!

Then an idea popped into my head. "Have you ever heard of the 'Whirlpool Theory of Layoffs?'" I asked, knowing full well he hadn't because it had just occurred to me. He looked puzzled, and said no. As he sat there, I told him to consider the following story.

"Most people know what a whirlpool in a river is like. It goes round and round with debris in it. The debris circles round and round, going deeper and deeper toward the centre until, suddenly, the debris is sucked down into the middle and disappears.

"But there is a second phase to the whirlpool. Look upstream to the pieces of stuff that are slowly being drawn by the river's current toward the whirlpool. Slowly, slowly that stuff is drawn toward the whirlpool. If the stuff reaches the whirlpool, it's sucked in and swallowed up.

"That's what layoffs are like. The people who are initially laid off are gone; they were sucked down the whirlpool and are not coming back. There's nothing you can do about it. Those left are the stuff upstream in the river. Unfortunately, people feeling sorry for those who have already succumbed to the effects of the whirlpool are probably actually feeling scared and sorry for themselves ... so worried, they aren't doing their job. If all they do is worry and fret and fail to do their job, they're allowing themselves to float downstream into that whirlpool, and they too will get sucked away in a secondary layoff.

"Me? I'm swimming like crazy, doing my job, proving time and again I am worth keeping, and getting as far away as possible from that whirlpool!"

I then told him to get back to work and start swimming like crazy! Last I heard before my retirement he was still employed and doing well.

CHAPTER 31
Port Angeles Pop Can

Anne and I are motorcyclists, but we aren't renegade "bikers." We drive what some motorcyclists who drive American made machines call "rice grinders"—a 1985 Honda 1200A Gold Wing Aspencade. I like to blame Anne for me getting this machine. Why? Consider that the first excuse in the Bible was used by a man against a woman to shift the blame to Eve: "…[Lord] *the woman thou gavest to be with me …*" (Genesis 3:12).

Earlier in the "I Was Outnumbered" chapter, this male co-author does the same thing concerning the purchase of the Gold Wing. It was insinuated in that chapter that Anne outnumbered me one-to-one, convincing me to buy our Gold Wing. So it's Anne's fault we own a motorcycle … right? It was also noted that I'd never been on a motorcycle, let alone driven one. There was a reason for this … a terrifying incident that occurred way before I was born.

In the 1950s, my dad noticed that Eaton's catalogues were listing war surplus Harley Davidsons at very low prices, and he mused about getting me one. Mom would have nothing of it. There was no way her son (or her husband) would have a motorcycle.

During his "volunteer" tour of duty in World War II before he met my mom, Dad was part of the Canadian Army Signal Corps in England. One night he was to deliver a message via motorcycle and, true to form, was racing along at probably too fast a speed on the back roads. Keep in mind that vehicles in England at the time had horizontal slit headlights, with a lot of the headlight blanked off to help prevent enemy night fighters in the air from seeing them. No moon was out, so it was very dark. Also keep in mind that some British trucks had a front cab with a top level with the box at the back, as well as a space in between the cab and box.

Dad roared around a corner and hit one of those trucks head on. His body flipped up, going through a 360 degree turn. At the top of the turn, legs straight down, he went into the space between the cab and box. Still turning, the top part of his body went ahead while his legs stayed straight, breaking them both. While recovering from his injuries back in Alberta, he met Mom. That's why Mom was adamant I never get a motorcycle, and that was why I had never been on a motorcycle!

After the purchase of our 1985 Gold Wing, an incident occurred partway through a long trip. It was "terrifying," but ended in a hilarious way. Anne and I tell the story to this day to laugh about motorcycles on ferries.

Our Wing provided us with many wonderful trips. This one took us from Calgary south to the Grand Canyon, over to the west coast of California, and back up #101. By that time we were in full flight marriage repair, and this was one very effective way of getting together. We were definitely close together as we drove along the roads through the United States on our motorcycle!

At the north end of Washington state, we decided to take the ferry over to Victoria, British Columbia. We had been on many British Columbia ferries, which were big, smooth, floating highways. Naturally we assumed any ferry from the States would be the same. We took the ferry from Port Angeles to Victoria. This was to become one of the most harrowing and funny motorcycle trips of our lives!

The first clue of trouble arose when we boarded the ferry. The wind had come up. They made us sign a waiver and tied—really tied—the Wing down to the lower vehicle deck floor. We went up to the observation deck. As we sailed over to Victoria, the boat started to toss and roll around quite violently. We didn't realize until we looked at the ship after getting off that it had a very wide top on a relatively narrow front hull. Rough seas caused quite a ride!

I ran down to the vehicle deck once as we crossed over the ocean to check on the Wing. It was okay—not moving, but the cars next to it were slightly moving. There was nothing more that could be done, so I went up and finished the ferry crossing with Anne.

We arrived in Victoria with no damage to the Wing and very happily drove off onto solid ground. Being only a half block from the British Columbia legislature buildings, we pulled over and parked the Wing there, heaving a big sigh of relief! Suddenly behind us from a side street came a scurrying line of Japanese tourists led by a Japanese-looking tour guide. They were all looking straight ahead so would have missed us, except the tour guide looked to his right directly at us and yelled in a deep, guttural Japanese voice reminiscent of a Samurai, *"Honda!"* The next thing Anne and I knew we were surrounded by about twenty Japanese tourists—none of whom could speak English—going over the Gold Wing with their eyes!

The English-speaking tour guide told us the 1200 motor was made in Japan then shipped to a factory in the eastern US to be assembled for sale as Gold Wing motorcycles in the same factory used to manufacture Honda cars. Apparently the 1200 Gold Wings weren't sold in Japan, as motorcycles with large displacements at that time were too large to be sold there. None of these tourists had ever seen a big Honda motorcycle. The guide asked if some of the older men could sit on the Wing and get their pictures taken. We obliged. They loved it!

After that rough trip and the hilarious circumstances of the Japanese tourists, Anne and I got back on the 1200A and proceeded on our way. Speaking through our communicators, Anne asked if I'd ever seen an empty pop can on a wave-tossed lake, and then asked me to think of a fly in that can. "That's what we experienced on the Port Angeles ferry," she noted. Hence the name "Port Angeles Pop Can!" Every year after when we'd go to a Victoria bed and breakfast, we'd look over the ocean at breakfast and see the Port Angeles ferry coming to Victoria. We took great delight telling everybody—especially Americans—about the circumstances leading up to the naming of the Port Angeles Pop Can!

CHAPTER 32
When to Be a Boyfriend

From the story of how Anne and I met, it's clear that it came easy for me to be a boyfriend. After all, I desired to court this beautiful young lady! Frankly, while I was pursuing her, she caught me. When we met we were both eighteen, and I desired to please that girl. I wanted to impress her with the way I served her, so I explored ways to please her while being very careful not to lose her. I didn't own her, but sometimes I behaved that way—which backfired until I smartened up! Her beauty was a magnet to me, so it would be a magnet to other guys. The need to understand what she did and did not want in a guy was urgent.

Discovering that she wasn't "high maintenance" was pure joy in my heart, as I couldn't afford a girl who was. It was a little puzzling that such a young-looking female looked so beautiful without makeup—wonderful, but unusual in the crowd I ran with. What you saw in Anne was what you got, and that was one of many personal reasons to pursue her.

Looking back now that I'm in my seventies, it was easy for me to be a boyfriend. Carrying her books, holding doors open, helping with her coat, holding her hand, putting my arm around her, hugging and kissing her all came naturally for me as her boyfriend. Frankly, it hadn't been easy for me before we met. I'd been taught to be courteous and polite, and before Anne that was mechanical to me. It was nice to do, but the actions meant nothing to me. With Anne, it went far beyond that. I really wanted to do all those acts! Anne made it easy by being obviously pleased by my actions, thus encouraging me all the more. Later in life I would find out she hadn't been treated that way by her previous boyfriends. We eventually discovered that there was a very special relationship between us, and my actions and the way she accepted them were part of the picture of the love between us. It all became a part of our pre-marriage life. It didn't become routine, as these were part of the joy we experienced with each other.

Then we got married. There is no question the love we had for each other was there, but our lives changed. Before getting my job in the oil industry, we were a very close team. Early in our courtship I told Anne that this relationship was going to be a team. It was. During my time in university, we were there together—not living together, but working together to build our relationship toward the day we'd get married. We both worked hard at this. After getting my job—a tough job for one not educated or prepared for it—we finally got married. Our team goals had been accomplished. Life now changed.

When a unit accomplishes a goal, quite often the unit goes into maintenance mode. You quit pursuing; you don't "follow up." Oh, we loved each other—passionately! When arriving home after being away for many days, the joy of being together was wonderful beyond belief. The sorrow of parting when leaving for another few days, or even weeks, was palpable. We looked forward to seeing each other upon our return. We then had children, moved away from the places we were familiar with, developed a home life, and got busy. Anne's boyfriend started forgetting to hold the door open or help her take off her coat. This wasn't really noticed, as we were busy developing a life for us and the kids. We were still very much in love, but the courting was over. In short, I began to forget to be a boyfriend.

As time went on and the kids grew older, we settled into a comfortable life together. The future looked great. Our finances were stable and growing, we became debt free, and our retirement plans were being successfully worked on. All our plans were coming to fruition. We hadn't come to the point of knowing the Lord yet, but life was getting very comfortable and predictable. Routine set in between the two of us. Then some things started to happen to me that led to the next change in my life.

I still looked forward to coming home to Anne. There were times I'd think about her in a very excited manner on the way home. I'd get out of the car and bound up to the door, looking forward to wrapping my arms around her, holding her in a big hug, and kissing her. Then I'd actually get in the door, hear kids fighting, see a mess, and find a hassled-looking wife struggling to get supper made and looking like she'd just had a fight with our kids. My excitement would drain away thinking about the tough day I'd had. I sure didn't want to have a tough day at home! Any thoughts of being a boyfriend went right out the door as I retreated to the front room to read the newspaper.

The next day while going about my business, my eyes started to wander. Those younger women sure looked attractive! I didn't pursue any of them, but they were eye candy to me. At home with Anne when the home was a disaster, I'd escape through the memories of those eye candies. This was dangerous. As time went on, even on vacation, I would look at younger women and forget about Anne. I didn't notice if she was looking at anyone else, or worse—was any guy looking at her? Never did I think that at her age she was attractive to someone else other than me. Talk about a one-way ego on my part!

When a situation like this develops, the closeness between a married couple fades somewhat, and a set routine emerges. Life gets less exciting. You quit getting excited, because you remember the disasters that greeted you when you came home. On the other hand, what was I doing to help the situation? Absolutely nothing; indeed, I was going backwards and didn't live up to being a husband. Was I helping this rushed woman, or just escaping?

On one occasion I came back from a long tour in the field and walked into the house to a wife and a couple of kids who obviously had been through "an incident." Anne looked at me with a wild look in her eyes, gritted her teeth, and asked me, "What would you like for dinner tonight, dear?" Just coming off a week of steak and accompaniments, I wanted no more of that. Never mind what Anne had been eating as a mother! I unthinkingly replied (without being sensitive and asking her what she wanted), "I would really like some macaroni and cheese dinner!"

You may guess that the mood around the home for a few days was pretty cold. Anne was absolutely tired of that; she needed to get out and go for a nice sit-down dinner anywhere but home. Someone had definitely forgotten to be a boyfriend!

Anne took a job when the kids were old enough to be left alone. This didn't bother me; she did very well, and I was actually very proud of her. She did so well that one day she came home and asked me if there would be a problem with her going out to Ontario to a worker appreciation convention with another co-worker in recognition of their good work. Without me.

At that point I suddenly realized how beautiful Anne looked. Inside I was in turmoil, even while saying there was no problem. Anne was a very attractive, late-thirties woman! The panic inside, quite honestly, existed because I'd done precious little to keep her as my wife. She went with my blessing, but it started me thinking about myself. To be honest, being a boyfriend didn't even come into my thoughts. Being too far gone to believe that a couple of older married folks—not that old, but not young anymore—could be boyfriend and girlfriend seemed pretty implausible. Nothing happened on her trip, so I was ashamed of my thoughts about her. On top of that, flaws in my parenting skills were also revealed during her absence.

A turning point was needed, mostly for me. If this occurred personally in a significant way, hopefully Anne would turn as well. It wasn't obvious to me how to accomplish this at that moment, but it came one day as I was scanning some of our colour picture slides onto the computer. By this point we'd come to know the Lord, and the kids were gone. The previous Sunday we'd heard a sermon in which *"rejoice in the wife of your youth"* (Proverbs 5:18, NIV) was fleetingly brought out. At first this seemed a little weird to me. Anne and I were no longer young. As I was scanning the slides from one of our vacations in Manitoba, I was thinking about how to do that. It still never dawned on me to be a boyfriend.

As I looked over the pictures, up popped a shot of Anne standing sideways outside Lower Fort Garry in Manitoba, holding onto our two very young children. Anne was looking back at me. She was wearing shorts and a blouse. My eyes opened up; I zoomed the picture in on Anne. My heart leapt! I shouted out to Anne to come and see this picture. She was busy and yelled "Why?" My answer just spilled out of my mouth *"I married the babysitter!* You have to see this!" Now she was puzzled and came into the computer room.

What we both saw was a superbly beautiful young woman in close-fitting shorts holding onto (babysitting) two young children, whose husband at the time didn't even see how attractive she was—not only to him, but to every red-blooded male who would see her! I'd been noticing other women when the most gorgeous young woman was right in my presence, in our home, sitting next to me, loving me, and being my girlfriend and my wife. I had totally missed the obvious. I began to rejoice in the wife of my youth at that moment. Instead of looking at what a beauty was there with me and appreciating her, I had been looking afar. Not only was this not loving, it was blatantly stupid.

The boyfriend in me welled up. Having a serious talk with Anne, I told her I wanted to be her boyfriend again but needed help. She would have to accept me as her boyfriend, not "just" as a husband. Frankly, it was awkward for both of us for a while. Now opening doors for her, helping with her coat, walking beside her instead of in a hurry ahead of her, and treating her like the jewel she has always been since the day I met her is great to do! I want to. She wants me to. It's fun! It makes us both feel decades younger.

Anne has the perfect ending for this story. When I told her I was writing this part of the book about being a boyfriend, she said, "When? Forever! And that goes for me as a girlfriend!" Guys and gals … take note.

CHAPTER 33
"Can't"

Anne and I reached a point in our lives where we realized we were well on the path toward being what we hoped to be as a married couple. We had worked through a lot of trials in our relationship and now wanted more than ever to enjoy life together. By this part of our lives we had purchased a used cabin cruiser boat, which was stored and used on the Shuswap Lake in British Columbia. It leaked—badly! Fortunately, it leaked not "up," but "down." When it rained, it dripped inside. It was also clumsy for the two of us to use, but we did enjoy boating, camping, and fishing on the Shuswap with this cabin cruiser. As we were now in a much healthier marriage relationship, we talked about this leaky part of our life. It was decided we needed to consider something better.

What we really wanted in a boat didn't exist. We didn't want anything bigger than a twenty-foot boat, but with an inboard-outboard propulsion system. And we wanted to sleep on the boat, with a cuddy up front like we had on our old boat. We also liked the barrel bucket seats on the cabin cruiser, and we wanted an alcohol stove, a big and a small ice box, a sink with a tap with water supply, and a table. Because of Anne's height (4'11"), we wanted something with a lower draft so she could net fish more easily. Oh, yes … we needed a compass, a search light to watch for rocks as we came into shore at night if needs be, a fish finder-depth sounder, and down rigging equipment. And dual batteries for the lights we needed for overnight camping, and a canvas top for nighttime sleeping, reading, and playing crib! Yes, we really thought this one out! Then something happened that threatened to throw a wrench into the whole plan. The oil patch suffered another downturn.

This is where an economically-minded, loving couple who were now fifty years old would have foundered if their marriage was in trouble or if they only thought of the immediate. We were that age; we were economically minded. We were debt free; we owned our retirement property. What to do? We asked ourselves one very vital set of questions: Would we go out and get our perfect boat if we were terminated from our oilfield service company? No. If we did buy it, could we make up our mind that this would be the last boat we bought, or if we got rid of it, would we buy another? Yes … and definitely no!

We made the scary decision to find this boat and buy it before possible termination came about. We committed to each other and the Lord that it would be our final boat. While this may not make sense to some, we took that leap of faith for the future.

But where would we find this type of boat? We could not! We approached several major boat builders and were snickered at. People either sold power boats for water skiing, or large cabin cruisers for what we were thinking. "No one" wanted to sell a ski boat that was a miniature cabin cruiser! Oh, really? What about us wanting such a boat? But these statements gave us direction. None of the boat builders would customize. Not one of them would even pay any attention to us. This would play out not too far in the future when we bought an SUV (see "Someone Had to Move" coming up). The word used in each argument from them was "can't." Anne and I now try avoiding four-letter (swear) words in our lives. To us, "can't" is a four-letter word!

Upon further research, and much frustration, we decided to try a local Okanagan boat builder, because they had advertised a 19.5 foot ski platform with a cuddy. An inboard-outboard propulsion unit was offered with various engine sizes. After that, most of what we wanted would have to be customized.

We approached them, and the answer to our query was to the effect of, "We don't customize."

"We will pay cash," we replied. Well, that changed things! The person we talked to said that their master builder was toying with the idea of building a boat just like we'd described! One problem, though … the boat platform we wanted to use was discontinued. Our hearts sank, but the person offered to check what they had and what the builder said.

We waited anxiously. They came back and said they had two shells of the model we wanted left, so the master builder could use one for himself and one for us! The boat normally would use long ski seats, but there was a way to put two swivelling barrel buckets in. Plus, they could do everything else—all for about 50 per cent more than the boat decked out to the hilt in a normal fashion. Sold! Except for one thing—they asked us what colour we wanted. Grey bottom and white top. "Oh, we can't do that. That colour scheme is reserved for our cabin cruisers!"

The "can't" word again! Speaking up, we noted this boat would be a miniature cabin cruiser, and we were paying cash. Upon some very quick thinking by the builders, the word "done" came out. One four-letter word to which we didn't object.

Anne and I left elated! Sure, we got an older design. It wasn't a newer ski boat design, but we didn't care. We decided on a V6 high output engine solely to give us a further eight inches of cabin room. This setup proved capable of going as fast as most V8s and slow enough to down-rig fish. Perfect—close enough! The boat would be built and we would pick it up from a local Okanagan retail seller of boats.

Our boat was built over the winter, with the plan for us to pick it up in May. But we got a call from the retail seller asking us to come out a month early. Not seeing the problem, I asked why. Well, it turned out the retailer was having a boat show. Families would come in, and the husbands would go to the big cabin cruisers and drool over them. They couldn't afford the price, so the husbands were steered toward smaller boats they could afford. In going to these smaller boats, they would pass by our completed boat. The husbands would see it and want our boat! The retailer wanted us to take our boat away so they didn't have to put up with this.

We found it funny that the boat sellers didn't realize a market just might exist for "our" boat! Not a problem for us—we now have a relatively unique boat. We later heard that people selling boats didn't want to market what we had done. This appeared to be the old "can't" attitude, in our opinion.

We made a decision for the future back in 1994 by not paying attention to the four letter word "can't." We still have our boat, love it, and use it over twenty years later. When people see it out on the lake, they are amazed. Anne and I didn't let a groundless concern get in our way—we stayed employed until 1998.

We had to buy a better SUV to tow it ("Someone Had to Move"), but like the boat we built, it was loaded, and we definitely plan to keep both vehicles for a long, long time!

Oh yes … how would you recognize our boat if you were on the Shuswap, where we use it? Well, it looks like a ski boat. It's 19.5 feet long and has a 1994 ski platform painted like a cabin cruiser. The colour and the interior are definitely unique, and its name is uniquely Edgson derived. Being as it comfortably fits two people and is just for us to use overnight for its designed purpose, we came up with the name *Just Us II*.

CHAPTER 34
Someone Had to Move

This story is one of many appropriate illustrations of how being boyfriend and girlfriend after you're married can positively affect others—even a new car salesman. After we came to know the Lord, we started getting serious again about becoming boyfriend and girlfriend. After many years of marriage, we needed a new vehicle—one which could haul a boat trailer or a cargo trailer. I was still employed as an oil patch salesman, so it seemed wise for me to talk to our purchasing agent and ask what he would recommend. At the time the company was using a particular major North American manufacturer for smaller vehicles because they had solicited quotes from the major car companies and got the best deal from them. Indeed, my next and last company car prior to my major, life-changing collision would be from that major manufacturer.

Anne and I decided we needed a big, two-door SUV to keep for many years. The purchasing agent recommended going to that designated manufacturer's dealer to see if they had something we wanted at the price we were willing to pay. So we did.

The price was very attractive, even with all the features we wanted. This was going to be the first four-wheel vehicle Anne and I owned that would have literally everything on it. The big SUV looked very good, with one exception—it came with standard bucket seats. I asked the dealer if we could get a split bench front seat. The answer was "no." Pressed, we said we'd pay extra for that particular seat. "Absolutely not," was the answer. We even suggested that he order a seat from one of their crew cab pickups (which had split benches) and fit it in the SUV in the dealership, noting we were willing to pay. Nope! Period.

Thanking the dealer, we went over to a Chevrolet dealer. After all, my current company vehicle was a big Chevrolet four-door sedan, which would eventually become my wife's car when we purchased it after the company gave me a new car from the above noted manufacturer. The Chevrolet dealer had a two-door Tahoe SUV, which was about $1,000 more than the other SUV. The demonstrator on the lot had bucket front seats with everything we wanted. Just like the other SUV.

We asked if a split front bench was available. The answer was yes, as that front seat was standard. We said this was great, and the dealing started. The price was pretty firm, because it was a very popular model in 1995. We said we would pay cash. While attractive to the dealer, there was no dealing. It was also noted the other SUV could be purchased for $1,000 less with buckets. Still no deal. Finally, we said we would purchase the Chev SUV as long as the split bench was in it. They tried talking us out of it, but it was our turn not to budge! It would take about three months to "special order." Fine! We came to an agreement, a down payment was given, and we left happy.

About two months later, I got a call from the car salesman. Everything was fine, but the fact we were willing to pay $1,000 more to get an SUV with a split bench front seat was driving him and his manager crazy! The SUV was on the way, but even people at the factory were wondering what was going on, so we told the following story:

"There was an old farmer driving down the road in his old 1953 Chev pickup truck (no bucket seats back then, only benches). The driver's window was down (no air conditioning) and his left arm was hanging out, resting on the window's edge. In his mouth he had a long straw on which he was chewing. His right hand was doing the steering, and his wife of many years was seated by the passenger window. Suddenly a convertible sports car with its top down sped by. The male sports car driver's girlfriend was firmly planted right up against the driver's right side. Seeing this, the farmer's wife of many years said, 'We don't sit close together anymore.' Hearing this, the farmer pulled in his left arm, took the straw from his mouth, looked around, and said: "I ain't moved none.'"

I then explained to the car dealer that my wife "ain't moved none." She and I were boyfriend and girlfriend, and we wanted to sit together, right next to each other, like we did when we first met. This surprised the car salesman, but he laughed about it!

It's both funny and sad to us when we think of how we moved apart, just like the farmer and his wife. The farmer had a point—he hadn't moved away in the truck, but the wife had. Probably he was like me and had become someone other than a boyfriend to his wife. Someone had to move back, and in this case, the wife did. In our case, I had to move; my attitude had to become one of a boyfriend once again. Anne very happily supported my move and moved back as well. I hope that farmer's wife moved; I hope the farmer moved. I hope they moved together like we did, literally.

Our 1995 Chevrolet Tahoe? We still have it over twenty-three years later. It gets poorer mileage than our other vehicles, but it hauls trailers, and we use it for camping out in the backcountry when we pick blueberries. It's in great shape all over. Just like our marriage now. We hope to keep it for at least thirty years. It's special to us … just like our marriage. It's part of the legacy of remembering to be boyfriend and girlfriend. To us, that split bench seat was part of growing back together in our marriage. We don't get rid of our good maintenance—we foster it. In life and in vehicles.

For those of you who are sales persons, there are a couple of lessons here as well. Neither car dealer was willing to move; we only bought the Tahoe SUV because it happened to come standard with what we wanted. Just out of curiosity, I looked into a body shop about fitting a crew cab split bench in the other manufacturer's big SUV after I had committed to the Tahoe. No problem! The bolt pattern would allow it. Keep in mind I offered to pay extra for this, as it meant a lot to me and Anne. The salesman didn't even offer to check into it. He was just set in his ways and wasn't willing to accommodate us. Too bad for him.

The Chevrolet sales person didn't ask either. If he had asked right away why I was so adamant, would that have become a bargaining chip for him? Would I have paid more? Most likely—we planned to keep the truck for at least twenty years. It was worth it. The $1,000 extra was far less important than the reason we were buying it.

Lesson for all you sales people: If the customer asks something out of the ordinary, ask for the story behind it. Just remember … perhaps Anne and I would be driving the other manufacturer's SUV today if someone had done this!

CHAPTER 35
Leaving Things in God's Hands

Once Anne and I came to know the Lord in late 1988, we began to truly appreciate what having a personal relationship with the Lord meant. We're convinced the Holy Spirit put a thirst in us to get to know Him better from that time on. We were still ten years from retirement and weren't even thinking of it when we came to know Him. At this same time, the oilfield service company I represented stepped up my responsibilities. Not only was my goal to get back several oil companies that had abandoned us in favour of our competitors, but I was to ensure the continued field sales over southern and central Alberta and Saskatchewan. Fortunately, the Lord gave me and Anne the strength to do this and do it well.

Our marriage had been getting a little rocky prior to coming to know the Lord, so one might think that the increased responsibilities would distract us from growing together in the Lord and each other. Quite the contrary. The Edgson team decided to have Anne come with me on the trips away from Calgary. Anyone who knows southeastern Alberta and south Saskatchewan knows how boring repeated trips in those areas by car can be! This was to our advantage, as we grew in the Lord and each other. We had plenty of time to talk about the Lord and with, and about, each other.

We started taking these trips together. Our company car had a cassette tape deck, so we purchased a set of Bible tapes to learn as we went along. We would also look forward to listening to Christian radio after 6:00 p.m. from Briercrest as we travelled in Saskatchewan.

We had very little idea as new believers about "leaving things in the Lord's hands." We wanted to do all we could for the Lord and were often impatient to do these tasks—Lord or not. As one might expect, we were sometimes disappointed and downhearted about our failures to serve the Lord effectively. Then the Lord gave us a lesson in His will and leaving things in His hands. In doing so, He also showed us how much He is in control and knows what is going to happen, even before anyone on earth knows. In all the potential places He chose to do this with Anne and me, he couldn't have found a more unexpected place, under more unexpected circumstances, than he gave us beginning in Shaunavon, Saskatchewan.

Anne and I had travelled from Calgary along the Trans-Canada Highway, then south to Shaunavon, Saskatchewan from Gull Lake along Saskatchewan Highway #37. It was a great paved road, and we had plenty of time to talk. When we were finished with my oil company field contact in Shaunavon, the plan was to go immediately to Swift Current and spend the night, as usual. We had done this trip many times.

This time I felt the urge to go into a farm tractor and implement dealership in Shaunavon and inquire about the cost of a small farm tractor, which we might be able to use on our acreage in the Okanagan in British Columbia. Anne looked at me like I had lost my mind. Why would anyone want to do this, especially in Saskatchewan, which was two provinces away from our Okanagan land? Nevertheless, she said to go for it, and my query went ahead.

The salesman looked at me in a funny fashion but went back to his office and figured out the price. This took a long half hour—a half hour less time for Anne and me to relax in Swift Current. Then he came out with the price.

I had been blessed with many interesting sales phrases prior to this point. One of them certainly applied to his price! Taking one look at the quote, I gasped and said to the tractor representative: "Lord, that is a vacuum cleaner price!"

He looked at me and said, "What?"

I explained that when I gave a quote that was really high to one of my clients, I would warn him that it was a vacuum cleaner price, which means that when he saw it, he would open his mouth, suck in air, and gasp mightily! The sales rep laughed and said the price didn't include shipment to B.C!

Remember the long half hour for later.

Anne and I jumped into my company car and proceeded north to Gull Lake. Leaving Shaunavon, we immediately slipped a Bible tape of the book of James into the tape player and listened as we went along on that clear, sunny day. Air conditioner going, smooth road, the Lord's Word, and a beautiful wife sitting right next to me … what more could a guy want? Total peace and relaxation. Expecting nothing.

The tape came to James 2:26, which said "… *faith without works is dead …*" I immediately hit the pause button and asked Anne: "I wonder what works we could do for the Lord?" She had no immediate idea, so I said "Well, let's just *leave it in the Lord's hands* and see what He has in mind." We continued with the tape lesson.

We reached the junction of the Trans-Canada highway at Gull Lake and turned east toward Swift Current. At this point the Trans-Canada was a four-lane divided highway with wide flat ditches on each side and between the lanes going east and west. It wasn't very far before we came upon an accident scene. At first the accident wasn't visible, but the many big trucks stopped in both directions were. To the south of the broad south ditch of the east-bound lane was a deeper ditch bordering a gravel lane just to south of it. In that lane's ditch was an overturned car. We were told later that the car had been going east toward Swift Current, somehow hit the right (south) shoulder of the highway, spun backwards and flipped, and skidded upside down in a southwesterly direction until it hit the second small ditch, partially shearing off the car's roof. The passenger, the wife of the driver, was wandering around alone in the ditch in shock. I parked the car on the highway, and Anne and I got out and went to the woman. She was uninjured but in tears, as was to be expected.

Soon the RCMP arrived. The constable quite rightly ordered the three of us out of the ditch. The wife refused. We tried to get her to move, but she was coming out of shock and wanted to see her husband. There was potential for a very ugly scene, so Anne suggested I talk to the RCMP. I suggested that I drive my car into the ditch and park far enough away from the scene to be out of danger. I expected him to tell me "where to go," and he did give me a pretty ugly look but said yes.

We moved our car into the ditch so we could see the upside-down car, but not the driver, out the passenger side of our car. The ditch was very wide, so we were far enough away to see the upside-down car without being in the way. In talking to the wife, we found out that she and her husband both knew the Lord.

Praise God! As we carried a Bible, Anne sat in our back seat with the wife and read Bible verses with her. I stood outside. Eventually, the wife was adamant about seeing her husband, who was still in their car. An ambulance was on the way from Swift Current, but she was getting impatient. Anne came and told me about this and informed me that she was going over to the upside-down car to see the shape the husband was in, which she did.

Anne came back, took me aside, and told me she didn't want the wife to see her husband. Anne had been informed that his head had been cut open, even though from her angle she didn't see any blood. He was in the portion of the car that had been crushed flat, so she could only see part of his head. The husband's arm was sticking out, so she took his pulse. There was no pulse; he was dead. Now we had a real quandary. We agreed this wasn't a scene for a distraught wife to see. The best thing we could do was pray and stall.

A farm tractor drove up. He had been ordered by the RCMP to come out, put a chain on the car, and turn it right side up. By now Anne, the wife, and I were back in our car. Both Anne and I were silently praying as hard as we could that the Lord Jesus would not let the wife see her husband at this time, in the shape he was in. Just as the tractor was pulling the car over, an old fire truck from Gull Lake drove up between us and the tractor/car, blocking our view! The wife couldn't see her husband as the car was righted. Then the RCMP officer came over and told us to drive out of the ditch onto the highway. The ambulance arrived almost immediately; the RCMP officer came over and said he would take the wife in his car to Swift Current, and we were left to praise the Lord. We were informed much later that the wife did not see her husband in the mess he was in. Praise the Lord!

Before leaving for Swift Current from the accident scene, I talked to one of the truck drivers who had happened on the scene as the accident took place. I asked him when it had occurred. *"One half hour before you arrived."*

Anne and I were stunned, realizing we had taken half an hour in Shaunavon doing a seemingly meaningless task. If we hadn't taken that half hour in Shaunavon, we would have driven by the accident point before it happened. The truck driver saw Anne and me looking both overwhelmed and joyful, and wondered why. I asked him if he knew the Lord. He did. We told him the circumstances about the half hour delay in Shaunavon. We all stood there hugging each other and praising the Lord!

If I hadn't felt the urge from Someone, who we believe is the Holy Spirit, to ask that price, and the tractor and implement dealer had not taken his half hour, and if the Lord had not known what was going to happen to two of those travelling down the highways who believed in Him, and if the Lord had not known my mind when I listened to the tape of James and would ask the question about how we could serve the Lord, would Anne and I have been there to serve Him the way we did? We had left things in the Lord's hands while listening to the Bible tapes. What happened is welded in our minds forever. We now take things to the Lord every opportunity we can, and if so compelled by the Lord, we leave it in His hands until He sees fit to bless us with his direction and answers, whatever they may be. Needless to say, we floated from that scene on the Trans-Canada Highway to Swift Current, singing praises to the Lord! In addition to the blessing of being able to comfort a fellow believer, Anne and I knew our rocky marriage was getting far less rough. The Lord used both of us; the Lord wanted us to serve Him together.

The Lord is in control, and we thank Him for enabling us to listen to Him and serve Him according to His will. We were impatient; we now seek out that will and wait for His answer even as we pray.

CHAPTER 36
Unexpected Lessons

Often in our lives something unexpected happens that leads to a blessing. As noted in the previous chapter, Anne and I wanted to do whatever we could to serve the Lord. We consciously left things in God's hands, and He used us according to His plan and will. From this we realized that those who had been forgiven much and handed their lives over to the Lord have a deep intimacy with Him.

There have been other times in our lives when we haven't made a conscious effort to connect, yet the Lord called us to help others then blessed us afterwards. One such event occurred in the Shuswap in February, 1994.

We love to point out to Alberta relatives and friends that our Okanagan Valley home is "Paradise on Earth." If you live in "Paradise," where do you go for a vacation? The Shuswap!

In 1984 we bought a used twenty-four-foot cabin cruiser boat from an oil patch friend and discovered a new water wonder world—Shuswap Lake. It's a two-hour drive north of the Okanagan with a cooler, moister climate and lots of sunshine. The four-armed lake is an endless water playground! We came to love fishing and camping in secluded Shuswap Lake coves. We enjoyed the wilderness peace and quiet rather than fast, noisy boats and water skiing.

We moored both our old 1984 boat and our current boat on the North Shuswap near a village and Provincial Park. We had taken frequent summer trips to our Okanagan acreage and the Shuswap after our move to Calgary in 1988. In December of that year, we made the most important discovery of our lives— Jesus Christ our Lord! From that point on, finding a good Christian church when we went on summer vacations became very important. This we found in a North Shuswap village two blocks off the lakefront. We could beach or dock our boat and walk to it.

We also drove 135 kilometres from our acreage to Sunday service, should we not be fishing and camping on the Shuswap. We often drove there from the Okanagan for the pure delight of the mountain scenery and a picnic lunch after the church service.

By 1994, we were focussed more on learning and active adventures than accumulating "stuff" and social climbing. Jim's widowed mother gave us each a 1993 Christmas gift of a nice pair of mittens with a $100 bill inside! This was a sweet gift, as we had never lived close to either set of parents during our years employed in the oil industry. We both needed a new winter jacket that year, and with the normal winter price per jacket being around $100, her gift was very appropriate.

Our busy lives put us off buying new winter jackets for a time. February Family Day long weekend arrived, and we still hadn't taken the time to purchase them. It was our custom to take a week vacation during this time to go to British Columbia to cross country ski and escape city life. The weather had been un-usually mild on the prairies. As well, there was almost no snow on the ground be-tween the Okanagan and Shuswap. Everyone was happily walking about in shoes and open jackets! We took our two-hour Sunday drive up to the North Shuswap Church with our picnic lunch in a cooler, *still* with two $100 bills in our wallets.

Church announcement time came. The first announcement noted a family had lost their home to a fire, and the church was taking up a collection for them. Second announcement: they were having a pot luck supper and missionary presentation that evening. Wow!

Jim and I looked at each other. The $100 bills were in our wallets. We were led to put one of those bills toward the family fund. Led ... absolutely joyfully!

We decided to stay for the evening function as well. It was pot luck, but we had an afternoon to get something. Kamloops was only an hour's drive west. We would browse in the city's mall for a couple of hours and return with some dinner buns as our contribution.

Driving to Kamloops, we noted there was no snow on the ground, just dust flying. We walked into the mall to see everything winter related marked down to the point of sell off. Jim and I each bought a warm winter jacket for less than half price. Even with taxes in, the total cost for both was $104! It was warm outside, but it was warmer in our hearts. Praise God! He had blessed us by keeping those Christmas gifts in our wallets until He pointed out how we should use part of them. Then he blessed us according to our needs. God lives, and His will is there!

God wants to talk to you in His love. He wants a committed love relationship from you. Through prayer and discernment, you can hear Him when He calls you. Obey His direction to love Him by likewise loving your brother in need, and He will take care of your needs! Jim and I know this first-hand.

CHAPTER 37
Successful Marriages

We hesitated to write this chapter because the road to our wonderful marriage in our seventies was at times extremely rocky! It seemed arrogant to even attempt to do so, yet we've been married for over fifty years at the writing of this book. We love each other, we have fun together, we are a team, we work with each other, we have learned and are learning from our experiences, and we comfort and counsel each other. We also find great comfort in knowing the Lord. Currently it is actually a quite successful marriage!

Whether or not you know the Lord, it's certainly possible to find success and have a successful marriage, but perhaps not always at the same time. This has been true for Anne and me, and I am certainly not ashamed of our marriage. The woman the Lord gave me, the wife of my youth, is greatly loved! So why not write about it?

Truthfully, we weren't prepared for marriage in 1966. We were in love, and we made sure we took the morally correct path and saved ourselves for marriage, yet we had no training in finances or what to expect once married. On my wedding day, I nearly ran before Anne reached the altar … until the pastor told me to turn around and look at my bride coming down the aisle. My heart melted. I needed her!

I was an exhilarated boyfriend who seriously courted Anne. I wasn't so great a boyfriend when I smothered her. She was and is gorgeous, so I was jealous. After all, other men couldn't be so blind! Anne tolerated this, but not all the time. She wasn't going to be my possession.

Once married, it was almost as if I said, "Well, project completed. On to the next task." I cringe at myself for thinking that now. Marriages don't fail all at once, but in many small steps. From the day of our marriage those small steps started. It's a testimony to Anne that she put up with the situation for so long. Eventually it got bad enough, we were just about on the slippery slope leading to a failed marriage.

Then the Lord stepped in and brought us both to Him.

Because Anne had tolerated me for so long, once we came to know the Lord and He started working on me, she found a new freedom to vent the frustrations she had kept to herself for so long. While she knew the Lord, she was having great trouble overlooking all the negative incidents prior to that highlight in our lives. We had been married twenty-two years before meeting the Lord. The next six years were rough.

Anne had had enough, and she was determined that our marriage would improve. We were both new in the Lord, but those twenty-two years of small, downward steps meant we were near the bottom in our relationship. Make no mistake—just because one has come to a saving knowledge of the Lord doesn't mean the consequences of past mistakes will disappear, no matter how small or large. There were two very important beliefs we had going for us, though: the definite realization the Lord was in control of our lives, and the commitment we had made to each other way back in 1963 before even going on our first date. We also heard an inner voice telling us to work issues out. My "lord and master" attitude had to go; Anne had to get over her anger for being held down those twenty-two years.

Noted elsewhere in this book are blessed circumstances that literally forced us to be close to each other, talk with each other, listen to each other, and grow together. We started travelling together in my company car on my sales trips in southern Saskatchewan and Alberta. Sound boring? It was not! Rather than just sit there bored, we looked around intently as we drove the back country of Western Canada. We saw all sorts of little things we both liked. We talked excitedly about them, just like a courting couple searching for something common to talk about. There were incidents put in our days that made us realize the Lord wanted us to be together ("Leaving Things in God's Hands"). Plus, Anne found a purpose in being with me on those sales trips ("Using 'Graft' Constructively"). We weren't only modelling a nicely married couple, we were being blessed by the Lord, causing us to actually be that way!

The company cars I drove had bench front seats of one kind or another. Anne found it very easy to slide over and sit beside me as we travelled. Keep in mind that we were in our forties at this time! As we began to realize there was actually something very special going on between us, we made the corporate decision to get our first fully-loaded, personally owned four-wheel vehicle specifically with a bench seat ("Someone Had to Move"). Sure, we were teased by those younger than us for sitting so close together, but that only encouraged Anne to squeeze closer!

We still had a lot of baggage. Some of it went back into our childhoods. Some of it came from my realization of how beautiful Anne was and my lack of understanding that she wasn't going to "fool around" on me—my jealousy. She got irritated with me for being jealous; I got angry over her not sympathising with my feelings! Here were two confused people thinking more of themselves than as a couple meant for each other. It was a serious learning time for both of us, no matter how much we enjoyed being together and even though we had been married twenty-two years.

Then something interesting happened. In our frustration, we hinted to others in our home church in Calgary that we were having trouble. Frankly, they weren't much help; indeed, some told us our situation was unlikely to improve. Two things happened. Upon hearing that last statement, I blurted out, "*There is nothing impossible for the Lord I know and love!*" This did not deter those saying the bothersome statement, but it was true.

Secondly, an elder of our church going to seminary gave us something life changing—some tapes on marriage. He had found them in a bin where people would swap good books and tapes they no longer needed but others might use. The tapes weren't just about marriages in trouble—the full gambit of marriage counselling was covered. They were quite funny; circumstances in those tapes mirrored some of the events that happened to us as we were courting, as well as after we were married. We could see that the husband and wife represented in the tapes really liked and loved each other. The feelings we had at the time were a combination of joy and … sadness. Sadness because we had let our relationship slip so badly. The joy part triumphed as we realized we had a lot going for us … a tremendous amount of *positive* going for us! Combine this with our Bible tapes as we travelled, our conversations, our realizations that we really were one and belonged to the Lord, and then add one more lesson. Two of the tapes dealt with how spouses should behave toward one another. Having a large remnant of ego, I decided to (read: Did not ask Anne. Note the problem, folks!) play the tape outlining how the wife should treat her husband. That tape was put in the player first.

It was all about how a husband should treat a wife! I had been snookered! It was obviously designed for an egotistical husband. I not only felt convicted … I *was* convicted.

Anne of course had seen the rather illicit motive behind me going with "her" tape first and was mildly ticked off. We played the husband tape next. *It was all for the wife*!

Here we had two rather sheepish people—Anne and me, who had unexpectedly been told how they should be living. Anne fell quiet. So did I. We were travelling between Regina and Saskatoon in Saskatchewan. The silence continued for quite some time. I really wanted to say something, but the words just wouldn't come. Then Anne said something that was a game changer:

"Jim, I forgive you."

I had to thank her so much. *I needed to hear that so badly!*

Was that the end of our learning? Not by any means. Garbage gradually accumulated for years had to be first shovelled out, and then the stains had to be washed. The Lord is doing the washing every day in our lives. The old "lord and master" in me is gone. It's true there are circumstances where a tough decision has to be made after full and equal input. I as the husband have to prayerfully make that final decision, but there is no blaming the wife. Any decision made by the Edgson team is now my responsibility. My wife and partner is protected in public, even if a bad mistake is made. We might have a private and considered conversation now that we are in our seventies when something goes bad, but that conversation does not spill out in public. There is no question we have an equal partnership in our marriage, with me as the husband being the one who takes final responsibility when something goes wrong. And frankly, there is no fuller joy than pointing out in public that Anne is the reason for the majority of the good things that have happened and are happening in our lives!

After all, the Lord made us one. Faith without works is dead, folks! And the faith the Lord has given us leads us to do His works, which preserve and grow our marriage while giving Him all the glory.

CHAPTER 38
Foibles

The two of us have some interesting foibles that can be both troublesome and funny … funny if you're the one hearing about them and not suffering the consequences! In my case, something had to be done to prepare myself for the foible to happen. That "something" was the purchasing of a watch. This particular watch has several features that are helpful during the day, months, and years it is worn. It gives the outside temperature, as long as you take off the watch and leave it away from your body for fifteen to twenty minutes. There is an altimeter based on the barometric pressure from the watch that is very handy when hiking. It's solar powered, which is fine as long as you have sufficiently long days or prolonged indoor exposure to light. These and other features are handy, but to me—and recently Anne—the watch helps explain a troubling physical happening in our heads.

When we lived in Calgary, something would happen to me especially in winter that was very annoying. Headaches occurred without any apparent reason. They would go away in a few hours without any medical intervention. They also very occasionally occurred in non-wintery seasons for no apparent reason.

Being the analytical type, I started observing what was happening around me when this problem arose. Was this a case of being confronted by an upset customer? No, they were handled. It also had nothing to do with eating or drinking. One thing interesting did pop up in the winter—within twenty-four hours after getting the headache, a chinook would occur. A chinook occurs in winter when the outdoor temperature rapidly warms up with a great wind from the nearby mountains, resulting in melting snow. It was said "chinook" was the First Nations name for "the wind that eats snow."

Since chinooks could definitely be associated with rapidly falling barometric pressure, the purchase of a wearable instrument that measures barometric pressure seemed appropriate. If falling pressure was indeed the problem, it could be anticipated. Mind you, monitoring this every second wasn't practical, so I needed an instrument that would plot this pressure over time.

I found such an instrument in the watch I now have. It gives instantaneous barometric pressure on demand, as well as plots the pressure every two hours. From this watch I observed that while there was no chinook occurring, as the pressure initially dropped rapidly, the wind would soon pick up and the temperature in Calgary would rise quickly. Now I can see a sudden pressure drop and prepare myself for the headache. Anticipating headaches associated with rapidly dropping barometric pressure makes them annoying without being too painful. Later when we were retired, Anne began to experience mild headaches with the same weather occurrences. She is now prepared for this, as we both monitor the barometric pressure off my watch.

Anne's main foible is a little deadlier. While appreciating the electricity of her kiss, it never occurred to me she could be electrically dangerous! This problem didn't become really obvious to me for some time. As noted in this book, Anne wasn't one for fancy things; she was and is "low maintenance." She is beautiful, so I wanted to get her something. She's not one to wear jewellery of any type, including watches, so I came up with the idea of giving her a wristwatch.

There were two problems with me doing this. First was where we lived at the time— Calgary, Alberta. Calgary has "interesting" winters. Besides chinooks, it experiences blizzards. The joke was that if you didn't like the current winter temperature, just wait twenty minutes and it would change! Calgary also has dry winters; the relative humidity can be lower than in Saudi Arabia. You really do need a humidifier in your home for winter comfort.

The second problem will be discussed a little later in this story.

The first watch I gave her died within two weeks, so I purchased a higher quality one. It died. Next I gave her a really expensive, battery-powered watch. It died! Then I bought the cheapest watch available. It died! No watch that I bought would work after a short time. To say the least, this was frustrating!

What happened next would bring the problem to a "striking" conclusion. We decided to buy a portable land phone that could easily be carried in one's pocket around the home. We purchased a nice, expensive flip phone, and then I went away on a short field trip.

Pause here. Our condominium in Calgary had shag carpet. It was winter. It was cold. Note from above ... that meant it was dry inside. Let us continue.

I phoned from my field trip on the way home to let Anne know her husband was coming back. I heard the phone ring, a click, then—nothing! Oh well. As I was only an hour away, I just went home. Anne was very upset as I came in the door. She reached for the new phone as it rang, and a lightning bolt came out of her finger when she was about four inches from it! That hurt! She picked the phone up; it was dead. No problem, dear! "I'll just take it in and see what happened."

The day after I took the phone in, I got a call at work. The repair person was wondering whatever happened to the phone. I asked why he would ask such a question. He'd opened up the phone and discovered that everything was melted inside. It was as if a lightning bolt had struck it. Of course, my honest reply needed to be that it had. The warranty would not cover such damage!

I went home and talked with Anne. She had been wearing fuzzy, comfortable slippers as she vacuumed the shag rug and walked across the room to answer the phone. The static electricity bolt that shot from her finger was so intense, it was blue in the middle. It burnt her finger, and it literally fried the phone!

It turns out this electrical "problem" was evident during Anne's teen years. She was killing watches even back then! Having issues like this are difficult to understand, so Anne didn't discuss it until after the "lightning" episode in Calgary, and the further killing of many watches. *Lack of understanding with the accompanying lack of belief was the second problem.* Both of us understand now that there is an issue within her body, which is of no medical concern. Anne is an electrifying person to me, and we both understand and accept what goes on.

The solutions to all of this? Anne doesn't wear a watch. Fuzzy slippers are gone (she wears leather ones now). We do not have thick rug anywhere in our home, and winters where we live in retirement in British Columbia have much higher humidity!

There are some positives to end the story. Anne eventually bought a cell phone when we retired to B.C., although reluctantly at first because we were concerned she would blow it up! The phone sometimes does weird things as she explores her apps on it. The barometric pressure problem actually led to the discovery that we could go into the mountains and find huckleberries at a certain altitude. Now when we go hiking in the mountains, we pay attention to the altimeter. Quite a few times we would see we were at a particular height when hiking mountain trails and, voila! There were plenty of huckleberries to pick!

Foibles understood, paid attention to, mitigated, and taken advantage of can be a fun part of life. Just don't wear fuzzy slippers on shag carpet in Calgary in winter!

The Retirement and Political Years
Thoughts and Events
1998 to 2018

CHAPTER 39
Advice

We are now in the period in our lives post-1998 after retiring from thirty-two years with the oil industry service company I had worked for continuously. We built and still live in our dream retirement home, a 4,700 square foot hand-crafted log home. It took two years to build, and my beautiful bride of thirty-two years at the time of retirement made it very clear she was not going to move again. The only way she'd move out of this home would be in a pine box. We will see what the Lord provides in this respect!

We have been married for over fifty years and have lived in the completed log home for over eighteen years. This in itself was a new experience, as neither one of us had lived in one place for so many years, either before or after marriage. We've had many more blessed experiences gained after retiring from the oil patch through volunteering, politics, and true (believe it or not) retirement. We have reached the point in our lives now where we believe continued advice from these experiences can be offered to hopefully benefit you in your day-to-day lives.

We all have either given or received advice many times in our lives. Some of it we deemed good at the time, some we didn't appreciate, some we didn't take, some we wished we had taken, some we gave, and some we should not have given. Anne and I experienced many of these moments in our lives. The suggestions outlined in this chapter were sometimes learned the hard way.

Let's start with receiving advice. Take into consideration your circumstances or situation when someone offers advice and accept it graciously whenever possible. Getting your back up leads to the undesirable effect of people not wanting to give you further advice, or possibly viewing you as someone temperamental and intransigent. Even if the advice appears wrong, mean-spirited, or even unhealthy, try to receive it graciously to avoid heated arguments. Note I said "receive," not necessarily accept! Take advice into consideration, even briefly. There may be a snippet of valuable information you can utilize to your benefit. If not, you can always silently hit the "delete" button in your brain afterwards.

Once you act on advice, the results are your responsibility. Case in point—I once acted on a stock tip that resulted in a loss of money when the stock was sold. The person who gave the tip didn't do the buying ... I did. The person giving the advice bears no responsibility for his or her actions unless there is some guarantee in writing. Verbal advice always contains a caveat—you act on it, you are responsible for the results. You may become wary of the person giving such advice, and you may make sure you get something in writing next time. After receiving bad advice, you at least gain a positive lesson not to repeat it!

Consider also how to offer advice from the point of view of a politician, which I was for a seven-year period after retiring from the oil industry. I made a point of offering advice in a way that gave clear direction, and no person or corporation received consideration without a valid business case for me to look at. After being convinced there was a valid business case that would benefit the constituency, the province, and/or the country, I would offer sincere and valuable direction that could be followed by the individual or group to help accomplish their goals. I preceded the advice with "I would recommend" or "I would *strongly* recommend." To those familiar with the way I dealt with people, no further explanation was needed. To fresh groups or people, it would be said, "If I say 'I would recommend' that means you're going in a positive direction and I'll be happy to support you. If I say 'I would *strongly* recommend,' you'd be foolish not to follow what was offered."

How you present your case becomes more personal when advising a friend or acquaintance. Be sure you have facts and information that can be substantiated. If you must offer an opinion, clearly state that it's your opinion. Beware of being insistent. Above all, don't start offering advice unless you fully understand the situation you are dealing with. If someone approaches you for advice on a situation that *in their opinion* is the fault of others, don't be too swift to advise if you don't fully understand the situation or the story from the other side. If the person seeking such advice gets upset with you for talking to the other side, back off or you could be in effect choosing sides.

Quite often you'll be asked if you've had a similar experience to what the person is experiencing at the present time. If you have, feel free to say so, followed by what happened in your situation, the results, how you handled it, and what you learned. Don't leave details out but discern what you say. If the person seeking advice listens to your well-articulated experiential advice, they'll get the point. Now comes the most important point: after relating your experience, you may make a recommendation, noting "But this is up to you. Please take this advice with the understanding that you need to make your own decision to do what's best for you."

I did this many times. I believe it's the best way to proceed, because while you're putting the entire responsibility to act on the person being advised, you're also giving that person the opportunity to gain personal experience.

I don't recommend pushing your view. We're not talking about building a case, but ignoring any questions or objections presented by the person. They may just have some valid points that need to be considered! Now is the time for you to listen and either polish your advice or further study the matter and come back again. Pushing someone could be like pushing the edge of a bedsheet— one side piles up, resulting in a messy situation. Worse, if you push someone who has a mind like a concrete slab—one who has firmly made his mind up— that slab could fall on you! Advise in a manner that doesn't cause the person to get their back up. Ideally, advice should be given under calm and considered circumstances, with both sides listening and receiving.

At times it may be inappropriate to offer advice. Sometimes friends have a falling out because one of them insists on proceeding their own way, no matter how negatively it affects other people, and friendly persuasion or even pleading has done absolutely no good. Indeed, the insistent one may actually get to the point of considering you the enemy! Those people are so self-centred, they'd prefer to lose and even denigrate their friends to get their own way. If you should experience someone essentially making him or herself your enemy, I suggest you never interfere with that person while they are in the process of destroying themselves. Leave them be. They've made up their mind; they don't want to listen to anything you have to say, and what they do is their own responsibility. Don't make it yours.

One thing I will *strongly recommend* (note how I say that) is to never demand. Unless you're a drill sergeant in a military situation, never demand! If you do demand, you're not advising—you're dictating. You'll find the receiving person may just tell you where to go. Further, no matter how valid your "advice" is, it could get totally ignored. If you demand and the person receives it graciously, then read the beginning of this chapter again. You may eventually notice the gracious acceptance of your "advice" is not only *not* acted on but is deleted, and you may be avoided in the future.

Giving advice is the act of carefully considering the situation occurring in the other person's life. You are doing this to hopefully have something received that will be beneficial to the receiver. It's not about you; it's for the receiver. Advice given knowledgeably, gently, and with due consideration for the person being advised is far more likely to be received gratefully and acted upon judiciously. And remember—be sure you are heeding your own advice!

CHAPTER 40
Beauty

Anne and I weren't computer conversant until recently. We never "did" Twitter and Facebook because they weren't all that private. As a politician, I saw fellow politicians hurt or wounded badly by what they naively posted on those entities. Nope! Anne and I didn't even text.

One day our daughter-in-law asked us if we wanted to see and have some pictures of our youngest granddaughter. Pause here for a moment. Anne was a "middle child." She has a brilliant older brother, who is Professor Emeritus at McGill University in eastern Canada. She has a younger sister whose teenage zest for popularity was considerable. Anne considered herself the type of girl whom no one really noticed. This is what *she* thought—not me!

We thought we knew our younger granddaughter, who is also a middle child. We thought she was a quiet, shy young lady. We had no idea how she fit in at school. While she was developing physically quite nicely, we didn't see her as outgoing. She was rather withdrawn whenever we talked to her. Interestingly enough, if she attended the University of Alberta, she'd be attending about fifty years after we'd attended. Note the word "if." When we thought we "knew" her, we had no idea if she would be able to attend.

Several things happened at the time of her graduation from high school. First, we were informed she was doing quite well academically. This we did not expect, "knowing what she was like" (in our uninformed opinion). Second, we were asked if we wanted copies of this young lady's graduation pictures. Third, we expected a bespectacled, shy, young girl. Fourth, we wanted to be polite. Is that not what grandparents are … at least?

Then we got the pictures. *Wow!* Was this beauty really our middle granddaughter? We eagerly attended her high school graduation in Edmonton to get to know her better and to encourage her.

She'd decided to forgo eyeglasses in favour of contact lenses. She had a part time job and worked hard to get nice looking clothes. She had gained a ton of confidence while doing so well in high school. Her best features were her smile and bright eyes. Unbelievably beautiful!

My first sight of Anne was from her back with a swept-up hairdo, long winter coat, and gorgeous calves below her coat. I went down to make a move on that girl because of her legs! Joe Cool in university, purely physical curiosity and attraction. As I approached her from the left, I saw the most beautiful female face I'd ever seen. It blew my mind! I lost complete control over what I was going to say. Our first meeting is welded in my mind, even though I got the feeling she would choose being home babysitting the cat over having anything to do with me!

Our granddaughter's smile and young beauty blew my mind again! Here I was standing at her grad next to the wife of my youth—whose beauty continues to grow—and a young, beautiful woman who is my granddaughter. It boggled my mind!

This bright-eyed teenager asked us if we texted, and we told her no. We explained why not but said we would try. We did—regularly! She broke *us* out of one of our shells. What another pleasant surprise!

Moving ahead a couple of years, our Bright Eyes sent one of her eagerly-awaited texts from university, with the subject of beauty brought up. By now, even though she was still in her late teens, she had gained so much confidence. We considered her an adult—one we were so blessed to be conversant and associated with. The word "beauty" remained in our minds after that text. I decided it was an appropriate time to discuss what beauty meant to me in my text to her from Anne's and my perspective of seventy-one years of age. Here is generally what the beauty part of my text said:

"Beauty. Let's talk about it. While there is lots of beauty in this world, let's talk about beautiful women. From GP's (**GrandP**a's) perspective!

"There are two really beautiful women in GP's life right now—GM (**GrandMa**) and you. I am not talking physical-type beauty—I am talking a beauty that goes way deeper. When I met your GM-to-be, I was stunned beyond belief (by the beauty of her face). When I saw your grad pictures, I was stunned beyond belief (by the beauty of your face). In both cases there was, and is, something there that in my mind defines 'beauty.'

"So what is it? GM was and is 'perky.' You are perky. Perky? Well, yours and her inherent enthusiastic love for life and both of your desires to serve others defines some of that inner 'beauty.'

"GM has a radiant smile that melts my heart. You have a smile that melts my heart. GM was a little unconfident when I met her. You were a little unconfident at first as well. GM developed her confidence over the years I knew her because she knew she mattered to me. You are developing your confidence, and we both love seeing your progress!

"You see, beauty is not static. It grows. Like your beauty is growing. GP and GM are aging together as GM's beauty grows in her. That is why I say the eighteen-year-old I met in 1963 is even more beautiful at seventy-one. Honestly.

"How do we express our appreciation of such beauty? Your GM looked like a beautiful little doll when I first met her. I called her 'Dolly' for years as an intimate sign of what I thought of her beauty.

"Perhaps you now understand why I call you 'Bright Eyes.' Same reason. Keep it up! You are truly beautiful to me and GM."

There was more to the text—there always is. Anne and I feel very close to Bright Eyes. She attended the same university we did. She is experiencing the same situations we did. Both Anne and I wanted her to understand our view of "beautiful." Mind you, both Anne and she seem to me as being beautiful in the physical sense as well. The most important part of their beauty is that it's of the type that will last and grow. The woman the Lord gave me is the wife of my youth. I rejoice in the wife of my youth! I also rejoice that the Lord put such a beautiful young woman on this earth as our Bright Eyes—one who has a heart to serve and benefit others and not just herself.

And … she taught us to text!

CHAPTER 41
Caring about Someone—
Can You Take It Too Far?

When we started our married and employed lives after I graduated from the University of Alberta, we soon discovered that the telephone could be a very intrusive irritant in our lives. This was before cell phones existed, and even before portable phones were common. To escape the effect of the phone ringing, we just … escaped! We took time off, which included time away from phones. Also, there was no personal Internet at the time. While the reader may think we were hindered in what we could do, we could look forward to some privacy occasionally. In today's world it's called wireless holidays.

While I was working, the company owned what personal life we had. You will recall a story from Anne early in this book about a guy working in the oil industry who's married to his company, and his wife is the mistress! Sad but true back then!

Today we have cell phones and texting as part of the blessings in our modern life. Anne and I have come to rely on our wireless devices, along with the Internet, because of their convenience. Most of the time we appreciate the speed of cell phones and the Internet and use them extensively. We keep our land phones because there's one big advantage they bring to people living in the rural forest interface. If an emergency occurs, emergency responders can pinpoint accurately where the person is located as long as that land phone is directly wired. Land phones work if the power is out, whereas portable land phones cannot be used if the power is out. Wireless devices do function if the power is down but cannot be recharged at home if the power is out. Hopefully in the near future wireless devices with built-in GPS locators will solve the location issue, but charging wireless devices will still require power!

We are seniors now. Anyone reading or hearing about the many scams and frauds going on realizes seniors are a target. We looked seriously at this and believe everyone, including seniors, must take personal responsibility for their actions as long as they are mentally capable of doing so. If we as seniors are not mentally capable, then we have a responsibility to consider getting caregivers or going to a care home. In the meantime, Anne and I have taken personal responsibility to at least mitigate fraud and scam artists. We also have taken measures to control how our phones are utilized—both cellular and land phones.

We have call display and voicemail on every phone, including and especially our land phone. We monitor who is calling on all our devices, and if we're not familiar with the caller, we let the phone go to voicemail. If the call is important, a message will be left. If unimportant, generally there's no message. Even if there is voicemail, we can swiftly identify a scam. We do not reply to scams. If we inadvertently answer a scam attempt, we hang up. No use being polite! Those characters have no character anyway.

We also genuinely care for each other. We've talked about what we would do if either of us were abducted, and we have a clear understanding of what we both expect the other will do should such a situation arise. We also care about each other's feelings. We bear in mind all the lessons we learned over the years about phones, and we do not let phones of any type rule our lives.

But can we care about each other too much? Can we decide something is just not important enough to communicate at a particular time? Do we use each other's feelings as an excuse to leave an issue for a later date? Does it matter?

One applicable instance is welded in our minds and is actually quite funny. It led to a calm and quiet discussion about whether we use caring for each other as an excuse for doing nothing for a period of time, because one of us deemed what was going on to be "not that urgent"? The funny part about this case is that both of us were rather sheepishly guilty in the end. We did get a big lesson from this series of events, which will help us in the future.

We needed some repairs on our water heater—not too urgent, but they were needed. As the boiler was about twenty years old, parts needed to be ordered. This was done, and we waited a long time to hear back. We went out for a walk on a Friday at noon, returned, and then ploughed right into some tasks we individually had to do.

Saturday rolled around and Anne checked the land phone. There was a message about the parts, asking me to call back. Anne knew the repair office was closed and that I was busy with some projects … which while interesting and exciting were not life and death events. Anne cared enough that I was enjoying myself and didn't tell me about the message, because neither one of us could call until Monday. She thought she would give me the message over breakfast on that day.

We had a great weekend. While Anne was preparing breakfast on Monday, I thought to phone the repair place before breakfast without telling her. I cared enough about her not to bother her as she was making our breakfast. When I phoned, they told me they had called on Friday and were expecting a return call from me! I called downstairs and asked Anne if she had gotten a voicemail message … she had. Amongst the confusion, we got the repair scheduled and settled down and had a discussion with each other.

Neither one of us had checked the phone when we returned from walking. Solution? First one taking their shoes off after getting in the door would pick up the phone and listen for the message signal. What if there had been a message about a loved one being hurt? Solution? It doesn't take any effort to lift a land phone receiver to see if there's a message waiting. We should also care enough about each other to communicate any message immediately. This will be done.

But how about me? In my rather misplaced sense of "caring," I placed the call without talking with Anne. Communication with Anne should have occurred either through a text (our house is big) or in person, indicating I was about to phone the repair place. Then and only then should I have placed the call. But this thought was ignored and my call went ahead. I did not communicate either.

The bottom line for both of us was that we should care enough for each other not to assume things. We should put communicating with each other first. Can we care too much about each other? Only if the care is misplaced! And that can be solved by timely talking with each other.

CHAPTER 42
Christmas Perceptions and Myths

Every year we are bombarded with messages on TV and other media about the "perfect Christmas" and how we all should buy, and give (after buying), and be with family (after buying). It has reached the point where most of us believe we must travel (buy fuel or transportation) to be with family or figure out some way to produce a great Christmas meal at home (after buying). Seldom in the mainline media do we hear about the reason for the season: *Christ*. Part of Christ-mass.

True, there are many stories in the media about those in need, which is a welcome change from the constant advertising that starts two months before Christmas. There are many needy people, and we should all figure out a way to help. But the rest of us have to … must … have a perfectly nice family "time" at Christmas. Right?

Or do we? Has there been a wonderful and peaceful time within your family over the year prior to Christmas? Is everyone in harmony? Or do some of you put on a nice smile, get together with a group of people who happen to be your family, open presents, share a meal, and then truthfully look forward to Boxing Day sales so you can get out and do something for yourself? Are you living a myth at Christmas because "it's the thing to do"? If so, you may be "doing the

Christmas thing" to be sure you "fit in" with the modern world's perceived way of "doing" Christmas. Nothing more.

If you're truly looking forward to seeing all your family, and they're all looking forward to being with you, that's absolutely wonderful! If you're celebrating the birth of the Christ child while gathering together, even better! If all is peace and harmony, and you and those you love aren't putting on a show for the rest of the world to see and believe that your lives are better than theirs, absolutely marvellous. Why marvellous? Because in our experience, the consumer myth of near-perfection out there is not always reality.

You can test to see if you're at the marvellous stage—it's what you do for the rest of the year. If you and those you love are always excited to be together, whether you come to them or they come to you, you just might be at the marvellous stage. Another possible test is to consider what you do on the day after Christmas. If you'd rather be shopping than with your loved ones, you just might not be at the marvellous stage.

Anne and I built a big log home in retirement. We used the ideas we got from lodges and resorts we had visited over the years. It has wood burning fireplaces in the great room and master bedroom … not gas-fired or TV illustrations but wood burning. We have a hot tub in the lower level and a quick exit from that tub to piles of snow outside if we want to get Scandinavian! We heat with wood through a boiler/furnace going to floor heat. We can put up really tall Christmas trees, although we've discovered that twelve feet is the practical limit. The main bedrooms have duvets; we have plenty of bedrooms and bathrooms for our family if they choose to visit.

We made a decision many years ago to build such a home because we had travelled all over Western Canada while Jim was employed. This retirement home was going to be our roots. Since we retired, moving again has never been a thought. We wanted to stay put except for the outdoor activities we enjoy so much, and to temporarily visit places we wanted to see and experience. We considered our family when we designed the log home. It was our hope if we provided a lodge for the family to come to, they would come and visit. There was one problem with this assumption, though.

Right out of university we went to work to pay off debts and make a living. But we neglected to note an important trend in our lives: *we were too busy making a living to have a life.* We transferred from place to place. True, we bought land and travelled, but the majority of the time the example we gave our kids was "work hard."

Guess what? Our kids are now *too busy making a living to have a life!*

Now we have this spacious lodge with just two of us. Do we downsize? Not our style. After all, we do have a lodge, and our kids, grandkids, and great grandkids are most welcome to come visit us and take advantage of our lodge. We travelled so much during our "employed" years, we don't want to travel in the winter farther than the local cross country ski hills. The lodge is here; if our kids and grandkids want to, they can come. In the meantime, we thoroughly enjoy what we worked so hard for! We do counsel our kids to make sure they have a good life with their family by working well and having family priorities ... not exclusive of each other.

But what about family time at Christmas? Shouldn't we go and see the kids eight hundred to a thousand kilometres away? Are we not feeling lonely at that time of year? Truthfully, no, and for two reasons: we don't want to travel that distance by car in winter, and we really dislike the rush and hassle of air travel at Christmas. That's for younger folks. We're in our big lodge with all the amenities; we are where we can enjoy winter. We also don't want our family travelling by car or plane in winter unless they want to, for the same reasons. We can safely visit them in warmer times of the year, or they can visit us likewise.

But aren't you lonely? Truthfully, no ... again! Our second and physically closer family is our church—a large one in Kelowna, British Columbia. They have six or more Christmas services over three days, all of them intense. We really love serving in all of them—Anne with children and infants, and me as a greeter/usher—like we do the rest of the year. We see the church attendees we either see or don't see during the rest of the year. All of us celebrating the true meaning of Christmas! Plus, we get to drive up and down one of the most scenic roads in the Okanagan every day, during which time we reflect on life on the way to church, and the blessings received from the services on the way home. By the end of the third day, on Christmas Eve, we come home—Anne thoroughly filled up with her grandma fix, and me having been filled by cheerfully greeting six-thousand-plus friends and people. Exhausted with pure joy, we relax in a hot tub and watch videos past midnight in our lodge. We are truly blessed!

Why do we want to stay home and serve at all these events? There are a lot of people out there who need to see someone who wants to serve them and/or their children. They need to see someone cares about them. They need to see there is someone who puts the Lord above shopping. Anne and I don't know what's going on in the lives of those we serve at Christmas. I personally hope that with a cheerful smile, a firm handshake, and a clearly meant "Merry Christmas" for those who attend, I will lighten someone's burdens, as will the message they are coming in to see and hear. Anne just hopes the children she cares for will see another loving grandma and look forward to the time they spend at Trinity.

We both hope we can bring smiles to busy people who are too busy making a living to have a life, or who have burdensome circumstances in life that need a smile and a welcoming greeting. We feel led to do this to help lessen those burdens at the special time of year we celebrate Someone who came to lift burdens from our souls. How can we be lonely or sorrowful when so involved?

You see, folks, there's a perception out there of how to celebrate the perfect Christmas. Most of the time that perception is something people try to create themselves. They sometimes have difficulty understanding why we don't behave the same way. When we explain our actions, some truly understand and encourage us. Others condemn us and shun us while pursuing what they think is ideal. No problem—let those latter types live a little longer and see how life unfolds.

Your kids grow up and move away. They pursue their own lives. You don't own them. They have a responsibility to lead their own lives, and you have a responsibility to let them do so. We hope and pray they conduct themselves in a manner beneficial for society, but we never expect our kids to automatically do things our way. We can provide advice if asked, but they have to make their own decisions. There are more than our children out there who can benefit from what we older types can offer.

As for us? We have no perceptions about others who experience Christmas in a way that is joyful and non-judgemental. After our three days of volunteering, Christmas day and the week following is our time to enjoy in the country away from shopping and crowds. Just us two… peaceful and quiet, loving each other. If the kids want to come out and see us, there's only one rule—the time you spend with us at Christmas will be peaceful and quiet, and all will take time to love each other!

Merry Christmas!

CHAPTER 43
"Constructive" Anger—Why We Quit

As already noted, we heat our retirement home with wood. Falling trees, bucking the wood, hauling it to a splitting site, and splitting and stacking the wood is great exercise. This labour also provides us with an opportunity to see things in our forest which we would miss otherwise.

We don't cut live trees unless there's a potential for them to grow up and be harmful to one of our structures or other property. Fir, pine, hemlock, and box elder (a soft maple) die completely. Fir and hemlock can stand dead for some time but should be cut fairly soon after dying so the wood doesn't partially or completely rot. Box elder dies, falls sometimes, but does not rot for quite some time. Ponderosa pine is a different story—when it dies, it must come down "yesterday" because it rots quickly and can fall just as quickly. Because pine is so sappy, it must be split and cured for over a year. Fir and hemlock require one hot summer to cure once split.

Our property has very little topsoil over hard rock. Fir trees in particular have spreading roots, which are sometimes susceptible to root rot. A big gust of wind will tell you which live fir trees have root rot. A live tree crashing down is particularly dangerous because you have no idea where or when it will fall!

Birch trees left wild in our area grow in clumps, much like willows. They start out looking nice and develop to the point where all the trees in the clump start competing for moisture. Then the trees in that clump start to die at the top. If you don't take a dying birch down, it will rot from the top down until it falls. Seeing this, we decided some time ago to cut the top-dead birches down, being sure to leave at least one or two healthy "sticks" to grow. After a year or two, one very healthy tree will likely be growing, so we prune all the shoots around the old stumps to "force" the growth through the healthy tree. After a while, the shooting will quit. If two birch branches are still growing, one is cut down. As a result, we have some gorgeous single birch trees growing healthy and strong.

All of this results in a lot of wood to be used. While we have a sawmill, we have more than enough beautiful wood to work with, so unless the dead or dying tree we cut is particularly useful for lathe work or other woodworking, it's turned into firewood. And therein lies this story.

There are many times in life when someone or something really angers you to the point you feel the need to vent your anger. One way to do this is to vent constructively. Prior to retiring, I would go out into my workshop and build something. If I was particularly angry, I would hammer something! Now that we're retired, we have a ready-made way of venting through working with firewood, should I feel it necessary.

Normally we split the firewood with an electric splitter. Doing this is rather benign and just involves a lot of lifting. But when angry, there is a different way. That's when the hand-held splitting hammer comes in! If we're angry at no particular person or circumstance, we can just go out to the woodpile with the splitting hammer (along with chaps, safety helmet, gloves, and hard-toed safety work boots) and carefully but purposefully hammer away. Great but very temporary therapy! If we were really angry at someone or some particular circumstance, we used to step it up a notch. We would give the wood to be split the person's name or the name of the circumstance. Then we would really put a lot of gusto into hitting that wood and seeing the pieces fly!

Strange thing, though … over the years knowing the Lord, we've gotten used to leaving situations in His hands. Our anger seems to be disappearing. Splitting a named log by hand is a form of taking vengeance on someone or something. Vengeance is the Lord's job. By splitting a named log, you're demonstrating that you have not forgiven that person yet. Rarely does one get lasting satisfaction by splitting a named log.

So today we generally just split wood to heat our home. If I feel the need to name a log and split it by hand rather than using our log splitter, it's time to take the matter to the Lord. But as noted elsewhere in this book—what you do is up to you!

CHAPTER 44
Do Not Back down from Your Beliefs

Sometimes you come across a situation in which you're forced to decide whether what you believe in is valid, or if you should back down from your belief. This could be called a crisis of faith, a possible mistake, or a possible misconception. No matter what the circumstances, taking the easy way out may appear safe but could be harmful. If what you believe in is real and you back down, you could be called a coward. If what you believe in is false, or not backed up by facts and information, it's nothing more than an opinion, and you *should* back down and get the facts and information to form a valid belief you can stand for.

Several times before coming to the Lord, backing down was common for me when it came to Christianity. There seemed no real analytical reason to justify what was being told to me about Christianity. As my nature was to analyze everything, I kept checking. Something was working in me that kept me headed toward the Lord. I just wouldn't believe what was being said at first!

It took a pretty big kick from the Holy Spirit to get me to acknowledge Jesus as my Lord and Saviour. His kick was very effective; I went from skeptic to believer literally in an instant. I wasn't effective in the world immediately, but I was a believer. I never experienced any desire to back down from the belief that was literally grafted into me by the Lord.

I want to share two cases in which backing down could have occurred—one case to hopefully benefit those who either know the Lord or who are searching, and one to show people who may or may not know the Lord how they need to gather all the facts and information to do something apparently radical to benefit others.

The first case came about while on my way home, driving along the Westside Road from my political job in rural local government. This was way after I had come to know the Lord and trust His work in the world and my life. A rainstorm had been predicted, which was welcome in a hot summer where forest fires were a concern. A nice dampening rainfall without lightning would help mitigate the threat.

My cell phone rang; I pulled over and answered. It was a local fire official. The local fire department had a practice planned that involved setting grass on fire in a large field near Okanagan Lake, then putting it out. The forecast rain would not allow the fire to be set, and the practice would be cancelled. Talking to me, the official asked: "Would you talk to the Big Guy up there and ask him to prevent the rain falling on the grassy field?" My first reaction was to consider this a rather flippant request of the Lord, but I said I would … and did. Backing down did not occur. My prayer went up.

What happened was hilarious. It poured—really poured—all around. Everywhere but on that grassy field. All around the field, but not on the field! The practice could go ahead.

The Lord has a sense of humour. As it had poured rain, the air was extremely humid. While the field was bone dry, the firefighters could easily start the fire, but they had a hard time keeping it going because the air humidity was so high. My prayer to the Lord was very specific, and He honoured that prayer. No rain in the field. Not once did I ask for low humidity! No matter—the practice went well, the Lord was honoured, He allowed me to ask Him in Jesus' name for something "unusual," I didn't back down, and the blessing taught everyone a lesson.

This first case reminded me of a second case that occurred before I came to know the Lord. The results led a Christian believer to see that I was worth saving, and to act on that lead.

There was a very good heavy oilfield in Saskatchewan close to the central Alberta border. It consisted of several widely spaced singular wells, each with quite a large vertical oil section. Some wells had obvious water zones; some had not so obvious water zones. The oil company that owned these wells had an office close to the field. My oilfield service company didn't get much work out of this office, as it was mostly a completion/re-completion office. Nevertheless, the people in that office had a thirst to learn how to interpret open hole logs (see "Know What You Have and Trust It"), which I gladly agreed to teach each time I came out from my office in Lloydminster. As time went on, I began to look at the field with singular wells, noticing something interesting that I communicated to the manager of the local oil company's office.

When oil reservoirs form, they don't do so overnight. It takes more time than most of us can comprehend. The reservoirs are there, generally filled with salt water. Oil and gas migrate in over much time, with oil displacing the water down and gas migrating up above the oil. In this reservoir, there was no gas cap. Multiple wells in a contiguous reservoir will probably have their water line at a unique reservoir depth, depending on how much oil had displaced the water. With singular wells, each well could be expected to have a unique-to-that-well water line if that water line existed.

The oil company's headquarters had clearly stated that these wells displayed all the characteristics of singular wells and should be considered separate pools of oil. This meant that little greater reservoir secondary recovery could take place. The singular wells status limited what could be done to enhance the oil recovery.

What interested me, and what I pointed out to the oil company's field office, was that all the wells with an indication of a water zone had the same top water level. In my opinion, based on all the facts and information gathered over the years, this meant the wells had to be connected with each other in a large pool. It was extremely unlikely all those wells could have the same water level if they were singular reservoirs. This interested the field office. If my interpretation was correct, many producing wells could be drilled between these wells, and much more oil could be recovered.

The oil company's field manager communicated my "theory" to the oil company's headquarters, and I was requested to come to Calgary to explain that theory. One Calgary oil company person was sympathetic, but some were not only unsympathetic, but quite hostile. The Calgary oil company personnel presented further information, which, quite frankly, didn't make sense to me. While I didn't back down, Calgary rejected my theory.

Going back to the oil company field office, it was noted that I would not back down. I wasn't aggressive, I just wouldn't back down. The manager of the field office told me Calgary was in charge of drilling wells, and his purview was completion and re-completions. I left rather saddened.

What the manager did next was surprising and took a great deal of courage on his part. He took some of his completion and re-completion money and drilled a well right in the middle of two "singular" wells, contrary to what Calgary recommended. This was very risky for him. His faith in me was about to be tested. He didn't back down, based on my not backing down.

A very successful well was drilled and completed. Everything was where "the theory" said it would be. The field manager went to Calgary and had … shall we say … a very frank discussion with the parties there. They granted permission to drill many more wells, all successful—based on "the theory."

From all this I was recommended for another hydrocarbon finding award—not for only one well, but for a whole field. The oil company field manager was careful to note that the people from the oil company had definitely not agreed with my theory; thus, the credit for many oil wells and the field was due to my careful log interpretation. Obviously I appreciated this award!

That manager didn't back down. He believed I was correct and backed me up. What was significant was that he and his wife knew the Lord and believed fervently in what He could do. That manager saw potential in me and Anne … not just because of my secular skills, but for the latent faith we had. Faith which could be harnessed for the Lord. That manager and his wife were among many the Lord used to bring Anne and me to His saving knowledge. We became close friends, even after he was promoted to Calgary.

CHAPTER 45
Dreams Can Point out Something

I was educated as a scientist. Over the course of my career in the oil industry, my ability to think developed and grew. While my co-workers initially analyzed me with the "driver" personality type, over time that morphed into a "driver analytical" then an "analytical driver" type personality. This last personality type showed strongest after coming to know the Lord, which was very fortunate because it led me to carefully examine what I truly believed in, making my beliefs stronger.

One aspect of my beliefs burdened me with uncertainty. It was the overall existence of the devil, the evil one. I was certain there had to be some sort of worldly "thing" or entity that fostered evil. This could be shown in me sometimes, even after coming to know the Lord. My analytical side just didn't see this evil influence outside of the individual human body. To compound this matter, discussion of the evil one and his minions was at best limited amongst Christians I knew. It seemed there was more fear in discussing these entities than the fear of the Lord Himself!!

After a while, true to form at the time, I left this concern with the Lord while I got on with life. I was confident there would come a time when the truth would be shown to me—in the Lord's good time.

My time of retirement came and went. Anne and I were fully engaged in our new lives out in British Columbia. We did run into some disturbing events in the churches we attended that seemed at odds with what we believed in, but we did our best through praying, reading the Word, and listening to discern and make sure the problem was not with us. My mother had died in Grande Prairie, Alberta, months before we moved to British Columbia. Even though at the time my sister Marg was a paraplegic confined to a wheelchair, she handled the estate affairs up there.

Marg had a "driver" personality if there was ever one. Even though she was in a wheelchair, she volunteered with the Grande Prairie Disabled Society, working tirelessly for them. Through that Society she accomplished great things. Mind you, the way she told me how she sometimes accomplished those great things was a little hair-raising in my opinion, but great good did occur! She not only worked successfully for a large forest industry company as an accountant, but she had taken charge of having a home built specifically for her needs. Marg was in charge but worked very well with people in the public and in her company.

After Mom died I called Marg on the phone every week for four years. She told me she had a housekeeper and was getting along quite well, thank you. The few times the Lord was brought up she was pleasantly adamant that she wasn't interested. I kept her in my prayers but didn't push the subject. I mildly pushed one other concern, though—her written, legal, and witnessed Last Will and Testament. I stated that anything less wouldn't hold up in court.

My mother had personally asked me prior to 1995, when I was still working in the oil industry, what I wanted to be included in her will for myself. "Nothing" was my answer, because I didn't need anything at that time. I had a great job, was to retire soon, and would be financially independent. Mom took exception to that. She wanted to give me something. I then told her my wish was that she will all her effects to Marg, who was in greater need than me, and I wrote a letter to that effect. Mom accepted this as long as she could give me something to remember her by. Sighing I said, "Well, you could give me the old washboard you used when you were first married. I would treasure that!" She agreed.

Later on, Mom presented me that washboard. On it was the inscription, "To my first born—a dear son. To show you the 'washing machine' I had when you were little. Love, Mom." Mom always managed to get the last word! The washboard is still prominently hung in our log home, long after her death.

When Mom died in 1998, everything went to Marg. My new desire was to make sure Marg had her legal, written, and witnessed Last Will and Testament, which outlined where she wanted all her effects to go. Anything discussed between us was just that—discussion. I stressed to Marg that I needed nothing. We both verbally agreed that she would put in her will that all her possessions would be liquidated and given away to charities she supported. Over the next four years, I phoned her weekly to see how she was doing. From these calls I got a vague idea of where she wanted her estate to go to. She kept saying she would do a proper will; I kept asking if she had done it. She avoided the issue as much as the issue of the Lord.

Each spring for three years I asked Marg if Anne and I could come up and visit with her. Each time she was too busy, or "this would not be a good time." No matter —the phone calls occurred weekly with a pleasant chat ensuing for about an hour. Then in January 2002, I told Marg we were coming up in May of that year. She briefly objected, but I used visiting my old high school stomping grounds as the reason. She relented, and Anne and I began to plan. We continued phoning Marg every weekend, plus we made sure we had all our paperwork up to date. Income tax deadline in Canada is April 30, so we made especially sure our tax returns were done well in advance.

What happened next was far beyond what anyone could have expected. Early in the morning of April 29, 2002, while still sleeping, I started having a dream—a very vivid dream in vibrant colour, complete with very clear sounds of someone screaming. The person screaming couldn't be seen, but some ugly looking, red, demon-like creatures were sadistically laughing and hauling someone down by the legs to a fiery, flaming bottom. I suddenly woke up screaming next to Anne and breathing heavily in a panicked, choking manner. Anne asked what was going on. I explained the dream as I looked at the time—7:00 a.m. Neither one of us had a clue what was going on, so I just said, "Let's leave it in the Lord's hands and go back to sleep." Oddly enough, we slept quite peacefully until about 9:00 a.m.

The phone rang. It was Marg's neighbour phoning to tell me Marg had died. I could feel the blood draining from my face, even as "When did she die?" blurted out from my mouth. Of course, the neighbour had no idea. I told him in as careful a tone as possible that Anne and I would be coming up right away after we took care of putting our cat in a kitty hotel and our affairs right so we could be up in Grande Prairie for some time. I made certain that the neighbour clearly understood one request: when we arrived, I wanted to know as close as possible when Marg died. The neighbour committed to have the attending doctor look at this closely.

There is an oddity between where we live in British Columbia and Grande Prairie, Alberta. If you look carefully at a map, the two positions are almost at the same longitude. Even so, Alberta is in a different time zone and one hour ahead of where we live in BC.

Anne and I hurried around and got our preparations done as quickly as we could. Marg's home in Grande Prairie was almost exactly one thousand kilometres from our home in B.C. We knew we'd be anxious and stressed, so the trip was bound over to the Lord as we asked for travel mercies, since we'd be travelling by car overnight. There was no point taking a plane and renting a car, as it was much quicker to take Anne's big car. As we travelled up to Grande Prairie, at least two hundred deer turned away from our car. We were blessedly alert and had no trouble getting to our destination.

We arrived at Marg's home and went next door to talk to the neighbour. He said that the doctor had determined fairly accurately when Marg had passed—*8:00 a.m. Alberta time.*

Anne and I were amazed! *That was 7:00 a.m. in B.C.* Exactly when my horrible dream occurred! The neighbour noticed we were a little concerned and asked why. We told him about the dream. And the timing.

We got some rest and began arranging the funeral. Both Marg and I had discussed how we wanted our bodies treated when we died. We both wanted to be cremated. That was easy. Now came the part where I became very insistent. I didn't care if Marg knew the Lord or not; she was going to get a funeral with Christ as the emphasis. We found a chaplain who very gently counselled me about it. I was insistent, so he honoured my request. The church was full, and the message gave honour and glory to both the Lord and Marg.

Then came the really tough part. When we arrived, all Marg's papers for her income tax were laid out on the table. She hadn't completed them, and her taxes were overdue. We got a lawyer and asked him to recommend a really good accountant. He asked "How good?" I said, "One who will work well with Revenue Canada," and one who would do everything legally and morally. He recommended one of the best accountants I have ever known! He started by doing Marg's taxes with the estate paying the fine.

We searched Marg's house high and low for her will. There weren't even any notes. She had bought a safe as I had suggested, but when we opened it there was nothing inside. Marg had been a superb accountant to everyone else, including the disabled society she volunteered for, but she was not good to herself in this matter. While there were blank estate and will forms around, Marg had never made a will. As the sole heir I would inherit everything. I could have accepted this legally, but it was not what my heart wanted to do.

I roughly remembered the causes she wanted her monies to be donated to from our many phone calls and talked to them all. None of them had anything in writing either. After I had seen all of them, I returned to the accountant and said I wanted to liquidate all Marg's assets and donate funds to those charities once everything was cleared.

The accountant asked me one question—if I was the sole heir. I affirmed this. He then asked why I wouldn't want to take the money for myself. I told him about all the phone calls Marg and I had over the past four years, and I was committed to honour her wishes as I remembered them. "In that case, you could more than honour her wishes, even beyond the amount of money in her final estate, if you would take the money, give it all away in her memory, take the tax benefit, and then continue giving away the money you receive back."

Wow! Marg's legacy could live on!

In the end, every charity I remembered Marg wanting to receive the money, did. In memory of Margaret Edgson. Plus, Anne and I made sure other charities benefitted beyond that. In all cases we went through trusted accountants to be sure we did everything according to the rules—rules we insisted would be strictly adhered to. We did keep some of the estate money to be sure we could have emergency money and continue donating to good, local British Columbia charities.

One request we fulfilled made us especially happy. The Grande Prairie Disabled Society was hoping to start a multi-storey housing project with housing for disabled people on the lower level. This had been their dream for some time, but they couldn't proceed unless they fundraised a large sum of money to qualify for grants from the provincial and federal governments. They weren't having much success, so I asked them what they needed and cut them a cheque. The Alberta and federal governments came right up to the table with the rest of the funds needed. My only request? Name the place "Margaret Edgson Manor." *Done!*

What happened next was funny. Anne and I were invited to the opening ceremonies and to tour the building. It was beautiful! The provincial and federal representatives showed up in suits, while Anne and I showed up on the Gold Wing with appropriate motorcycle gear. Marg was never one for "suits." The way Anne and I were dressed at the ribbon cutting was more than appropriate!

What happened here? Marg's passing resulted in a large amount of good here on earth, both in Alberta and a small part of British Columbia. A lot of very needy people were served. Marg's name is forever emblazoned on a building. What else happened as a result of Marg's passing? There is no doubt in my or Anne's minds now about the evil one and his minions. While we do see evil happening, we also know the Lord is definitely in control and will ensure good triumphs according to His will and for His glory, as it was done after Marg died. Once again, we were honoured by the Lord when He saw we were willing to leave events in His hands so He could show us His love by eventually revealing His will. He further blessed us by directing our memories so we remembered where the monies would go, hopefully as per Marg's wishes. The most important point was the certainty both Anne and I have about the existence of the devil. That being said, the evil one may … may … have won one battle with Marg, but in the end so many more people benefitted from Marg's legacy! Evil certainly did not triumph—the Lord did!

We don't know if Marg came to know the Lord before she died. This we do know—if we need to know when we get to heaven, He will let us know then. In the meantime, if anyone doubts the devil exists, send them to us and we will tell them of the events of April 29, 2002.

CHAPTER 46
Fire the Tires

We live in the British Columbia interior off a windy, paved, two-lane road that follows along Okanagan Lake. Travelling this road is an exercise in the pleasure of actually driving while enjoying wonderful, back country scenery. The road is not straight! We are motorcyclists, and experiencing "the ride" is something we both look forward to. Even when driving our smaller car, the scenery and the drive are worth it!

In the winter, vehicles require proper winter tires. Obviously, we put our 1985 1200A Gold Wing to bed each fall, looking forward to riding it again in the spring. Even though we are in our seventies, we're like a couple of kids looking forward to this annual event! I used to train motorcyclists, so I put myself through many "parking lot" refresher exercises in the spring after thoroughly checking the condition of the old Wing.

As for our Subaru and Smart Car, we change to the appropriate rims with proper tires first in the fall for winter, and then in the spring for the rest of the year. From doing this on our Subaru, we learned a life lesson that is sometimes missed.

We believe in buying vehicles that will last. We have a thirty-plus-year-old Gold Wing— bought new, kept "new." We have a twenty-plus-year-old 4X4

Tahoe—bought new, kept "new." We have a ten-plus-year-old Subaru—bought new, kept "new." We also have a ten-plus-year-old Smart Car—bought used, kept "new." All have their purposes; all are paid for. All have good, appropriate rubber on their wheels.

When we change out the wheels in the fall and spring, the tires are checked to see if they are safe before the wheels are cleaned and waxed. Proper tire rotation is followed according to the types of tires and the vehicle operation manuals. The cleaned tires and rims are stored properly when not on the vehicles. I point this out to illustrate that all proper procedures are followed to ensure the best outcomes. Sometimes those outcomes aren't all that desirable—whether with tires or with life in general.

We put a set of high end winter tires on the Subaru. Over the course of four years, these tires were monitored, maintained, used, and stored properly based on what we knew and were told. We were a little concerned when we changed over to these tires in the first season because they were a little rougher-riding than the summer tires we'd changed from. We sought advice from those who sold us the tires and installed them. As balance wasn't an issue, we were told to put it down to "those tires are that way." We lived with the issue.

We didn't experience that problem with the winter tires installed on the Smart Car. Different brand of tires, but still high end.

The next winter the Subaru's winter tires seemed to get rougher. Balance wasn't an issue, so again we lived with it after getting advice. The third year got worse. The fourth year was really bad. Then a pull and pulsing sensation to the left occurred, which hadn't shown up in previous years. None of this was observed with the summer tires.

Even though there was well over half the tread left on the winter tires, I insisted a more thorough professional examination of the tires be done. The result was a diagnosis of tread separation. Changing the winter tires out to a different, lower end brand resulted in a smooth, straightforward ride. Problem solved!

We had tolerated a situation that could have had serious consequences. We had taken the advice of the people who knew tires up to a point. When problems got so bad we had to finally rectify the issue, we took the line of professionally finding out what was going on, and finally decided to "fire the tires."

This learned lesson brought to mind some corporate and political instances where someone should have done the same thing. Sometimes it's necessary to "fire the tires" before problems get worse. We had procrastinated with the Subaru's tires because we were told not to worry about them. Are any of us procrastinating by not dealing with people who are less than suited to the job at hand? The following example is typical of what has occurred many times in my career.

A person assigned to a job in a particular area wasn't doing well. They thought they were doing well, but it was obvious to most others that this person wouldn't follow procedures, was disruptive, and blamed everyone else for their ongoing problems. There are either defined or probable ways to mitigate such a problem. It was obvious the person's immediate superiors had to get involved, since the problem person didn't improve.

The immediate superior had a performance review at his disposal. Any problem person should not be allowed to continue on the way he or she is going. The performance review should make it clear where the problem or problems exist and chart out a path of improvement to be followed. The situation should be discussed with the employee, who should commit to improving within a defined time period.

The problem that occasionally arises is that little is done by either the problem person or the immediate supervisor. In this situation, the problem person was transferred to another area. The problem hadn't been solved. It had been transferred.

Hopefully when this occurs the new immediate supervisor recognizes the situation and does a performance review with a committed time period to improve. This new performance review should be independent of the one conducted at the last place. Hopefully the committed improvement will be strictly adhered to. Sometimes it isn't, and the problem person is transferred again. Eventually this method of "disposing by transfer" finds an end, and the problem person is terminated. In this discussed example, this was the end result.

The problem was finally discussed when the situation created undesirable results. The problem person expressed surprise! He believed he'd been transferred because his talents were needed elsewhere. He said he wasn't aware of any problem. This situation could be the fault of the immediate supervisors not addressing a problem and developing a plan to either rectify it or terminate the problem person.

A person with glaring deficiencies should be made aware of those deficiencies and given a time-specific plan to improve. The plan should clearly outline that failure to do so will result in termination at a specific point. People with serious deficiencies should not be transferred. Why is this not always done?

Some supervisors are "nice guys." Pals. Buddies. They don't want to hurt anyone. They just want one happy crew. Unfortunately, problem people put a drag on good workers, and morale may suffer. Rather than deal with the problem, the immediate supervisor just "transfers the problem." In this case, the immediate supervisor is not doing his or her job. If this occurs, that immediate supervisor should also be put on a timed notice and dealt with according to the communicated objectives.

In the meantime, though, the problem employee has been transferred, and the new immediate supervisor sees that he or she has just received a dud. If that new supervisor does his or her job, they will monitor the newly transferred employee and communicate effectively with that employee as quickly as feasible. The employee should still be given an opportunity to rectify his or her problems, but with a time constraint.

Often the top superiors have been monitoring the situation and are aware of the problem person; they are also aware of the procedures and processes that should be followed. The top superiors expect the immediate superiors to utilize the procedures available to at least mitigate the situation.

If effective action isn't taken, the problem person could realize he or she has a problem but that the people he or she works for are doing nothing. Emboldened, that problem worker starts to take over meetings, often in a demanding way, testing the waters to see if the immediate superiors will do something. Seeing nothing substantive being done, the problem person gets more emboldened. Eventually the problem person does something which is either out of the ordinary or blatantly ignores a process by going over the head of the immediate superiors and lobbying the top superiors to get what he or she wants. This type of problem needs to be addressed at some point before the cancerous nature of what is going on spreads further in the organization. There comes a point when you need to "Fire the Tires."

I've seen this problem both in my corporate and political years. I was fortunate to have been given notice early in my corporate years—a notice that changed my attitude and gave me focus, waking up my latent ability. I wasn't terminated, and thirty years later I gave one year's notice and received a very honourable retirement after thirty-two years with the same company.

Giving responsible professional appraisals, just like giving professional advice on tires, does have good outcomes. Delaying those appraisals in either case could be very damaging.

CHAPTER 47
Handling Evil

There were times in Anne's and my life together when evil events occurred, both before and after coming to know the Lord. Most of these could be considered minor events and easily handled. Before we came to know the Lord, we'd heard of the devil. Some people said there was no devil, just as there was no Jesus. Some were so terrified by the thought of the devil they choked up and wouldn't talk about him in any way. Me? Well, as stated elsewhere in this book, I am an AA—an **A**nal **A**nalytical. Desiring to understand situations, I don't form an opinion unless I see some verifiable facts and information. We both eventually came to believe there are evil influences in this world that go beyond just saying "evil is part of human nature." Also, we observed how some people we would have labelled "evil" changed after they became devoted Christians.

Once we became Christians, evidence mounted that these evil events were being driven by something like the devil. Reading the Lord's Word made it very clear the evil one existed and had powerful influences. This was much easier for us to see after 1988, the year we came to know the Lord. In addition, this evil was increasingly apparent everywhere in the news.

The first evidence of personal attacks came shortly after coming to know the Lord. Many annoying, niggling, little events started to happen to us, both individually and as a married unit. We'd been told to expect this as new Christians. The effects were generally trivial, so we could hand them over to the Lord and move on with our new lives. Still, there were those who professed to be Christians who urged us not to even talk about the devil for fear of having him or his minions influence our lives.

Years later we experienced something that on the surface appeared terrifying. This incident needed to be told, but it was difficult to relate until our church discussed *"Put on the full armor of God, so that you can take your stand against the devil's schemes"* (Ephesians 6:11, NIV). As the discussion progressed, this terrifying incident, along with the perpetrator, came to mind. To illustrate, a brief description of both the incident and the background is necessary.

The perpetrator was a constant complainer, running down those who didn't agree with the way he conducted his personal affairs. His idea of "working with people" was telling others what to do and expecting them to do it. He had little respect for his immediate superiors or the organization they belonged to. Eventually, the person left the employ of the organization.

One day Anne and I were returning to our car in a public parking lot. After we parked, this person parked right beside us. When we returned to our car, he started yelling nasty things at me, which grew in intensity to vile swearing that neither Anne nor I had ever heard, even in the oil patch before we knew the Lord! He jumped out of his vehicle and stood about three inches from my face, yelling and screaming at me. I locked eyes with him so that the rest of his body wasn't visible. Anne, terrified and standing near me, at first thought to speak, but something inside her told her to just stand still. She noted later that the perpetrator's fists were clenched. She was also amazed that there was no movement or reaction from me.

This was due to the strong belief in my Lord's ability to control any situation. I sent a silent prayer up in a sky telegram, asking Him to control *my* actions to His honour and glory, which He did. I kept constant eye contact without blinking. When the perpetrator saw nothing was being accomplished, he got back into his vehicle, still yelling and swearing, as we finished loading our car and driving off.

The event caused me to forget to breathe for a couple of kilometres! I pulled over, took a breath, and thanked the Lord. What had happened was something more evil than I had ever experienced before. This incident was reported to the police, discussed with them, and left with them.

In my distant past, before knowing the Lord, the urge to strike back at least verbally would have been strong. Such action would only have perpetuated the evil. The valuable lesson learned from this incident is definite proof the Lord is in control of everything on earth. His followers must realize that. When they do, the Lord will bring about circumstances to clearly illustrate how He wants events to unfold. Sometimes this won't be evident right away. The story related above shows how a potentially dangerous incident was thoroughly handled by a Lord who is in control. The result for me was an increased desire to take it to the Lord before doing anything and seeking His guidance and control in all that I do. In my opinion, this lesson illustrates one of the best ways to handle evil!

CHAPTER 48
Forgiving and Forgetting

Most would agree that the act of forgiving is a necessary one. If someone wrongs you, and you do not forgive, you may at the very least build up a resentment that can threaten your mental well-being. This applies to Christians and non-Christians. Forgiveness doesn't "belong" to either group. It's something that needs to be done.

Forgetting upon forgiving is an act Christians espouse, yet some professed Christians say they forgave, but they will not forget. To someone like me, this statement can be very disturbing. I used to be guilty of doing that. Now both Anne and I see how this necessary-to-us act blesses us in sometimes wondrous ways.

In the recent past, I struggled with grudge harbouring even after coming to the Lord. This was troubling when it occurred. My analytical mind wondered what was wrong within me. Note that I wasn't holding myself responsible for keeping a grudge. Something was wrong within me, but I wasn't taking personal responsibility for the grudge. I needed to correct this and hopefully be blessed by doing so.

After coming to know the Lord, two events showed Anne and me what forgiving and forgetting is all about. While this applies to us in a Christian sense, others may want to consider the suggested solution.

The first instance occurred when a Canadian born Japanese man married a Canadian Caucasian woman. His father and mother had been forcibly moved inland after Pearl Harbour, and there seemed to be a family prejudice against him related to his race. For a while Anne and I were among the only ones who would talk with them. While they were hurt, they didn't let it bother them. Eventually the others clearly came around. After that, we never heard of prejudice against them again. This was the first great example we saw of forgiving and forgetting. We didn't understand it, because we didn't know the Lord at the time. Even then, the act of forgiving and forgetting seemed wonderful!

The second incident was actually a string of events caused by one perpetrator. The major incident concerning us was the verbal assault in public described in "Handling Evil." While I had to report the incident to the police, the person was forgiven. I couldn't allow myself to forget for quite some time; however, Anne and I did our best to remove ourselves from any dealing with the individual.

Over many months, my attitude began to change. It was obvious to others that the individual had more targets for this wrath. People started tiring of the ranting. The perpetrator frequently blamed others for his personal shortcomings, and then began making untrue statements. Others recognized this and backed away.

As more and more people of influence backed away from the perpetrator, his anger and frustration grew. People at first ignored and then started not tolerating the individual. It got so bad, no one of influence would take the person seriously. He changed his tactics, but the apparent hatred and ranting continued. Eventually, as one person of influence noted, if the perpetrator had argued white was white, no one else would agree! The perpetrator had become essentially ostracized by some influential people.

What happened? After we forgave, Anne and I set up boundaries. At first we removed ourselves from any association with the person. While we may have been a target, the perpetrator couldn't directly hit us, even verbally. We then forgot but didn't allow ourselves to be drawn into those circumstances again.

Other people of influence did likewise. The more the ranting and hatred occurred, the more other boundaries went up, but not everybody forgave! As a result of this lack of forgiveness, the perpetrator became less and less effective at influencing people of influence.

Anne and I watched all this evolve with great awe and wonder. We had forgiven a terrifying incident requiring the eventual involvement of police, yet the Lord ensured that by us removing ourselves—not running, just removing ourselves and allowing us to forget—we had become reasoned in the eyes of important influencers because of our perceived calmness.

Were we actually calm? In public, definitely. At first we spoke often with the Lord, asking Him to help us and leaving the perpetrator in His hands. As time went on, more influential people let it be known that they respected our positioning. We praised the Lord for honouring us.

Forgiveness is a necessity—no matter who you are, or your reasons for it. Forgetting goes hand in hand with forgiveness, no matter what your motivations. We believe boundaries must be set, however, to avoid future involvement in the same problems.

I once was told an old saying that notes that one must be careful of a caged tiger. A tiger roaming free can be dangerous. If you forgive and forget by using boundaries as above, the roaring tiger may develop his own cage. As he does that, he could get angrier … until the cage he's building around himself closes in on him to such an extent he's in a zoo with everybody observing him at a distance, safely out of harm's way.

Forgive: be understanding. Forget while being aware and prepared.

CHAPTER 49
Fortunate Experiences Do Occur

Sometimes in our younger married years we have to give something up because we are mommies and daddies and have a higher responsibility to our children. As adults we may pout because of this, or even regret having gotten ourselves into the situation. As we age and our wisdom and experience grow, there may come a time when we realize we are indeed fortunate we actually gave some stuff up. Such was the case with me and my Triumph TR250 sports car.

While the first part of this story occurred between 1968 and 1970, the final lesson occurred in 2015 after I retired from both the oil industry and politics. This is an ego story, folks! It's a contrast between a nice-looking sports car and a Gramps Mobile.

Our first personally owned car was a used Triumph TR4, complete with wire wheels—a fun car whose wheels were constantly out of balance! It was quick on acceleration, and it was cold in the winter (even though we had a hard top we put on in winter). It was really rough riding, as befits a car meant to handle like a sports car of the day. *I loved it!* I'm amazed Anne tolerated us having that car. We drove it to Expo 67 in Montreal, Quebec from Edmonton, Alberta, and then on to Houston, Texas. While we had the wire wheels successfully balanced before the trip, we ran over a railway track and they went out of balance again! Our trip to Houston and back to Alberta took place with shaking wheels. Add to the Expo 67 Houston trip the fact Anne was expecting.

Time to buy a better car. What did this loving husband with a newborn get for that car? A new 1968 Triumph TR250 sports car. No question of ego here, folks! By now I had a company car. A point to note—Anne couldn't drive at the time. Another point—we didn't drive the TR250 in winter. It was the car we "owned" when we experienced the life changing event that led us to selling it ("Bank Manager Tough Love").

That TR250 was a beautiful looking car. It rode smoother than the TR4, but it sure did not handle as well as the TR4! It was cold ... like the TR4. It was fun with the top down, but with a baby we couldn't have the top down much. The 250 also leaked electricity. I had to charge the battery all the time. It also leaked oil. I had the oil leak looked at, and while it did improve, it still leaked. It was expensive to maintain ... really expensive. It had solid wheels this time with wheel covers that had faux bolts that loosened and rattled! It overheated in slow moving traffic. But it looked so nice, and it was so ... well ... sports car like! But we sold it.

Over many years we had various vehicles. We finally smartened up and bought practical and useful vehicles. We eventually got a 1995 Tahoe, which we still have and use. We got Anne a 2007 Subaru Forester, a wonderful vehicle that handles almost as well as the TR250 and is a car we're both glad we still have. Being a politician and needing a dedicated car for that job, I got a 2006 diesel Smart Car. This car really surprised us! Not only does it get sixty-eight mpg, but it handles like the TR250, rides like the TR4, and has heat and air conditioning—which the two sports cars either did not have or had inadequately!

I should be satisfied, shouldn't I? Well, even though we have a beautiful 1985 Gold Wing motorcycle we both enjoy, when an opportunity for latent ego pops up in a male, it still may happen. A friend of mine heard me talking about my old TR250 and just happened to mention he had a restored one stored at his place. A red TR250 with black upholstery—just like the one we used to have! At that time, our granddaughter was coming out to visit. I mentioned this to my friend. "Bring her over and look at the car," he said.

Keep in mind he was looking to sell the car to buy another. Also keep in mind my ego was excited. I could afford to buy that car now; "we" could have some fun with it!

Our granddaughter arrived, and she and I went over to my friend's place in our two-seater Smart Car. He had the TR250 out in his driveway, top down—a spitting image of my old car. I admit I was excited! My granddaughter and I sat in the car and had our pictures taken. Fortunately, reality started to go through my mind.

I noticed a mat under the car to prevent liquid leaks from marring the concrete. My old TR250 leaked oil. The hood was up and the battery was being charged. My old TR250 leaked electricity. The friend was going to let me drive it, but it was threatening rain. I didn't drive my old TR250 in winter or inclement weather. The car was beautiful, but when would I drive it? When my granddaughter was here? Maybe a few times in good weather? I certainly wouldn't want to get the finish marred. Where would I park it? Would I use it more than the Gold Wing, which we don't use enough as it is? Where were my priorities?

I didn't make an offer on that car. My granddaughter and I got back in the Smart, my Gramps Mobile, turned on the air conditioning, and enjoyed the old sports-car-like drive on the Westside Road back home. I explained to her the Smart had everything the TR250 had—the handling and the fun, but it also had heat and air conditioning, and I could drive it year round. The cost of maintenance was far, far less than would have to be paid for the TR250 today. It was almost like I was apologizing to her for what I was saying.

The young lady understood. She likes the Smart Car. She is one smart lady! Don't ever think that young people don't think better than we do, especially if you talk with them. Give them an opportunity to talk and give you the pleasure of listening to them. Fortunately, I did that day. Fortunate experiences do occur!

CHAPTER 50
Hammerhead

Many tasks in life are either necessary to do, or a good idea to do. They may require effort and time, so aren't always looked forward to until you actually complete them and see the benefits. While completing these tasks, difficulties can be encountered. Yet you persist and finish the task. Finishing the task may require a fair amount of perspiration and may result in some sore muscles, both below the brain and in the brain.

Anne and I live in a nice, 4,700 square foot log home we had dreamed about for years. It is beautiful, but it is huge. The lower level—some would call it a basement—is "stick built," meaning it's built conventionally out of concrete and lumber. One big log character post with many natural scars and weird growth holds up a beautiful, laminated wood beam, but otherwise it's conventional. All the pipes and wires are hidden, so the ten-foot ceiling looks clean and high. The main floor has horizontal logs for the walls and logs for ceiling joists, with a twenty-seven-foot-high great room complete with fireplace. A character post in the great room holds up the fifty-foot-long roof beams—one going north-south and one going east-west. Upstairs is post and beam. The main bedroom has its own fireplace along with a built-in entertainment center. There is an en suite bathroom with a footed iron bathtub.

We heat with wood using a wood burning boiler feeding floor heat to the lower and main levels. We call the boiler "old voracious" for good reason! We burn clean—from the boiler in the lower level to the top of the chimney is forty feet. That means we need to get firewood. A fair amount we get from the 3.6 acres of property we own. We get more from wood providers. Splitting that wood gives credence to the advice given as to why to split your own wood: that way it heats you twice! It's also tough work retrieving the split and cured wood in the winter from our three three-cord sheds. We placed these sheds far from the house in case we have a forest fire in the summer. The sheds may burn, but they won't take the house with them!

During the winter, we use a five-foot toboggan fitted with two one-foot shelf brackets at the back to hold more logs. We can stack this toboggan quite high so we have enough to fill our big steel construction wheelbarrow high. We put a cumulative quarter of a cord of wood in the house each time we bring wood in. All winter we have to load firewood on the toboggan, haul it through the snow to the lower level of the house, unload the wood into the wheelbarrow, bring it in to the furnace room in the middle of the house on the lower level, and then unload and stack it. To store that quarter of a cord of wood requires eight of these trips. You're perspiring a fair amount when all is done!

Falling trees, bucking the wood to be split, splitting and hauling that wood, and then stacking it is tremendous exercise. You're pretty weary at the end ... so weary sometimes you're more than grateful to be done the job. That is when Anne and I say we've done a "hammerhead job." Why? Because sometimes the job seems like hitting your head with a hammer—it's so much fun when you quit! That phrase also applies when we hike up mountains or go on a very vigorous exercise bout. But do we cherish the memories, and do we ever get exercise making those memories. Plus we heat the house along with keeping the heating cost down!

CHAPTER 51
How to Lose People

There were times in our life when it seemed like something unpleasantly silly happened that could only occur once. As you get older and remember events, you often find these seemingly silly events aren't that unique. This was true for us.

I worked for thirty-two years for one of the oil industry's biggest service companies, the last twenty years in marketing, sales, and service. Toward the latter third of my career, I was given responsibility for quite a few oil companies that didn't use our service company for one reason or another. It was my job to convince them to use our services in a legal, ethical, and moral ... yet significant ... fashion. This was no easy task.

One fact was evident before even starting: these customers used to use my company but turned away from us. Others in my company told me their excuse: we were too expensive. Note the use of the word "excuse."

I approached my task by becoming familiar with the operations and procedures of the potential clients *as told by those potential clients*. I learned very quickly that all of these clients were quite satisfied with our competitors, in some cases to the point where they wouldn't even consider using anyone else. I often didn't need to ask what happened, as some made it abundantly clear as I walked in the door the first time! But one point wasn't clear to me: why. This one word was the best technique in the arsenal of ways to market my service company.

Accepting immediately how those companies felt about our competitors was the first step. This surprised some of them, which I in turn found surprising as well. The clients asked things like "Aren't you going to tell us about how great your products are compared to your competitors?"

That was a trigger point in my thoughts. Before answering the question directly, I'd ask: "Is this what others in my company did before?" The answer most often was yes.

"What did you think of them?" I'd continue. Words like "arrogant," "self-centred," "stupid," and "careless" came at me. Obviously the people before me started their visit to these particular clients by making claims about our company in an attempt to bolster their case, before even thinking of the client they were facing and his thoughts. Our people weren't looking at the reasons why the potential clients were using our competitor, other than perhaps the competitor was cheaper. Our people weren't working with our clients, gathering information, analyzing that information, and then moving forward in a client-centric fashion. The clients were surprised that I accepted their feelings about our competitors, because they had become familiar with my company's attitude as expressed by those who preceded me. I then made it clear that I felt uncomfortable trying to sell them something unless their needs were understood, and until it was understood if my company had any services we could provide for those needs.

That was the beginning of mutual understanding for the majority of those potential clients. As I visited them more often, they began to realize that I, and hopefully the company I represented, cared about them and their business. To carry this to the ultimate, I developed a personal policy to try and *not* sell them something unless it was fairly certain our product would benefit their company.

This was just the beginning of my quest to understand the oil company's procedures and operations. Clearly there was a problem with these companies using some of our services, especially since quite often they used to use us and then stopped. As I gathered more information, I learned that my company was actually very well thought of, but our manner of conducting business, as represented by our marketing people either intentionally or unintentionally, had upset the potential clients. That issue needed to be resolved before seeing any positive results.

I asked those clients to tell me what had happened. Only after the potential customer and I understood that they and their procedures were respected, plus they expected my representation to be there to offer genuine help through our products, did my company start to get business. Through this process I learned something surprising yet sad. Our service company came across as not caring and presumptuous that we would be the organization used by the oil companies. We took the oil companies for granted.

Digging deeper by talking to both our people and the oil company people was the next step. It was true—our company did take these clients for granted. We didn't follow up; we waited until they called us. We delivered results and discussed them, but between service jobs we were noticeably absent. Little or no attempt was made to ask if any problems arose. This resulted in us losing their business.

The competitor was there, hungrily looking for business. Quite often the oil company's problem or concern was of a simple but puzzling nature, and easily solved. Who was there asking questions? The competitor. Guess who got the business? Eventually the client realized the attention he needed was given by the competitor. To make life easy, he switched his business. That client noticed something else—my company did not follow up. We waited. The client saw this, perceived we really didn't care about his business, and decided not to use us again.

Once I learned this and became familiar with the various clients' businesses, and once clients saw that I genuinely cared for them, the marketing process began. Not only did my service company get business back, but we regained it quite significantly. On top of that, I co-authored technical papers with some of those companies. Not only did the oil company and my service company benefit, but the industry as a whole benefited.

To me it was easy to see why the client left. My service company had representatives who, for whatever reason, came across as not caring through their presumption. This lost us a lot of business. Worse, it took a lot of work to get their business back! For me, while difficult, it was a career builder. Through digging for facts and getting information about the oil producers and how to better serve them, I became a pro in the eyes of that industry. Even with my BSc education.

The same attitude that lost my company business can bring trouble to our private lives as well. Let's look at another case in point, which took place when Anne and I retired from the oil industry. We acquired our properties in the

Okanagan between 1970 and 1972. We purchased six adjoining lots over two years and eventually consolidated them. Even though we didn't live there until 1998, we joined the local community associations to familiarize ourselves with local events. We became lifetime members of the local seniors' association, and the longest continuous paid up members of the local community association at the time of writing this book. We cared. Whenever we could, we attended community events. Wanting to serve the local community played a part in me getting into politics. We enjoyed doing this, and in turn the community enjoyed our participation. Anne volunteered on a regular basis to help serve lunches on Wednesdays. People loved her Saskatoon pies!

Attitudes changed due to external rumors and whispering by disaffected people when I was elected as the local politician. Anne and I kept trying to be part of the local community, and as time went on it became clear that the community expected us to show up. If we didn't, we got some very nasty comments about it. One day we showed up at a major banquet and felt shunned. We did find some people to sit with and enjoyed their company, but it was obvious to us that we weren't part of the scene. We stayed away for a while, and no one seemed to care. We then showed up at another event and felt very uncomfortable—almost like we weren't welcome, although no one said so.

In the meantime, another church group in Kelowna had been asking us to come to their monthly brunch/sing along/testimony time. As these monthly meetings were on a Wednesday, the same time as the local Wednesday lunches, we had politely turned them down. Sensing we were becoming less and less part of the picture in the local scene, we decided to skip one local lunch and attend the Kelowna lunch. We not only felt welcomed ... we were uplifted!

We then made a decision that unless the local group approached us, we would stop going there on a regular basis. We would attend once in a while, but not if it interfered with the monthly Kelowna event. This carried on for about three years after I retired from politics.

People in all forms of life desire to be wanted and respected for who they are, what they represent, and what they do. People will gravitate to other people and situations that satisfy their needs and wants. For any group or company to succeed—indeed, survive—this fact must be realized on a regular basis. There is no room for neglect. Before you blame someone else, look in the mirror. If you intend to not be part of something, don't be. But if you intend on having someone continue to be part of activity that will grow your business or your community, then you must absolutely not be part of any neglect that could drive them away.

Eventually the local group started asking why we were no longer coming, so we (especially Anne) told them. We finally decided we should "check things out" again, and we were very warmly welcomed! The local group didn't let the situation stand—they were concerned and showed it. This brought us back.

I could say it was unfortunate in one way that our marketing representatives didn't follow up, but it was fortunate in the final sense because the leaders in my company saw what had happened and determined the best approach was to inject my "older blood" into the situation and see what resulted. As noted, it was a career builder for me.

One final lesson: make sure what you do is of value to all those who want to trust you, and always keep their trust alive!

CHAPTER 52
I'm a Responsible Driver ... or Not!

I like to believe I'm a skilled, responsible, and professional driver ... most of the time. At least that's what my ego tells me ... most of the time! It's true that I'm now a very skilled driver the majority of the time, but this doesn't mean all the time ... just most of the time.

My eyes constantly scan to observe everything. My peripheral vision is more than adequate. Sensing motion out of the side of my eyes comes naturally. Driving a well-tuned vehicle helps me love driving. Awareness of all the gauges, sounds, and feelings of the vehicle I'm driving also comes naturally. Knowledge of the roads being driven and the driving laws enhances the driving experience.

Taking care of our vehicles is a must. If a vehicle is taken care of, it will take care of me. The awareness of how I gained my skills is constantly in the back of my mind, and getting there wasn't always pleasant. Earlier I shared the story of a horrendous collision and how my ego got me into it. Complacency played a huge role in causing that and other collisions. We didn't own one vehicle prior to 1992 that wasn't in at least one minor scrape with me at the wheel or handlebars.

Why do I like to believe that I am a skilled, responsible, and professional driver? I do my best to learn from all my experiences, coupled with ongoing learning from professional sources. Let's take a look at one of the occasions when a very valuable lesson was learned. And no … it wasn't the incident that taught me the lesson, it was what my wife said when the incident occurred. Her words were far more pointed than any collision could have been.

I have deliberately travelled many times in my oil patch career in southern Alberta and Saskatchewan during a blizzard—a complete whiteout blizzard! And yes, driving into a ditch because the road was not visible has occurred! That particular incident taught me to "feel" the road better and slow down to a crawl when travelling in a blizzard. I learned to travel so slowly I was hardly moving so that I could feel the edge of the road. This rate of travel was so slow it would have made more sense to not be on that road, but there was a personal challenge at the time that I wanted to live up to. Sound like ego?

The other lesson learned was to observe the snow in front of me. If it was coming directly at me, there was no truck in front of me. If the snow started to swirl, there was a moving truck in front of me—even if the truck's lights couldn't be seen. When this occurred, my male logic kicked in with the rationale that "if the trucker knows what he's doing, all I have to do is follow him!" This meant that if the truck went into a ditch or off a bridge, guess who was right behind him? But what the heck … I only followed a truck into the ditch once!

More ego? And what about cars driving ahead of me? Let's examine the one case that finally taught me the most valuable lesson ever learned about deliberately driving in a blizzard—from the hands (or mouth) of my wife.

Anne and I were on Highway #1 in an almost whiteout blizzard. We travelled that stretch of road in good weather many times, and I "knew" the feel of the road. In my mind at the time I wasn't speeding; we were going about sixty kilometres per hour. Occasionally I glimpsed lines on the road and shoulder. The snow was blowing so hard it wasn't accumulating. We were on a divided four lane highway, and there were two wide lanes available just to me. It was night— pitch black except for my low beam headlights. No one else was dumb enough to be travelling that night! Except me … with my wife. In hindsight, I must have cared more about my male ego than my wife!

"Do you feel comfortable driving in these conditions?" Anne asked.

Good question, so of course I gave a dumb answer. Observing farm lights off to either side, I stated, "As long as I can see farm lights, we're in good shape."

Suddenly all the farm lights disappeared. The blizzard had picked up in ferocity. Now we were in trouble! I slowed right down, and we were blessed because the farm lights became evident again. What Anne said next was the most important thing I could have heard in our circumstances: "Jim, there are nights when we shouldn't be on the road. This is one of them."

That hit home … and hard. What was I doing with the woman I loved so dearly, deliberately driving in a situation where it was almost certain I wouldn't be able to see beyond the hood of my car? Right after I realized this, the blizzard slacked off, and we drove quickly to our motel.

That night my analytical mind went through several iterations of driving scenarios and what I should do if those scenarios arose.

Number 1: Blizzards do not last forever. Generally they're gone in a day or less, so do not start the trip if severe whiteouts are forecast. Phone people who are expecting you, explain the situation, and set new appointment times.

Number 2: Keep in mind the topography you will encounter on your trip. If you're on flat or relatively flat land without any significant trees around, observe winter weather conditions and act accordingly. Heavy snowfall on Canadian prairies may not be a problem if there's no wind. If there is a wind, that heavy snowfall will essentially become a blizzard. Also, if there is heavy snowfall in such a situation, even without wind, bear in mind that every time a vehicle passes you in either direction, an artificial blizzard will be generated and you will momentarily lose sight of where you're going. If you decide to hit your brakes while temporarily blinded by either an artificial or real blizzard, and if there is someone of equal intelligence (sarcasm intended) behind you, your vehicle will most likely be hit by that vehicle, because it was also blinded!

Number 3: You're driving along and a sudden snow squall comes up. You dim your lights. You can see the road, but just barely. You're tempted to continue or pull over on the shoulder immediately. Both require some not-so-obvious further thought.

If you decide to pull over on the shoulder, keep in mind that you're not out of harm's way if a driver behind you has decided to continue by keeping his eye on the white line between the main road and the shoulder. His vehicle may run right into your parked car! Even if you're not at fault legally by being on the shoulder, there will certainly be damage to you, your passenger, and your car. Ideally you should know the road and where the pullouts are. If at all possible, drive to one and stay there. If you don't know the road and the snow squall was predicted, you shouldn't be on the road.

Number 4: Bring a warm sleeping bag and candles with you. If you stop either on purpose or due to a collision, do not run your car! If you don't use candles or any other form of heat that requires oxygen, you can leave your windows mostly shut. If you use candles (in appropriate containers), you'll need to leave a window partly open for oxygen and the candle exhaust. Running your car could kill you if the exhaust is either leaking or blocked and fills your car with carbon monoxide.

This is by no means a complete list. You can get more helpful ideas from professionals and other experienced professional drivers.

A fair amount of people have "gotten away" with not following the above. Statistically, the more you drive, the more likely you are to have a collision. To make those statistics worse (more likely to kill, hurt, or maim you), all you have to do is not think and experience examples like those listed above. And remember: what you actually do in these situations is entirely your responsibility. Safe driving!

CHAPTER 53
I Can't Do My Job

It's interesting how one's professional job can be similar to a political job. One of those similarities takes the form of the statement, "I can't do my job." Oh, it's rarely directly stated that way, but good leaders can spot the true meaning of what someone is saying when an excuse is made. A good leader looks for someone who not only does their job but is constantly learning about and improving in their job.

I was amazed at how some professional, well educated people in the oil industry demonstrated a lack of willingness or ability to learn how to accomplish tasks given to them. I wasn't amazed at how short a time those people stayed employed.

After growing out of my junior years on the job, I could do my job. When a project was difficult, I worked with people to find a solution—but my job could and would be done. One example of this is how my nickname "Snake" came about.

During a sales meeting, one of my company's younger salesmen said he couldn't sell to a particular client because that client didn't believe he needed "anything fancy." He wasn't going to use our services because our competitor sold a much cheaper solution. Hearing this, I offered to help. The younger salesman and I sat down with the client. I asked questions because I wasn't the least bit knowledgeable about that client or his business needs. It soon became obvious that more than a "simple solution" might be needed, and the discussion opened up to a particular service and the interpretation we provided. After the resulting sale, the two of us were walking back and the young salesman said, "I bet you sold magazines at one time!" I replied to the affirmative. Indeed, I earned my high school two magazine sales records in the 1960s in Alberta. The conversation stopped at that point.

After the services were successfully run and the results interpreted, the client told the young salesman, "You know, that Edgson is a snake oil salesman!" Thus the "Snake" moniker— one I wore proudly until I retired.

The situation in local politics was similar—work with people, and you accomplished a whole lot of good for your constituents. True, there were many obstacles to some of my ideas. There was also staff who enjoyed explaining what could be done and where there were difficulties. Note what I just said: "there were difficulties." Very rarely did these difficulties prove insurmountable. Some work was required to fit the legalities and processes in place. Sometimes the processes had to be altered, which required board input along with a well-considered business presentation to get a favourable decision. Most of the time goals could be reached.

There were also many training opportunities for local government people, which I took full advantage of and applied. Many legal training sessions provided valuable input so I and others could fully understand what could and could not be considered, even before bringing an idea to the board table.

During my political tenure, the vast majority of ideas I brought to the table were either approved or deferred until a better business case was built, which, when done, resulted in the board's approval. Very few ideas were not approved by the wisdom of the board.

Anyone dealing with a local government board or council must remember one point: Once the local politician puts a proposal on the table, it is no longer theirs—it belongs to the board or council. They will allow and encourage debate before deciding what is to be done with that idea. It's their decision, not the local politician's. Once this is recognized and respected, the local politician will find it easier to bring well thought out ideas to the table for consideration and work to get them approved.

On the other hand, if a local politician doesn't do their homework and doesn't bring well-considered ideas to the table, and especially if that local politician either ignores or belittles staff's advice, that person should not be surprised by the board or council turning the proposal down. Indeed, if the idea is deferred, the local politician should be relieved, do further research, engage staff, and bring back a well-considered, modified idea.

One should definitely not go to the media and say something to the effect of, "I can't do my job" (because of the board or council). If you don't adhere to working with people before, during, and after bringing an idea to the table, then you're probably correct—you can't do your job. Indeed, you shouldn't even be sitting in a chair at the table. Essentially you are stating that you are incapable of doing your job, and by that admission you should consider removing yourself from that job before you are removed at the next election.

If anyone implies they cannot do their job as an excuse for not getting something done, they could be correct. This applies in local governments and businesses. In business, the people who continually offer this excuse will probably find themselves unemployed. In local government, the people who offer this excuse just may find themselves un-elected the next trip to the polls. People are not looking for what you cannot do; they are looking for what you can do. Ignore this fact at your peril.

CHAPTER 54
"I Don't Think." "I Don't See."

When I became a politician, I often heard two phrases: "I don't think" and "I don't see." I'd heard these phrases before; actually, they were used to death! Once in politics, it became apparent to me who used those phrases and for what purpose.

When someone uses one of these statements, it appears that they're trying to state they are at least knowledgeable, and at most an expert, on whatever follows the particular phrase. It's as if they're trying to show the listener that they know more than someone else, and that other opinions should be negated.

When in training to run as a local politician, those phrases most often were used as a put- down. The person using the phrases would leave you hanging as to why they said them. The obvious conclusion was they had no idea what they were talking about and just wanted to make themselves look good while making the person they were talking to look bad. Many times there was no reasoning behind the phrases. I soon realized how to deal with the situation when these phrases were spoken.

When an obviously puffed up person would make one of these statements in response to myself or anyone else, I would change the direction of the conversation by saying, "Have you ever noted when someone says 'I don't think,' they probably haven't?" One of three reactions followed.

The first was a kind of "harrumph" reaction, followed by some gibberish that showed the person hadn't thought at all about what they'd said, followed further by a statement of embarrassment before physically exiting.

The second reaction was, "You know, you're correct. Let me make it clear what I do think and why." That I encouraged, and usually a good debate followed with a great conclusion. To be frank, such a person rarely if ever used the "I don't think" phrase again without a follow-up.

The third reaction was dumbfounded silence, followed by something like, "I'll make sure of why I think the way I do in the future." This I also encouraged.

Similarly, those who state in an arrogant or huffy manner, "I don't see," without further explanation are leaving themselves open to rebuttal of a more direct nature, such as "You are absolutely correct. You probably don't see, but not for the reasons you're giving. I'd like to suggest you make an effort to look!"

Interestingly enough, the three reactions for the "I don't see" statement are mostly the same as the "I don't think" phrase.

For those who appear genuinely puzzled and note "I don't see" or "I don't think," points of clarification should be offered. A rebuttal should only be offered if either phrase is used as a put-down with no further clarification.

As a politician, I welcomed input and valid discussion at all times. What was not welcomed was unthinking and unseeing statements that were put forth with little or no basis, hindsight, or foresight to them. If the statements came out because the person had an opinion, I would have preferred that they state it as an opinion so I could help them understand what was going on. Saying one of the noted phrases to try and show others you have a better idea, without stating the reasoning behind the better idea, is just a display of ego. While polite in most cases, I generally flushed my brain of such empty thoughts.

Instead of "I don't think"—think! Instead of "I don't see"—see! If you don't think something is correct, or cannot see why it should be, seek further explanation. After getting all the facts and information, develop an informed statement or discussion point. We all lose with opinions empty of factual information. We all gain with informed discussion points that hopefully result in clear conclusions.

CHAPTER 55
Knowing in One's Head Vs. One's Heart

Those who are familiar with the New Testament know that the Israelites were expecting a Messiah as prophesized in the Old Testament. What many, if not most of them, were expecting was a Messiah who would lead them in defeating the Romans. When it became obvious Jesus wasn't what they expected or wanted, some turned on Him, which ultimately resulted in His crucifixion.

Christ came for something much different from that. Besides coming for atonement for our sins on the cross, Jesus came for our hearts. Why would the Israelites object to that? Consider this: The Israelites were God's chosen people, and they knew that. Someone telling them that they needed to accept Christ could rankle them. If they were "the chosen ones of God," why would they need to do anything further to get to heaven? Those who thought this way would see it as insulting, indeed blasphemous, to even consider such a thought! Even though it was stated in the Old Testament "*and through your offspring all nations on earth will be blessed*" (Genesis 22:18, NIV), some Israelites would find the idea that other nations could be saved both insulting and blasphemous. In short, they "knew" something in their heads. They did not "know" something in their hearts. Some of God's chosen people had a very unfortunate attitude stemming from what they "knew"—an attitude that wouldn't allow their hearts to open up to the message of Christ. Does this happen today for others? It would appear so.

We have already described how some people make up their minds about something so definitely that they have minds like concrete—thoroughly mixed up and permanently set. While there are many concepts on which one can become properly educated, or definitely experience in a fashion to yield a well-based opinion, quite often what they "know" is based upon either false or misleading information, or an opinion based upon what "everybody else" is doing or believes. When someone does something "everyone else" is doing, they risk following mob mentality—especially if the alternative means giving up some perceived personal freedom or taking on some additional responsibility. If the "easy way out" leads where everybody else is thinking (possible mob thinking), it seems easier to follow and believe in. If this happens to someone, their heart could become closed.

We can see this in democratic elections when candidates make promises that are either impossible to keep, or appeal to the prevailing opinion. Occasionally there is a pervasive opinion that there is "a need for change," even if the current government has done almost everything possible to provide a good living and services to those they govern. The politicians who use the "need for change" argument are particularly nefarious. They pursue an agenda that often leads to a change alright—sometimes for the worse once they come to office. Suddenly all those wonderful promises seem to fade away! The "new" policies seem to either follow the policies of the government voted out or, worse yet, they result in worse living conditions and unacceptable services. When this happens, the mob turns and the offenders are voted out again. This is still a form of mob rule.

In order for democracy to work effectively, the electorate needs to be educated and well informed—*personally* well informed. If the electorate doesn't work to become informed, but just waits for someone to inform them, they could easily succumb to mob mentality. If an individual or group of individuals chooses to "just let things be," they are uninformed and irresponsible.

There is always the complaint "voter turnout is low." Who is responsible for that? Every eligible person in a democracy has a personal responsibility to vote and make a well informed, well considered vote. Not voting is laziness. Not voting because you cannot see a reason to vote is essentially saying you are uninformed or lazy. Even worse, you are agreeing to let others lead who may not have your needs in mind. There's an old saying: *people get who they deserve after an election.*

Remember … if you've made up your mind based on false information, or information you want to believe in your heart but doesn't take into consideration the facts before you, you could be leading yourself and those around you toward potentially dangerous results. You may be hoping to "defeat the Romans." You may be leading an innocent to his or her death. Indeed, your misinformed mind may be leading you and those you care for to a life all may find unsatisfactory. Seek all the facts and information. Examine all facts and information. Discern. Examine historical information to see what was done before and the results of the actions, and then proceed with the heart knowledge you have done everything you can to make an informed decision. Don't go down in history as "part of the mob."

CHAPTER 56
Lighting Strike; Being in a Hurry

Many stories can be told about the results of an action done in a hurry. The consequences vary widely and can be quite disastrous. The reader may have gotten to the point where they have become so saturated by such stories, the stories and their morals are just ignored. We suggest rather strongly the reader take this weird experience Anne and I had on the Shuswap Lake in British Columbia to heart, and do your best to plan accordingly, heeding scientific evidence concerning boating during a storm.

Pause here and consider several points. First, plan your actions so you don't get caught short of something. Secondly, if an electrical storm approaches while vacationing on a small boat, get off the water! Thirdly, if you haven't planned, and you're short of something as a storm approaches, do not ignore the first points. Wait until the storm has passed!

You may think, as some impatient young people and older people are wont to think, *It will never happen to me.* I am analytical. The odds of something happening to you increase as you continue to "tempt fate." Eventually you'll experience something potentially hazardous as you ignore good, scientific advice and common sense.

The background to this story is the Shuswap Lake in British Columbia. This lake forms an "H" with a narrow connecting water path between the two "vertical" arms called the Cinnemousun Narrows. At "The Narrows" is a provincial park with docks on both the north and south sides for use by small boats other than houseboats. Houseboats can beach off the ends of the park where there are no docks. Above the docks on the shore are picnic shelters with roofs, tables, and fire pits. The Shuswap eventually drains into the Thompson River and is said to change water every sixty days. It moves, albeit slowly. Anne and I have been out visiting the lake in the spring when there is still some thin ice on it and have seen the ice slowly moving in a westerly direction with the current.

The Shuswap can get some very big storms. We've been on shore when we could hear and then see an electrical storm approach and hit. Being a narrow mountainous valley throughout the "H," the sound effect is quite excitingly loud. It can rain violently! Most of the time it's relatively calm—a very enjoyable lake on which to boat, swim, and fish.

At The Narrows are two floating stores for fuel and ice, along with various supplies and needs. They are very popular. When we're on the Shuswap, we use them to fuel up and get ice for the ice boxes on our boat.

Now for some minor science. When something moves or rotates, a very small electrical charge is set up (see "Foibles" earlier in this book). One normally doesn't see this charge because it's so small. Even if a moving or rotating object is in the water, that small charge is being generated. Want to increase that charge, even a small bit? Speed up the rotating or moving object.

Lightning is the result of the completion of an electrical circuit between where the bolt begins and ends. There has to be some electrical charge existing or set up for that circuit to eventually complete. Because of this, it's strongly recommended that when a storm is approaching, especially an electrical storm, you get off the water. If docked, I shut off electrical circuits on the boat in a storm.

If you're fortunate to be in a valley that amplifies the noise of an approaching electrical storm, pay attention! One time on the Shuswap, Anne and I decided to tie up at one of the southern docks at The Narrows. We chose a sheltered picnic site relatively close to the dock and unloaded what we needed for supper from the boat. A storm had been forecast, and the sky was darkening. We set up the BBQ in the shelter and started supper. The rain hit ferociously! We could hear the thunder up the northern arms of the Shuswap, so we sat under our shelter and waited for nature's light show after supper.

The rain slacked off a bit. Suddenly a speedboat came from the southwest arm, going full tilt past us, straight over to the floating stores on the eastern side of The Narrows! It probably came from a houseboat around the corner where they could beach legitimately. We waited a little longer, then the rain picked up and noise from the lightning grew closer. We could see the flashes and hear the sounds of thunder up the two northern valleys, so we sat back and continued to enjoy the show.

Suddenly the boat came roaring back from the stores, heading toward the front of the dock where we'd tied up our boat. The rain picked up and hit hard. What happened next took only milliseconds, but our eyes and brains seemed to process everything. As the boat rapidly approached off the northeast end of our dock (prop rotating rapidly), the water close behind the boat seemed to instantly form a large bowl. That bowl was filled with what appeared to be orange-red fire! Then from the middle of the bowl a white peak of water formed, with the bowl staying in its round shape, even though there was wash from the speeding boat. The peak joined up with a lightning bolt from the sky just as the loudest explosive *bang* we had ever heard simultaneously went off! The noise rattled everything on the shelter's picnic table. It even rattled my glasses and took away my breath! This all happened right behind the speeding boat. The "bowl" disappeared and the water calmed right after the lightning strike.

After gaining my composure (immediately after the boat sped off), I looked at Anne and asked "Did you see what I saw?" She answered yes. She'd felt a pressure on her chest from the shock!

In review: The boat was on the lake during a storm—a very definite, well heard, well seen, electrical storm. This was the first wrong action from a safety point of view. The second error was that the boat was going at a high speed, so the propeller was rotating rapidly. Third, the bowl formed right behind the boat and wasn't dissipated by the prop wash, probably because everything happened so fast, in milliseconds. Fourth, we can only surmise that the charge set up by something on, or because of, that boat probably started at or near the boat, but because the boat was moving rapidly, the effects of that charge happened behind the boat. This all seemed to have contributed to the lightning strike forming where it did. It was the only time in our lives we ever saw a lightning bolt originate from water.

Anne commented that the colour of the boat operator's seat was now probably brown! I replied that the person operating the boat under those conditions should count him or herself fortunate the bolt didn't hit the boat. Anne asked what I thought would have happened in that case, and I said we probably would have seen boat and body parts flying!

Enough science and emotion, folks! Stay off any lake when a lightning storm is occurring or approaching. We don't want to pick up your body parts or have to take our boat in for repairs from flying pieces of your boat after it explodes!

There's never a valid reason for being in such a hurry that you put your life or the lives of others in jeopardy because you forgot something. Wait out the storm! This storm passed thirty minutes later.

CHAPTER 57
Living with Retirement

While writing this book, the word "are" popped up in our minds, used in the context that occurrences "are" what they are at the time they occurred. As time went on, several lessons were learned about so-called "retirement" that caused us to change the "are" to "were," as many circumstances have changed over time—some to the good, some to the bad.

Anne and I are respected, as we try to tell it like it is and gently speak the truth. We attribute this to our relationship with the Lord. This relationship is not only precious, but it allows us to be at peace with events in our world today. There are times when some disturbing things happen—disturbing in the sense that the things we have cared for and been blessed to work to accomplish are denigrated by the actions of others.

We worked hard to accomplish our tasks to a point where others could move forward with confidence and continue those tasks after we moved on. Sadly, both in the oil industry and in our retirement years, quite often the continuation of these blessings was not forthcoming due to ongoing actions of others.

There were many cases in which our successors benefitted from our experiences. There were also far too many situations where others did not heed the benefit. It was fairly easy for most discerning people to see why there were failures, or near failures, in those cases. These were brought about by people who either didn't think or wouldn't work with people.

One example out of the oil industry occurred when I worked with a client who was assigned to me by my service company. That client hadn't used us much previously. Through patience, persistence, and understanding, this client gradually became quite a good client. Everybody in my company was apprised of how this was accomplished, as there was no real secret to the process. Care for them. Listen to them. Work with them in such a way that both the company and the client prospered. I understood that certain procedures the client followed, while not always to the liking of my company, were legal and could be easily worked with.

When I announced my retirement, this client was very upset with me. He even called the president of my company and demanded that he persuade me to change my mind! Thanking the client for that, I committed to work with them until I retired, plus work with my replacement to be sure he understood how to maintain the good relationship that had developed between me and that client.

I did this and followed up a year after my retirement. My former company had gradually lost that client. The problem was as noted above—there were some procedures followed by the client that weren't necessarily to the liking of my company, and my successor and his successors didn't want to work with them the way I had. Other clients who had been won over to my former company who preferred to use the same procedures began to fall away as well.

Sad, but true. The term "working with people" always requires you to apply patience, persistence, and understanding. The key word here is "apply." After leaving the oil industry, I often heard that I was missed and that people wanted me back. While that seems nice to me, it was rather disturbing, because while I had no intention of coming back, I still cared. So much it sometimes hurt. I noticed something, though—the respect people had for me grew as my successors were lesser regarded.

After retiring from the oil industry, I developed an interest in becoming a local politician. I spent the eight years prior to becoming a politician on a commission, six of them as Chair. During that time, I learned a lot through working with provincial and federal politicians and bureaucrats and by attending—on my own initiative—local government board meetings. Others noticed this. By the time I was elected to represent a rural area, I had acquired personal training, which was now bolstered by more formal training. I worked well with and supported staff, and never slagged them in public or private. If there was a problem, I took it to the boss of the staff, the CAO. We dealt with the issue quietly, away from the public. If I couldn't support the issue, affected staff were taken aside and their perspective listened to. If I didn't change my mind, I assured them that I would not slag them at the board table. As a result of this, as well as honestly and diligently working with all levels of government, many truly productive events took place.

When I announced that I wouldn't run again after seven years of local politics, people were genuinely concerned about what might happen after I left. I stated that my decision was irreversible. Several sources exerted pressure on me, and I noted that if any particular potential successors were as bad as people thought, the future opinion some would have about me would not be all that bad! Puzzled, people asked why. Simply put, if they were that bad, I'd look all the better, as people remembered what governance was like when I was there!

After I left local politics, members of the public and politicians would come to me with fire in their eyes, saying they wished I was back or that I was sorely missed. In some cases, it was noted by others that all the good things done during my tenure to bolster the community appeared to not only have disappeared, but relationships appeared to have gone backwards. I asked them what they meant by this, and they explained that there was little or no working with people, in the sense that the parties listened to each other. Board meetings were being disrupted and staff weren't getting their work done and were being slagged.

In the case of the oil industry, what happened was very subtle. Good advice given during the time I was part of the picture was quietly ignored after I left, and situations deteriorated. In the political case, results weren't so subtle. Working relationships with both staff and other local politicians seemed to have deteriorated. Before I retired from local politics, many wonderful benefits were enjoyed—not only to my constituents, but to those in the region and the province. All anyone needed to do was work with local politicians and staff to see how all this was accomplished and to continue and hopefully improve what had been done.

My political job and my oil industry job were, in principle, not all that different. They were service jobs. I was not "the boss." I was "the servant," but I wasn't a slave. In both cases, I had to work with people. In one case, those groups were my superiors and my clients. In the other case, they were the board and my constituents. In both cases I was not the boss; I was a team member. I wasn't weak—I had to be strong to stand up to the yelling and screaming of my clients and my constituents. I had to work with my board and my bosses to convince them there just might be a better way. If either my bosses or my board deemed they had a better way, I learned to work with them and still reach goals to the benefit of all. Simple!

When anyone in the oil industry or the political arena comes out with a hard-headed attitude that they are the boss, or that they know better, they shouldn't be surprised to find themselves butting their head against a wall. There is no use getting mad about it!

In both of these situations, Anne and I were bothered. We'd seen how we were so blessed by being effective in both cases, and although we're no longer in either politics or the oil industry, we're ready to provide guidance based upon how we were successful to anyone who asks. One caveat, though—whoever asks the question must listen. If they don't, they must take full responsibility for their own actions.

We were blessed by the wisdom gained through our life work together. We both hope we continue to strive to be wiser as time goes on.

CHAPTER 58
Many Moves, Much Learned

Anne and I came from families that moved around a lot. Anne was a "railway brat," and I was a "post office brat." When we married, we became "oil patch nomads." This chapter examines some of the lessons we learned from our experiences as nomads.

Early in our married life, we bought six individual lots in British Columbia, which when consolidated gave us about 1.5 hectares—3.65 acres to be exact. People ask why we bought so much land in British Columbia prior to retiring. There are several reasons, all from lessons learned as we moved around.

Anne's BSc Chemistry boyfriend-turned-husband took a job in the oil industry right after graduation in 1966. She hoped he would settle into a nice, stable job where there were little or no moves. Indeed, she communicated this emphatically several times prior to agreeing to marry the guy! Instead, she married a nomad, just like her dad. After it became evident she was going to move more than her dad had, she made it clear our marriage stability may be in danger unless the Edgson team found some roots for retirement!

Lesson one: Give the wife and the Edgson team hope that at some point (upon retirement) roots would be put down. Get an address that would be stable upon retirement. We bought our retirement property.

Prior to acting on lesson one, we made a few moves that taught us some interesting lessons. For example, when you buy a newly built home, there's a strong possibility that the house may be located in a different spot from what was indicated on the site plan. While we occupied our first house, our neighbour built a fence based on his site plan. After the fence was built, I checked out the property pins. The fence was over a foot onto our property! On a city lot one "plus foot" could be quite significant, and it was.

Lesson two: Make sure you know exactly where the property lines are before you buy a property/house. Make sure your neighbour knows as well. We did this for our retirement property, but to be absolutely comfortable with our decision, we bought six lots. Reason? We knew who our neighbour was going to be—us! And should anybody "accidentally" encroach on our property, who cares about one foot on a large consolidated lot?

We bought six lots in the early 1970s and left the lots separate for a while. The regulations at the time were pretty lax compared to today's standards. One of our lots was two hundred feet wide with a little brook running right through the middle. In 1970, we could have built right up to the brook. In the late 1990s, we couldn't build within one hundred feet of our brook. In other words, the lot in question was sterilized because of its two-hundred-foot width.

Lesson three: If you're only buying one lot in the country, make sure you understand what the rules are at the time of purchase (get a lawyer, which we did), and build before those rules change. They will change!

When we bought our first two of six properties, there was no water, electricity, or even good roads. But we bought those first two lots anyway.

Lesson four: If you don't have services, you'd better realize you cannot build until those services are available (get a lawyer). We had faith that in the twenty-five plus years left prior to retirement, required services would be provided. They were installed, but this was a gamble we took. Others may not be as successful.

If you're not sure what you want but you want the security of having a retirement spot, you must make a decision—lake front, scenery, depth of property, and more. Anne and I looked at lake front property on a very windy and wet day. Most of the properties had a small strip of land on the lake with the vast majority of the property behind that being sloped (almost vertical in some cases). Access could be difficult, plus you were limited by "lake front/road back." Importantly, should a storm occur, you'd get all the fury of that storm coming off the lake, which was happening the day we looked so long ago!

Lesson five: If you want depth of property with much less sloped land and some buffer from lake storms, you should purchase above the lake. There is land with benches above lakes.

Lesson six actually evolves from this as well: If you want scenery, you should purchase property where you can control the scenery to some extent. In our case, we bought quite far above the lake—three lots up and three lots down, all adjoining. Mind you, one of those upper lots was eventually sterilized by the brook flowing through it. Plus, the lower lots were very sloped—essentially cliffs. But we owned the cliffs! Any trees that would grow tall over twenty-five plus years could be controlled, thus preserving our view overlooking the lake from "up the hill."

While our lots had varying topography, we eventually decided where we wanted to build. It was a beautiful site with a great view! We could control the growth in front of our home because we owned the lots in front. There was only one ... albeit major ... problem. The perfect spot for our home was smack on a property line. We owned both lots, but that property line legally existed.

Lesson seven: Be sure where you want to build. You may have to buy a couple of lots and consolidate, which we did. We actually consolidated all six 0.6 plus acre lots into one 3.65 acre lot. The middle of our log home runs right along an old property line.

Regulations change. As noted above, if you buy property and don't build on it, you may get caught with a property you can no longer build on, unless you convince the regulating authority to allow you to construct your building. They will likely require expensive consulting work to be done, which could make it financially difficult for you to build.

Lesson eight: Buy enough property so you can place your building where you want, unless you're willing to or financially capable of putting it within regulatory requirements. In our case, we were so far away from any of the consolidated property lines, we could build almost anywhere we wanted. This will in all likelihood not apply in an urban setting.

When we were considering buying our retirement property, we were made well aware of the fact that we were going to build in an area on top of solid rock ... well, not quite! The rock was one to two feet down and fractured. The area we wanted to place our house on was sparsely vegetated by big trees, which turned out to be an area with a fractured rock "dome." This was easily moved by a large excavator back hoe ... to a point. That point, fortunately, was where the bottom of our lower floor was to be built. We did notice that where we wanted to place our house close to the cliff was actually scree slope with rock rubble, so we moved it back five feet to be sure the lower cement pad of the house was on solid granite. The deck is built on the scree slope.

Lesson nine: Building a house on a solid rock foundation is tricky unless you have room and regulatory space to move the foundation prior to pouring the cement if needs be. Make sure you have sufficient land to do this. Building a log house resulted in a beautiful home for us. The cost was more than expected, it took two years from start to finish, and the logs require a lot of maintenance.

Lesson ten: Go in with your eyes wide open when contemplating building a log home. Get an estimate and add 25–30 per cent to it. Some people fail to do this. There are incomplete log homes that take more than two years to finish to testify to this. Keep in mind logs shrink, so choose your construction method carefully. Use a reputable log home builder and be aware of those who say "they can do it cheaper." Building a log home requires careful research and clear understanding of the finances and pitfalls. We were careful, we could afford it, and we love our beautiful home.

These homes need a fair amount of ongoing maintenance. Anne and I tell people that if they plan on living in a log home beyond age sixty-five, they better be in good shape (we are currently in our seventies). In addition, if you're building a complicated or multi-storey log home, you should consider purchasing a good set of new or used scaffolding, as we did.

One person we met bought a nice looking, non-log home and didn't use a lawyer because they were trying to cut down on expenses. When they registered their new-to-them property, they discovered that there was no building permit! A caveat was slapped on the home, requiring whoever purchased the home next to upgrade to the local standards of the purchase date. That one "economy" turned out to be costly, because the caveat will remain until the required work is done. This could be a negative point should the current owner wish to sell the home without the repairs being done.

Lesson eleven: Use a lawyer. We always insisted on using a lawyer for our many moves. We have never been disappointed.

After our first home and subsequent moves in the oil industry, we bought what we needed and could afford to live in where we worked. We generally selected a home of 1,000–1,400 square feet. This was not the norm for my oil patch colleagues. Generally they bought big, sometimes ostentatious, homes. Until we were in our early forties, whenever we bought we had a mortgage, but one we could afford. After that time, we were debt free and bought homes for cash. The people we knew with large homes generally had large mortgages.

We bought relatively small homes prior to retirement because our research showed that these homes would sell easily—a necessity for us because we moved a lot. Indeed, we never lost money on any of our homes. We came close, though. In the worst case we only gained 2 per cent on one home, but we never lost. Those with large mortgages were not so fortunate. Large homes don't sell well if the economy is poor or if there's an industry downturn. On top of that, if a mortgage makes up the vast majority of the purchase price, and the market or economy falls, you could get nothing back if you're unfortunate enough to have to sell … if you can sell at all.

Lesson twelve: Buy what you can afford. If you're not going to move for a fair amount of time—like ten to twenty years—you can possibly wait things out, as long as you have a job. If you have any doubts about any of this, it might be better to rent, or buy a home suited to your needs, not your ego. An ego-bought home is a very poor investment in the short term. In the long term, it may be okay … if you're willing and able to live in that home until the mortgage is paid.

Our big log home is free and clear of any encumbrances. If we're so fortunate to live here until we part this earth, we do not care what our heirs receive for it!

We built a log home in an interface forest, where forest fires can and do occur. We heat with wood. Our wood sheds are at least one hundred feet away from the house, so they will burn in a forest fire without taking our home with them. We live in a subdivision with a fire department and a good water system, and our home has a steel roof. Our garage is "stick built" about one hundred feet away from the home. It has fiberglass shingles.

Lesson thirteen: In an interface area, the best material to build a home out of is concrete with a steel roof, as concrete and steel don't burn. The second best option is a log home with large logs and a steel roof. Forest fires on a slope generally burn through a particular place in about twenty minutes. The big logs may scorch, but because of their size, they probably won't ignite. "Stick built" buildings will probably go up in a major fire, so we don't count on our garage surviving such an event.

Lesson fourteen comes out of this as well: It's our firm opinion you should build in an area with a fire department accredited by the insurance underwriters. This is the case where we live in British Columbia. One should check to see what accrediting agent is necessary where you live. Frankly, you can buy insurance anywhere—with at least a couple of caveats. First, if you mislead an insurance agency about having a fire department (for instance telling them you have a fire hydrant nearby), you risk the insurance company refusing to compensate you in a loss. Be absolutely sure (like through a lawyer) what you need to tell your insurance agent.

Secondly—and in our opinion the most important point—if you don't have an accredited fire department nearby, it won't matter much if you do get an insurance payout after you lose all your memories and most of your irreplaceable keepsakes.

Wherever we moved we immediately changed not only our address but our insurance and vehicle licenses. It galls us when we see someone who lives in British Columbia with "foreign" (other province) license plates. They may be skipping some local taxes, which means we honest types have to make up for it.

Lesson fifteen: Pay your taxes where you live. If you don't want to do this, we suggest you move to the place where you are paying your taxes.

Everywhere we go we hear those who crab and complain that it was better where they came from. For many years people from Alberta would say B.C. meant "Bring Cash." It was true at the time that Alberta was better off financially than B.C. As time went on, though, our relative taxation went down as we in B.C. tried our best to become more fiscally responsible. Alberta, in our opinion, had plenty of money but squandered it. Suddenly Alberta was in trouble financially, while B.C. was much better off in the early 2010s.

Some people in my company who were transferred stateside bragged about lower taxes in their new places but found out a big truth very quickly. The cost of schooling, fuel, power, and other essentials turned out to be far greater than in Canada. In fact, the total cost compared to living in Canada was about the same in many cases.

When we were planning our move to British Columbia, we priced some material out in Alberta compared to the cost in Kelowna, B.C. To our absolute surprise, we noticed at the time that the cost of most of the identical items we were going to buy in Alberta was actually 6 per cent higher than in B.C. before taxes! Once the 6 per cent provincial sales tax was added in B.C., the prices were the same. While this may vary from place to place and from item to item, one should not make assumptions. And of course it can depend on what the provincial government mindset is at the time.

As for land taxes, we currently pay less than half of what would be paid in Alberta. Mind you, we are in a rural area in B.C. In Calgary the home we had was less than one third the size of our current home, and the lot was less than

5 per cent of what we have in B.C. Be careful of judging your current place by your former place.

Lesson sixteen: If you liked where you came from, and if it is truly better than where you currently live, why not move back? Why are you living somewhere where you aren't happy? And—most importantly—why didn't you do your homework before you moved to your current location if the situation is so bad? Do your homework! You may find you're much better off where you are.

Anne and I pay cash for all our transportation. Our beautiful boat, bought new, is over twenty years old. We use it for fishing and camping in British Columbia. It is a custom boat for which we spent roughly 50 per cent more than the basic boat would cost at the time, but which would cost now about four times the total price we paid for it in 1994. Our motorcycle is over thirty years old and runs and drives well. We use it for the pleasure of motorcycle touring. The current model costs well over three times as much as what we spent. Our big SUV is over twenty years old and looks and drives like new. We use it for going back in the mountains, fishing, and berry picking. The current model is at least double the price. We have a ten-year-old Subaru that looks and drives like new, and the current model is about 1.5 times as much. We use it for shopping and for icy roads; it gets thirty-four MPG. Our eleven-year-old diesel Smart Car is like the old Triumph sports cars—fun to drive but with air-conditioning and far less maintenance. It's good for those trips where we don't have to do major shopping, but you'd be surprised at how many groceries we can fill it up with from major box stores! You cannot get a new diesel Smart Car now in Canada, so you cannot get the sixty-eight miles per imperial gallon we get from it— which is handy fifty kilometres out in the country. It's actually cheaper to keep all these gems than drive into town, rent, use the rental, then drive it back and come back out—both in time and in money. All our vehicles are tuned well, so they're low polluters.

Lesson seventeen: Why not buy new then keep your vehicle for a long time? We've saved a huge amount of money by doing this. Besides, we have a vehicle to suit every one of our needs and desires—all paid for. We don't have to dispose of batteries from a new electric car when they die out. We also ask you to consider one other point: How much does it cost to build, and how much does it pollute when you do build a new vehicle? Do your homework and get what you need for your situation. Keep your vehicles well maintained and consider keeping those vehicles for *at least* twenty years.

A lot of people complain about the water and its cost wherever we go, yet they'll go out and buy something far more than they need and pay exorbitant prices. As a politician, I was confronted by a very angry guy over the $1,200 a year he was going to pay for water in our sparsely populated, rural area. Thinking as he pontificated, my mind noted that if we had more people, the cost would be less. I thought at least we had good and dependable water, unlike some others in rural areas who had wells that were running dry. Then blessed with a line of thought, I commented that the pickup truck he had looked very nice. All the accessories he had on it, including roll bars, big tires, extra lights, riser kits and the like, were noted. He paused and looked obviously pleased.

"How much did it cost?" I asked.

"Forty thousand dollars."

"Oh, and you have it debt free?"

He replied no, he was paying about a thousand dollars a month on it. I then asked if he used this very pretty truck for his job.

"No, I just wanted it."

"You're willing to pay a thousand dollars a month for something you want and may not need, yet you're complaining about paying a little more than a thousand dollars *a year* for something you do need, like potable water?"

The conversation ended and he left.

Lesson eighteen: Get your priorities correct. Just like those who bought homes they couldn't afford, or didn't use a lawyer, or didn't do their homework before they spent money—if you don't get your priorities correct, don't blame others for your shortcomings or problems.

Oh … and about that moving concern in our marriage? We have been married over fifty years and happily counting. The nomads are now firmly in place!

CHAPTER 59
Modern Solution to Those Twitterpated

Elsewhere in the book it is noted the girl I met and married really affected me in a wonderful way, right from the first time we met. There was no question in my mind after a couple of weeks that she was the girl I wanted to marry. We had one problem, though. We met in Edmonton, Alberta, at the University of Alberta. Anne lived in Edmonton, and I was in residence at the university because my home at the time was in Grande Prairie, Alberta, about 430 kilometres away. That wasn't a problem during the academic year, but between May and the end of August, I was away in Grande Prairie.

They say that absence makes the heart grow fonder. That was so true in my case! I'd never been affected by a girl as I was and am by Anne. I did the only action that seemed sensible to me at the time: writing letters to her every day!

In those days stamps cost five cents. That didn't bother me, nor did the cost of paper and envelope (probably because I didn't care). I just wanted to show Anne that she was not only cared for … she was needed. That continued right up until just after moving to Dawson Creek for a time in my new job after graduation, when we finally set a date to get married on July 15, 1966.

Anne has always teased me that I was, and am, "twitterpated." I offer no apologies for my condition. That girl is needed even to this day! Now that we're in our seventies, I chuckle at myself over the cost and time spent writing letters to my beautiful girl back in the 1960s. I chuckle until I consider the cost of writing letters today. Ho boy! If there's some poor twitterpated sap university student like me out there, the cost would be almost prohibitive now! I realize that there's a modern and appropriate solution for those who are far away for a spell—a solution that my granddaughter taught me: texting!

Texting daily requires no pen, ink, or paper of any kind. Anne and I text each other within our yard and home. Doing so replaces walkie talkies on our acreage, and it's almost instantaneous. For the twitterpated male, there's less anxiety over what he sent to the one he loves being favourably accepted, as the answer comes back rather quickly. You don't have to wait to sit at a desk or table; you can text when the moment hits you!

When I realized this I initially felt a little sorry for us old types who had to use pen and paper. But why? I was committed to Anne then and I wrote. My commitment to Anne exists now and the writing still occurs (texting, that is). The key here is that we were and are committed to each other. If you have a very inexpensive method of expressing your feelings to the one you love, that's all the more reason to express your feelings right off the cuff, so to speak.

One caution—if two lovers get a little more than just gushy romantic, remember to hit the delete button after the message is sent! The temporary nature of texting is definitely an advantage over more permanent writing. Anne still keeps one letter sent from northern British Columbia where I finally stated a very definite need for her. That in itself is not bad, but how you state it may be!

CHAPTER 60
Old Realities and New Realities, Learned Lessons

Early in the 1970s, Anne and I bought retirement land in the Okanagan Valley in British Columbia. During the mid-1970s, we'd take trips out to the land at least once a year to dream a little of our future. We'd come to the head of Okanagan Lake and travel south along Westside Road until we reached our subdivision. Along the way, we'd look forward to seeing one lone, very large and magnificent pine tree on the east side of the road along the flats prior to climbing up to the area where we had land. The pine was tall, thick at the trunk, green-needled, and clean of any lower branches. It stood as a huge statue showing us we were near a place dear to us.

One year we came out, looking forward to seeing the lone tree that meant we were close to our land. We could normally see the tree for quite some time before we reached it, so we were watching for it in the distance. This time it wasn't there! We couldn't think of any reason why someone would cut this giant, so we began to wonder what happened as we approached the place where it had stood. What we saw initially shocked us. It hadn't been cut down—it had fallen. While the huge trunk looked solid on the outside, it was severely rotted inside. The outward appearance belied the fact that, in reality, the inside was so rotten it wasn't strong enough to withstand a big wind, so it broke apart and fell. Its outward appearance hid a rotten inward reality.

This life lesson taught us a couple of things: One, beauty truly can be only skin deep and hide interior flaws; two, beware of someone who has a handsome appearance, physically or attitudinally. One should watch for inner rot.

Several times I observed this both in the oil industry and the political game. I can hear you say "Well, that's to be expected in those situations!" It's true that oil patchers and politicians are prone to such traits, but not any more than other types of people. At times I observed people outside of these two entities behave poorly—in some cases worse than those we saw in the oil industry and politics.

We loved to see people who professed to be environmentalists smoking cigarettes and travelling around in either big, fancy vehicles (planes or cars) or oil dripping, smoke-belching beaters! The outward appearance they gave as being caring people who were concerned about the environment belied the reality that they were far worse polluters than the rest of us.

Another comparison of realities came about when we bought our British Columbia land early in the 1970s. While today our decision to buy seems very astute, the reality of how it actually happened was very different. I was educated as a chemist. When Anne and I were courting in university, she was attracted by the prospect of her fiancé getting a job as a chemist and not transferring around. Her personal family life had been one of many moves with her parents, so this potential stability looked attractive. It was the hoped-for reality. Then I went into the oil industry upon graduation, and we got married. The hoped-for reality faded quickly away due to the intensity of the job and the many transfers that were part of it.

Very early in our marriage, this job intensity drove us to jump in our car near the end of February and drive to Banff to take some brief time off, as far away from the job as possible. We took a motel room in the place we'd stayed as part of our brief honeymoon, expecting to stay a few days. The first morning we got up and decided to drive west along the Trans-Canada Highway "for a short trip." The day appeared beautiful as we left. We had a second-hand Triumph TR4, which was great for bare roads. As we neared the Alberta-B.C. border, a blizzard set in behind us. |Being the "wise" types we were, we decided to keep going west for a while until the blizzard quit. It didn't. Note that I didn't say "smart" and that the word "wise" is in quotation marks. We were obviously neither wise nor smart!

We decided to keep travelling into British Columbia. The blizzard continued until we turned south at Sicamous off the Trans-Canada Highway to go down to Vernon. We stopped and phoned Anne's grandfather in Vernon from that turnoff, asking if we could stay at his home for the night. Of course! From that point south, it started to rain … pour, actually. We had a peaceful night in his house on Kalamalka Lake in the Okanagan.

The next morning, February 28, 1967, we woke up to warm weather, no snow on the ground except high in the mountains, daffodils popping out of the ground, and Anne's granddad out golfing. I immediately commented, "We have to get a piece of this action!"

At first we did nothing about this statement. Then in 1968 a new reality set in. Anne was not seeing the path she'd hoped to see in her life—a stable, non-moving home life. It turned out we made sixteen moves in the first thirty-two years of our marriage! In 1968 she dropped a pretty big hint that our marriage wouldn't last unless I could find her some roots. She was willing to wait until we retired, but those roots had better be there.

The rapid appearance of instability was not what either one of us expected. The new reality was far more moves than she'd experienced prior to getting married. We decided to apply a learned lesson—live with what you are given and turn it into a newer reality. As noted previously, we bought six adjoining lots in the Okanagan, consolidated them, and eventually built our beautiful log home on property overlooking Okanagan Lake. We control our view over the lake (three of the original lots are below the top three where our home is), there are magnificent trees, and we have a pretty cascading brook flowing through the property. The newer reality had to wait thirty-two years, but we are hopefully in our final home while we are active.

There is a dark side to the title of this chapter, though. The last part of this story has been observed several times by us, both in the oil industry and in politics, so we will discuss a blended story from both entities. We have observed "pillars of the community" with inner decay, well respected by many, including ourselves. The more we observed these types of individuals, the more we saw some disturbing things. Employers were constantly complained about— sometimes blatantly, sometimes in whispers. We advised them to learn to work with people, but they claimed that they were working with people, but their employers would not work with them.

It also became clear that if others didn't do as these people wanted, including their superiors, they desired to get rid of them. In many instances this wish actually happened, but eventually their actions brought about their own downfall. Then new realities set in. Past and present actions were scrutinized, and their employment ceased.

A different reality became evident with their replacements. These were different jobs in different places, yet the common facet was that growth and prosperity occurred under the replacements, benefiting those served. As was the case so many times, new realities set in. In the many instances where persons were impacted by people who "told people" versus "worked with people," the people dictating were gone, replaced by case-building, working-with-people types.

Many of us learned that someone who is effective working with people is not the same as a person who tells you what to do and expects you to do it. Learning to accomplish a task in a legal and moral way, within limits of regulations and practicality, are necessary first steps. "Working with people" means using this information and working with others to build a business case that can be presented in a convincing fashion to benefit those served. On the other hand, a person who dictates what will happen without a valid business case is not "working with people." That person is dictating. If that person is dictating to their superiors, they should expect to fail and fail often.

It is said a willow tree will bend in high winds. It may lose some leaves, but it stands after the storm. On the other hand, much more handsome trees—like an oak or an inwardly- rotten but majestic pine—are uprooted and blown apart in a high wind. Being inflexible can result in self-destruction. Learn to work with people in a way that benefits all concerned.

CHAPTER 61
Peace in Our Time

Peace in our time. For those who are either old enough to remember the 1930s, or those of us who are students of history (particularly World War II), we're familiar with the Prime Minister of Great Britain prior to the Second World War, Neville Chamberlain. We're also aware that he had a document signed by Adolf Hitler giving Hitler something he demanded in return for "peace in our time." Hitler promised that if Chamberlain agreed to give him some territory, he wouldn't make any more demands. The result? Hitler saw that those he opposed were weak, and he not only went back on his word, but he maneuvered the world into war—a war in which he made it quite clear he planned to dominate the world. Chamberlain appeased Hitler to get "peace in our time." That infamous appeasement tactic failed badly.

Before we judge Chamberlain too harshly, let's stop for a minute and ask ourselves if this was unique to him. Do we ever corporately or individually do the same thing? When someone comes to your door with a local gripe and asks if you will sign a petition, you may listen to what the petitioner says and may be wise enough to actually read the material. But if you're busy at the time and don't want to be bothered, you may just sign the petition, just wanting to get the petitioner off your porch and out of your life.

Peace in our time.

Later you may hear that what you signed for has greater implications than you thought or were led to believe. Again, you are busy, so others will take care of the issue. You just leave it.

Peace in our time.

Or maybe you actually think no harm will be done by supporting what the petitioner said would be done. You don't know, and you're too busy to find out further details. Let others, or the government, take care of the problem. What if a government council or cabinet just wants "peace in our time" as well? What if they just give the petitioners what they want? What if later you find out that the project you were told would "save taxes" actually costs you more? What if the government decided to get "peace in our time" and now you suffer?

Stop for a second here. Is it the government's fault if that happens? Yes, if it is shown they took the easy way out. But what about you? Did you not take the easy way out as well?

Consider an example from the corporate world. Often the people hired do not work out very well and are actually a potential liability to the company that hired them. What do some companies do? Rather than keep that potential liability in their present locale, or admit they made a mistake in hiring that person, the company transfers them to another locale. Often this only compounds the problem, because that potential problem is now a real problem. So that person is transferred again. And again.

Peace in our time.

If the employee is truly beyond redemption, they're eventually terminated by someone who doesn't shirk from looking at all the facts and who has the company's best interests in mind.

Unfortunately, "peace in our time" is a common mindset. But should we be too critical of the companies who do this? Are we also guilty of this at times? Anne and I do not sign petitions. If we're even a bit swayed by something, we dig in and check out the situation. Most of the time what we're being asked to sign is either a baseless or ill-informed opinion. If we believe something is wrong, we talk to the entity responsible, listen carefully, if necessary talk to other entities that are better informed, and then respond by letting people know our position—if necessary in a signed letter. We have found too often that door to door petitions appeal to "the mob." Petitions are often too simplistic in their thinking.

The "peace in our time" attitude is not the property of only Neville Chamberlain. It never has been, nor will it ever be. Ask yourself if you're getting caught up in this attitude as well. If so, you may experience a localized World War II result. If you take time to look at a proposal carefully before committing, you, and hopefully many others, will get rid of this appeasing attitude to the benefit of your community and the world.

CHAPTER 62
Projects Take Time

Following "Peace in Our Time," which is partially about avoiding personal responsibilities, this story also shows that practising such avoidance can result in projects being ridiculously delayed. It also demonstrates that proceeding in a manner to best serve others takes considered time once started. This involves patience, working with people, tenacity, and the necessity of developing a good reason or business plan to show why a project needs to be done. Two examples will be discussed: first the water systems in a rural area in the Okanagan, and second, a secondary highway between Vernon and Kelowna. Both take place in the beautiful province of British Columbia and both of which I was involved in before, during, and after my time as a local politician.

Many people thought we were crazy when we purchased our properties in B.C. because there was a rather primitive road south to Kelowna, and the lots were not serviced. The upper three lots didn't even have a road when we bought them. They were inexpensive, but the prevailing opinion of others was that it would be better to put our money in stocks.

As noted elsewhere, owning these lots ensured that Anne would realize one of her most important goals—a place to set down roots. To me, this was worth far more than we paid for the properties. It was also important to both of us that we got the type of land we wanted to build on. The desired natural features of the properties were difficult to come by back then, and in all probability would be even more difficult to find in the future. Even if others thought this was a bad investment, we truly were happy when we bought those lots.

Shortly after we purchased all the lots, the developer put in a water system. While this was thrilling to see and obviously made our purchase more meaningful to us, there was a concern. Part of the system built across the top of our three upper lots was less than impressive. We were sure some poor sap of a local politician would have to bear the responsibility for upgrading the system someday, but at the time this wasn't a concern. We had a family to raise and a job to perform. We had plenty of time to get our personal act together before the water system warranted any of our attention.

There was a road from our subdivision called the Westside Road leading both to Vernon and Kelowna. From the time of our property purchase, we reached our lots by driving down this road from the north. It was paved to a point then became what we in the oil patch euphemistically called "Texas pea gravel"— boulders and pit run rock that came right out of the "gravel" pits without crushing. It was rough!

The Westside Road continued south past our subdivision, leading to Kelowna, but was not what you would call a regular road—not even a regular road with Texas pea gravel. To call it a goat trail would be insulting the goats! We decided to do that southerly drive for fun while visiting our lots in the early 1970s.

As we bounced along with two young children, we came to a point where the trail split and went around a big pine tree. Obviously this trail was "built" with a minimalist approach. It took forever to get to Kelowna, and we drove back at night. While we bounced along, we did note that there were no lights along the road, and few lights across the Okanagan Lake. Other than the wear and tear on us and the car, the trip was interesting and beautiful.

Obviously this road needed to be improved. Some poor sap of a politician would probably be involved overseeing this road upgrade, but for now, I wasn't concerned.

By 2003 the Westside Road was improved. It had been entirely paved! There were several areas where it appeared the pavement was just laid down on a widened Texas pea gravel road, but there was pavement. One three-kilometre section blasted out of the side of a mountain along Okanagan Lake initially was built by relief crews in the Great Depression. This section, subsequently paved, was narrow and twisting. If two opposing big vehicles met on it, one would possibly fall off a cliff into the lake. On top of that, sections of the pavement had deteriorated to the point where the potholes had become worthy of being called depressions!

As Anne and I became involved with our Member of the (Provincial) Legislative Assembly, we brought this up to him quite often. The Westside Road was a secondary road and a very small part of the road infrastructure in British Columbia, so getting money to do anything but patching was a problem. I was also Chair of a local government Commission and received much feedback about the road, which I passed on to my MLA.

That summer as we left for vacation, I received an urgent email from one of the members of our Commission. The Westside Road had fallen into the lake in one area, blocking traffic in both directions. I immediately fired off an email to our MLA, noting a rather selfish point: I hoped the road would be fixed before we got back from vacation! The MLA sent a follow-up email, asking me when we would return. On our way back from vacation, the MLA emailed the road was open.

By now it had become obvious the Westside Road needed more attention. Our MLA asked me to organize a citizen's committee to report to him to recommended improvements for the road and to work with the Ministry of Transportation (MOT) to see how this could be done. Initially six members worked with the MOT (later the Ministry of Transportation and Infrastructure—MOTI), and while the money was still very scarce, the MOTI and the Westside Road Improvement Committee (WRIC) worked diligently to plan for the future, when and if funding became available.

WRIC continued to work with the MLAs of the day and the MOTI to support the MOTI from 2003 up to and including the writing of this book. I was the de facto spokesperson for WRIC, which had no hierarchy. Its purpose was to improve the road, not seek glory. The monies eventually were granted because of MOTI's diligent planning and the building of a valid business case.

One day at a community fair, the Premier of British Columbia noted that I was being called "Mr. Westside Road," as I was so involved with the WRIC and the MLAs. I thanked her for this, but it must be remembered that I was part of a working team called WRIC.

My time as a member of WRIC spanned from 2003 to the writing of this book. I was the local politician from 2007 to 2014. I smile about this, because it was noted above in this story "some poor sap of a politician would probably be involved overseeing this road upgraded." It turns out one of those saps was me! On top of that, this project did take time—over fifteen years and still ongoing!

The water system also became an issue during my time as a politician. It was leaking and there were pressure and other problems causing concern. Remember the statement above in this story about Anne's and my observation when the water system was installed above our lots: "We were sure some poor sap of a local politician would have to bear the responsibility for upgrading the system someday." Well, guess who? Me again!

Little money had been put aside to upgrade the system, new regulations were coming up regarding water systems, and there were infrastructure concerns with the system, so major upgrades became necessary. Major costs would be borne by the local taxpayers. Taxes for upgrades had been kept low until there came a point when they had to be raised … and raised by a large amount. It certainly appeared local residents didn't realize that keeping taxes low for "a short time" would end up keeping them too low for too long, making the necessary jump in rates quite large. Ouch!

To ease the tax pain with the water systems, I insisted the rates be phased in. This was still unpopular. People naturally noted the rates had been kept low for so long. Why could they not be kept low now?

Some facts to note here. First, upgrades take time … and money. Delaying them only makes costs escalate. The price of each individual lot we bought in the 1970s has gone up over fifteen times in forty plus years. The delay in providing money for the upgrade and maintenance of the water system since the 1970s made the current work fiscally astronomical. Both the Westside Road improvements and the water system improvements are ongoing and taking quite some time. Just sitting around and "keeping taxes low" might work until some poor sap of a politician finally does the obvious and helps get plans in place to ensure such wild jumps are mitigated in the future. In these two cases, I was one of those "poor saps."

Secondly, for those concerned about getting major infrastructure projects fixed—and now—they need to be constantly planned for. Today few people care or realize how much the Westside Road has been improved, yet some of those same people wanted that road fixed immediately back in the early 2000s. Those same people are still upset about the costs of fixing the water system today, because they don't want their taxes raised.

In my office in Calgary I had a framed piece of paper that stated "Your poor planning is not necessarily my emergency!" Lesson: plan, budget, work with people. To this day the Westside Road Improvement Committee has been the lone major citizen-driven entity that has seen what was a trail even the goats wouldn't want to travel on become a scenic and drivable secondary highway. Others outside of WRIC, MOTI, and the MLAs may try to claim credit, but check and qualify what they are saying.

Oh, and the water system Anne and I had concerns about? No need for us to buy bottled water—the system is great! A word of caution here: When you are young, be careful when you say "Someday some poor sap is going to have to …" That poor sap might just be you!

CHAPTER 63
People of God

This story is partially a sad one, but one that must be written. While the vast majority of those who profess knowledge of the Lord lead wonderful lives that give honour and glory to Him, there are those who profess the knowledge yet cause one to think otherwise. It's unfortunate when people who do not know the Lord put their search on hold when they see the hypocrisy of some professed Christians.

Anne and I will start with a couple of examples from when we were young people. The first took place when we had just met and had not been going together for a year ... way before we knew the Lord. It still lives on in my mind as one I wish to emulate. The other example makes me shudder every time I think of it. It took place about two months after the first. Amazingly, these two examples became the forerunners of many examples to follow, even to this day.

The first and best example was Anne's maternal grandmother. I only saw this lady once, but the memory is welded into my mind to this day. She was an elegant lady with a successful marriage and life. Only after her death did the trials and tribulations she'd experienced become apparent to me. All were overcome. I met her at Anne's home and was immediately imbued with a sense of respect for her and Anne's grandfather. Anne's grandmother was a little more awe- inspiring to me. She was calm, polite, and very respectful. Anne's grandfather was fun!

The surprise of my life came about with Anne's grandmother. She was all she appeared to be, with a fun-giving twinkle in her eye that became evident by something she did involving Anne and me. Anne's grandparents were visiting during one of my visits with Anne at her home. Anne was drafted after lunch to wash dishes, allowing her mother the chance to visit with her parents. For some forgotten reason, I didn't offer to help but stayed out in the living room talking with the crowd. Anne's grandmother suddenly came up to me and said, "Jim, Jim … come quickly this way!" I followed her, having no idea what she was talking about. She excitedly led the way toward the kitchen. Then she whispered for me to peek in at Anne as she washed dishes.

"Oh Grandma," Anne said.

Anne's grandmother admonished her to keep on working, handwashing a glass milk bottle. What I saw was cute, funny, and sexy! As Anne shook the bottle side to side, her beautiful rear end shook side to side as well in the opposite direction to her hands! Both Grandma and I laughed. That rotating rear end looked fascinating to me! From that day on, I appreciated seniors who were full of life and didn't hesitate to enjoy moments without being stuffy about it. Anne's grandma was fun!

The other example involved an old lady who provided room and board for a male university student. I stayed at Athabasca Hall on the University of Alberta campus during my first year at university. Neglecting to register there for my second year until it was too late, I had to look elsewhere. An older lady off campus had accommodations. Meeting her with my parents, my first impression was unfavourable, because she obviously wasn't particularly happy boarding students. Immediately she came across as judgemental, leaving me feeling unworthy. Having failed to find a suitable place to stay earlier, I had little choice. Besides, my parents liked her because she appeared to be a strict disciplinarian. Just the type to keep my mind on my studies!

My first breakfast was a greasy plate of fried eggs and sausages. Supper was a greasy form of fried food. The next day was the same. Finishing my supper was impossible. The boarding lady saw this and criticized me. From that point on I spent hard earned money on meals on campus—money that could have been better used for my education and taking out my girlfriend. Since my parents had connected me with her, I couldn't complain to them. I didn't realize that my parents had set up a communication system with her to monitor my activities.

Not showing up for supper and coming in late after eating on campus resulted in a report to my parents.

That fall Anne had gone out to Vernon, British Columbia to look after her frail grandmother prior to entering nursing school in Edmonton in February of the next year. I went home for Christmas to Grande Prairie soon after she came back to Edmonton. I was greeted with a chewing out, because my parents believed I was out with my girlfriend and not eating the boarding house meals. I explained why, and my parents essentially called me a liar. Reminding them that I couldn't be spending money on my girlfriend because she had been out in Vernon from the middle of September to the middle of December was of little use.

I resented all the spying going on. To this day I have a huge distaste for grumpy old people who gossip and delight in putting young people down. I cannot stand greasy food now, especially greasy sausages, which remind me of those suppers "offered" fifty plus years ago. Irrespective of those experiences, two types of old people became evident—wonderful people who are fun loving, understanding, and encouraging, and those who are nosey, grumpy gossipers who go out of their way not to be loving, understanding, or encouraging. In a word—curmudgeons.

Today Anne and I know the Lord. The Bible speaks of Pharisees. Saul, who became Paul, was a wonderful example of how God's transforming powers could change someone who was extremely knowledgeable about the Old Testament yet had closed the eyes of his heart to its real meaning until he was on the road to Damascus. Saul fiercely persecuted followers of Christ prior to that point in time. We have two people—one who did not have a personal relationship with the Lord, and one who came to that personal relationship. Indeed, the Holy Spirit-inspired writings of Paul speak of all the Lord means to Anne and me, plus provide direction to where we should go to learn—not only through the Word, but through others inspired today by the Holy Spirit.

We have known many people who are lovers of the Lord in every sense. Missionaries we met many years ago on the Shuswap in the Okanagan not only inspired us but fervently prayed four years for Anne and me to come to that saving knowledge. When we did, it inspired them! Through the Lord using them, we wanted to move forward in our lives and be wonderful examples of God's work in earthly man. Those missionaries were fun loving, wonderful people whom we will never forget as we go forward in life.

Then there were those who professed knowledge of the Lord yet wouldn't tolerate you searching in God inspired ways to grow in Him. They were judgemental, legalistic, gossiping people who frowned on someone holding up their hands in praise and getting tears in their eyes when something they learned moved them to do so. Worse, when I became a politician and wanted to go to church to publicly worship the Lord with other believers, some church goers wanted to "take advantage" of the politician and grill him on subjects other than the Lord. When I made it clear I came to worship the Lord, not to politic, they ignored me and kept on discussing politics. They ignored my strong suggesting to meet me during the week outside of church. It got so persistent, we left that church when the pastor retired. One of those trying to play politics stated that we shouldn't make the move because our new church wasn't in our community. Same denomination, different place!

The problem even persisted in our neighbourhood after we transferred to the other church. We still lived near the "old" church. One day during the week when I was away, Anne attended a community meeting near where we lived. A member of our former church confronted her about politics, corporations, local and regional government, and how awful they all were. Anne tried to defend both her and me, but the person started yelling, so she backed off. Arriving home and hearing this, I phoned up the person and gently explained where that person was off base. The answer was a mumble and a hung-up phone. The sad news—actually, the good news in a way—is that the person refused to speak to us or look at us for quite some time. From this experience I learned one thing: some people put their hate of politicians and corporations ahead of their love for Jesus.

In one case we had God fearing and loving people who inspired us and were used of the Lord to help draw us to Him. They remain an inspiration to us as we continually grow in the Lord. In the other case, we had someone who professes a saving knowledge of the Lord yet has not let go of their hate of certain types of people. It doesn't matter if those hated people actually did the community some good … that person disliked those people so much, they behaved like they weren't inspired by the Lord. Such behaviour can turn people off the Lord.

Another example was pathetic yet sadly humorous. Anne and I still chuckle about this incident. We were at an excellent church Christmas dinner, and an older woman complained she didn't like it. When asked why, she said the turkey was chunked, not sliced. When that same woman found out she was sitting next to a politician, she asked "You're not one now, are you?" After replying that I was, she declared that all politicians are crooks!

That person was being served and was complaining about how she was being served. She also would not let go of a prejudice—even though she didn't know me, she decided I was a crook. The wisest thing for me and Anne to do was leave her with the Lord.

Anne and I seek out those who are community builders, and we avoid the unrepentant community bashers—those who are so self-centred, they build themselves up through gossip and prejudice. To this day, any conversation we have with our grandchildren stays between them individually and us. We made it clear to their parents that this is so, and we won't tolerate anything else. We will not tolerate being spied on, nor will we be spies. We like to listen; we like to have fun; we love to encourage; we love seeing others grow. We offer advice in confidence, but the final decision has to be owned by the person receiving the advice.

Even though it seemed we were not blessed by some of those negative experiences, we were blessed by them so that we could understand how to avoid negative conduct in our lives!

CHAPTER 64
Ready to Retire

Within a week of Anne and me meeting in university, true commitment to her welled up in my heart. After my second year at school—our first complete year of going together—I decided I needed that girl and I wanted to marry her. Over the next year, we discussed this. It turned out that while chasing her, she caught me! Anne was not a high-maintenance girl. When I tried to shower gifts on her, she said the money was better spent getting an education so we could get married after I got my degree. More than once I heard that she did not want to be bought!

I could afford to put some money toward a wedding and engagement ring, having a part- time job at a liquor store in Edmonton. I felt awkward doing this because of my upbringing and my desire to be as much a gentleman as possible. At first I just wanted to go out and buy the rings, but I realized this was truly a partnership, even though we weren't engaged, and would become much more of a partnership after we were married. I asked Anne if she'd feel comfortable helping me pick out the rings. Typical Anne ... she totally agreed, because she didn't want me to spend too much! She wanted a symbol to show we were truly engaged and then truly married.

We went to a high-end jewellery store in Edmonton to pick out the rings. The fashion of the day for the engagement ring was one huge solitaire diamond in a high setting. Anne pointed out that this wouldn't be suited to someone barely five feet tall! We picked out a beautifully simple set of diamond rings plus two plain gold bands. I used a lay away plan until her twenty-first birthday, when I formally asked her to marry me and she accepted.

Next we began to look at our future. I was approaching graduation and some pursuit other than being educated (not realizing that this "formal" education was only the beginning of my education). I had no idea what kind of job I wanted but was fairly certain about one thing: the job prospects with my BSc were very slim and not too enjoyable. Retirement wasn't even on the radar. I would consider it around age sixty-five … or so I thought. What I needed was a good paying job.

After I viewed several prospects at a job fair, two companies offered me a job: an oilfield service company and a company in northern Manitoba. The service company offered first, and I accepted—not because it was a chemist job (it was not) but because of how they sold me on working for them. They promised a company car, benefits, good vacation time increasing in length the longer my employment, profit sharing, and a retirement age of fifty-five with full pension. They showed a movie describing the job. Honestly, the movie showed a terrible life on the job—muddy; long, variable hours—not at all a cushy job until I had completed several more training phases (education by the service company). Frankly, what I saw was gross but intriguing! I did ask one question: What if I wanted to work until sixty-five? Their answer was simple but scary: "You won't. You'll probably burn out before then."

I talked with Anne about this job, describing the conditions in the worst way possible. She actually found it a bit exciting, as did I! I accepted, my degree was finalized, we got married, and I started my career. Within a year, Anne laughingly slugged me on the shoulder.

"What was *that* for?" I asked.

"You lied to me!"

Startled, I said "How?" Anne replied that the job I had painted for her was much worse in reality.

Still, retirement was way off. If I retired at fifty-five, I'd be with the company for thirty-three years. The prospect of retirement wasn't even in our thoughts. We had debts to pay off, kids to raise, and life to be busy with. Many years later it would be remembered that I was too busy making a living to have a life.

My career and marriage precluded me even thinking about retirement. Fortunately, I was accumulating profit sharing, which wasn't available until I quit or retired. We had no financial plan whatsoever; we were living from paycheque to paycheque. It never dawned on either of us that we couldn't handle an emergency. Our bank manager gave us some severe advice (see "Bank Manager Tough Love"). We eventually became debt free after applying his advice.

Still, retirement was a long way off. We had time to prepare, which means we concentrated on getting debt free first and then tentatively started thinking of retirement. We bought land and we bought and sold houses as we moved about. The pension we were building up plus the profit sharing was our main retirement plan. They came with the job ... as long as I had the job!

Anne and I began our journey with the Lord on December 7, 1988. Both of us were forty-four. This was a blessing in many ways, and it saved our marriage. We also realized we were potentially ten and a half years away from retirement. We started to change our lifestyle, aided by our growing knowledge of the Lord. Age fifty-five was close, and we were debt free. What could go wrong?

Well, something did go wrong. One day around my fifty-third birthday, I was coming back from a royal butt chewing that had been delivered by a very irate client who had received terrible service from one of our field crews. A personal policy of mine was to get reports from the field if our field people had performed a problematic job. Their report had not been received. On a routine next-day follow-up, the bad news came directly from the client, and he was not happy. Taking the verbal beating face to face, I committed to finding out what had been problematic and getting back to him in twenty-four hours. I left the client's office upset and was walking back to my office in downtown Calgary. Suddenly my whole left side went numb—nothing would move on the left side. No pain, just immobile numbness. Being a typical male and with my cell phone on my right side, I took it out and phoned my wife. Explaining the problem, she called our doctor and set up an immediate appointment for me. I didn't think to call 911, just a silent sky telegram prayer to the Lord. The numbness disappeared! I went to my car and drove straight to the doctor. Tests revealed that it had been a stress-induced panic attack. Fortunately, it wasn't a stroke.

This was a very clear message from the Lord that I should retire. Anne and I knew we were two years away from full retirement and would suffer a penalty on our pension. Nevertheless, I gave a one-year notice. Every one of my clients and those at my company were shocked; they knew how I loved the job. I was respected in the oil industry. While my company accepted the letter, they didn't immediately accept my resignation, expecting me to change my mind. That did not occur. Retiring on Anne's birthday in 1998 would leave us a little under one year short of a full pension.

We were both surprised by what happened on retirement day. The timing of Anne's birthday was planned—it was my intention to give myself to her for the rest of her life! This was to be only partially true. Details will be described later.

We spent a few weeks ahead of the retirement date "burning off" some accrued vacation time. On "retirement day," we drove over to my oilfield service company on our Gold Wing to sign the necessary papers, get our handshake, and ride the motorcycle off to our land in British Columbia. Prior to going on my vacation, the oil patch seemed quite busy. When we returned from vacation, and prior to going to my oilfield service company, we found out there had been quite a severe downturn. The company I was retiring from had to lay off many of their employees.

I was ready to retire from the oil industry, so we went in to complete the retirement paperwork, say our goodbyes, and (literally) ride off into the sunset … on our Gold Wing! Arriving at the backside of the building on the Wing, in our leathers and helmets, we met the secretary of the president, who apologized to us about all the layoffs and the severances they were giving out. "I'm sorry that we cannot give you one, because you first gave a notice of retirement."

"No matter," I replied, "I'm so happy to retire anyway. I've had a great run!"

Anne and I went upstairs and signed all the papers. As we were leaving, my boss said, "Just a minute. The president wants to see you before you go." He escorted us into the boardroom and asked us to sit down, saying that the president would be right down. He handed me a big, brown envelope and said "You can have this if you want." He then left us by ourselves.

We were shocked when we read what was in the envelope. We were being "offered" a half year's salary and full pension benefits! Then the president came in. He wanted to see someone who had "lasted" thirty-two years, because most employees in my employment class quit or were fired before or at fifteen years. At this point I couldn't stand it anymore. I blurted out as I held up the brown envelope "*What* is this all about?" His answer was surprising.

"Well, you had given notice so you weren't eligible for any benefits. Three of your co-workers approached me and told me that the Snake had given his life to his job, and he deserved a severance package. I felt like tossing them, but I was curious, so I went down to talk with your boss and found out how good you were. We're now offering you that package."

I was stunned. The president stipulated that there was a condition—I couldn't work for the competitor for a couple of years. (Not that I wanted to, but he didn't need to know that!)

I blurted out, "What about the guys who stood up for me?"

"Are you kidding?" he replied. "Anyone with that much guts deserves to stay employed!"

My signature was required, which was gladly given. Anne and I rode off into the sunset, jubilant … ecstatic! I was retired from my oilfield service company.

I wanted to retire, we were financially prepared to retire, but I was not mentally ready for it. Within six months, I was restless. Making a couple of trips back to the oil patch to help train some heavy oil people helped somewhat. I began volunteering locally. Getting very involved in provincial politics and volunteering on a local rural commission was a productive way to at least partially accept retirement. I quickly became the Chair of the commission and, working with members of the team, soon made it a well-respected commission both with the local government and provincially.

An opportunity came up to become a local politician, so I ran and became a rural representative in our local government. I held this position for a one-year term and then two subsequent three-year terms. This job was surprisingly similar to my job in the oil industry, even though it paid one-eighth as much. I enjoyed it immensely! Anne and I became known as people who wanted to serve the citizens of our region, province, and country. People of all political views across B.C. knew us and respected us. Life was great … with one exception. I realized I had accomplished all that I wanted to get done. We both were approaching seventy years of age.

When I left the oil industry, I wanted to retire but wasn't mentally ready for it. In my seventh year as a local politician, I again wanted to retire. After prayerful consideration, I received peace about retiring. Wanting to retire while being ready to mentally retire made a big difference. After a battle with my ego, I retired.

Not to say that we faded into the sunset! Phone calls started to come in asking me for advice and to volunteer. Anne and I prayerfully chose projects to concentrate on, including the priority given to our home church in Kelowna. Now we are busier than ever! But as Anne points out—we are now working for ourselves. In addition, we're using our motorcycle, boat, canoe, and all the other items we let collect dust while waiting on our retirement. We are now truly ready to retire, which is the place we must be to fully enjoy it!

CHAPTER 65
Precious Moments

There are many times when events occur in our lives that bring joy into our hearts and give us pause to think how precious those moments are. Two of these moments occurred within a week near Christmas one year. One of them had its roots in my youth. It was about believing, while the other moment was a simple little phrase uttered out loud by a young child at a Christmas play depicting why Christ came to this earth, born as a child of Mary.

There have been many times in our Christian lives when we've tried to explain to people something from the Bible, or an experience when the Lord used circumstance in our lives to show He is with us all the time. As Christians, we understood what we said, yet those we were talking to just gave us a blank look. Some of those people weren't believers; some stated they were believers. Most of the time we took such a reaction personally, thinking we didn't explain ourselves clearly.

This greatly concerned me one time when a precious moment occurred around Christmas. I pondered over the circumstances and silently asked the Lord to make my words clearer and to help me understand why such simple concepts seemed so unclear to the listener. "If this is my lack of belief, or knowledge, or my inability to explain things in a way to give You the honour and glory, please come into me and help me serve You better through what I say and do."

Prior to going further, I offer some background explanation.

Every year Anne and I watch *The Polar Express*.[1] It's cute, but we know the real reason for Christmas. While the story is about a young fellow who is starting to believe Santa Claus doesn't exist, that isn't the reason I like watching the video—far from it! When I met Anne, it became clear she was a railway brat. She had grown up literally next to the tracks, sometimes living in a little prairie railway station. She grew up in the steam age with a father who served on the Canadian National. She gets a thrill out of hearing steam engines and, to a lesser extent, big diesel railway engines.

I was a post office brat. While my parents had moved me to Edson, Alberta on a Canadian National train pulled by one of CN's big steam engines, I didn't get my real initiation into those engines until I started delivering newspapers as a boy in Edson. We newsboys picked up the *Edmonton Journal* from the CN passenger train during its stopover on its way west from Edmonton to Jasper. Edson was an old Grand Trunk railway town, complete with a big GT station and round house. Engine switches occurred there for the mountain part of the trip as the papers, passengers, and freight were taken off. The first time I went to pick up the newspapers I looked east toward Edmonton and could see the steam train literally roaring toward Edson's station from many miles away, smoke blasting straight up in the air. The train came in rapidly past the station platform and gracefully came to a stop with the baggage car in front of me. While all the unloading activity was going on, the engines were switched. On went one of CN's big Mountain steam engines. For whatever reason, the train reversed. Back past me went this big Mountain steamer with its white painted, steel-tired wheels slowly turning. All the rods and levers gently and rhythmically doing their job fascinated me!

The big Mountain steamer reversed beyond the platform quite a distance as I watched, transfixed. The smoke stack gently spewed out white smoke. Suddenly it blasted out a huge puff of smoke straight up! For a fleeting moment … milliseconds … there was no sound. Just as suddenly, there was a huge *chuff*, which nearly knocked me off my feet! The smoke and chuffing gained speed, and the big Mountain engine roared by me with those big, white, steel-tired drivers rapidly turning and all the connecting rods and levers flailing rhythmically, pulling the train onward to Jasper. I just stood there in awe! That was the beginning of my love for steam engines.

---

[1] *The Polar Express*. Film. United States: Robert Zemeckis, 2004.

Then I met Anne, the railway brat. After that, whatever knowledge I had about steam engines blossomed. I became really intense, devouring all the information possible about any and all steam engines. That's why I like to watch *The Polar Express*. The graphics and sounds of the steam driven train are superb, especially of the engine itself. While the rest of the movie has an interesting storyline, I watch it to see the images of a very realistic looking steam engine. The part about the young non-believer and how he comes to believe in Santa is just that—a nice story. Then the Lord blessed me by opening my mind. The young non-believer can't hear the reindeer bells, because he doesn't believe. When he comes to believe, he can hear the bells! This was the poignant moment for me.

Prior to knowing the Lord, and for some time after while working out my many pieces of baggage and non-beliefs, I often didn't understand the Bible. As the Lord taught me, I began "hearing the bells." Today, I hear most of the bells, and when I don't, I look deeper into the Word.

My love of steam engines led me to understand why some people don't get what Christianity is. They don't hear the bells—yet. If they know the Lord and don't hear the bells, they need to do more searching in the Word and hand their lives over to the Lord. We all must do this.

If people don't know the Lord, they may not see or hear the Word except from those of us who believe—until they come to know Him. It's not up to us to open their ears but to be the workmen and women of the Lord through spreading His Word. Let the Lord draw them to Himself, as well as help them hand over their hearts.

The other poignant moment came from a young child and taught me how vital it is to show the world the reason for Christmas. Our church in Kelowna holds multiple presentations of the Christmas story each year just prior to Christmas. In six or more identical services, between 10,500 and 13,000 people attend. One year, part of the show clearly presented the whole reason why Christ came down to earth for us. The show itself was very professionally done but wasn't "heavy." To set people's minds at ease, carols were sung and stories told that clearly showed that some people, even believers, could be a bit confused about who Jesus was. In a sometimes humorous fashion, this point was clearly presented. Just short of twelve thousand people attended the six services. As I stood at the door wishing people a Merry Christmas and urging them to come back, I was overwhelmed by their extremely positive response. That wasn't the "poignant point," however—it came from a very young child in the audience.

Part of the story concerned the creation and the fall, which showed why Jesus had to come to redeem us. As creation was unfolding in the play, the actors "grew a tree" in the Garden of Eden as giraffes, elephants, monkeys, birds, and all other creatures were being put in place. In the next part the serpent tempted Eve. When Eve bit the apple, thunder and lightning flashed about. There was a slight fog on the floor. As this terrifying event was happening, a hidden actor in the tree was spalling off foliage. When the tree was completely defoliated, everything stopped and became deathly silent.

Not a sound came from the audience. The scene was so well done, everyone just took a deep breath and watched to see what would happen next. It was as if there was a sudden burst of steam exhaust for a boy long ago in Edson just before the blast of sound coming forward that nearly knocked him off his feet.

From the audience in one session, a little child's voice chimed up, loudly and clearly through the expectant silence:

"Uh, oh!"

This was so poignant and so appropriate! What had been portrayed on the stage would have far reaching consequences for humankind. What was going to happen was going to be catastrophic and would need Christ to come to redeem us. The audience gently laughed at the innocent words; some clapped. It was as if some little child—mankind—had just broken everything and all they could utter was that one simple phrase. The Lord had used a young child to show all of us there what had actually happened to give rise to the need of a saviour. The Lord's bells could be loudly heard!

CHAPTER 66
Riding off into the Sunset

As told in a previous chapter, Anne and I rode off into the sunset, jubilant and ecstatic! We were finished in the oil patch. What happened literally during the first week of retirement made us realize that our new life would be far different from past experiences.

We did indeed mount our Gold Wing in Calgary and ride off into the sunset—to British Columbia. We weren't in a rush; we wanted to take our time after thirty-two years of the oil industry to experience the life we'd looked forward to. We stayed in bed and breakfasts and motels; we toured southern British Columbia. We took ferry rides along the southern main highway of B.C. We were relaxed. We travelled between July 31 and August 5, 1998.

We knew we were retiring around the time of year when B.C. was hot. But who cared? There were plenty of lakes we could cool off in should we decide to take a swim. We were adventuring into something we believed we would enjoy, and we'd planned this for years. Our log house design was finalized, and we loved the thought of our new life and our new house. What could possibly go wrong? We were fifty-four and entering into situations we had never experienced before.

As we approached our land on August 5 down Westside Road from the north, we saw the smoke from a forest fire south of our property. All that wonderful hot, dry weather had rewarded us with a forest fire close to our new home! We had no idea what to do. We went to our land and made supper in the garage we'd built in 1988 to store the material we'd need as we built our house. We didn't unpack the Gold Wing or cargo trailer. Someone came by and told us we needed to evacuate because of the proximity of the fire. This was new to us, so we asked where and were told to go north toward Vernon where they had set up a check point. The authorities would direct us from there. We didn't panic. We were more curious than anxious. It was all so new to us!

At the check point we were told where to go in Vernon. We went and parked the Gold Wing and trailer. We were in full black leathers. Anne was left with the Wing while I went in to see what was going on. Once in the building, I saw a long table with alphabetical letters in front of several sections. Going up to the table with a big "E," I politely said my wife and I had just been told to leave Killiney Beach and wanted to know what we were to do next.

The lady said "Name."

"Jim and Anne Edgson."

"Address." We hadn't moved from Calgary yet, but we did have a B.C. address because we needed an address to build the storage garage. I didn't think to give our Calgary address, so I gave the address of the garage.

"Would you like to get a room?"

"Sure!" To be honest, I thought the lady was going to make a reservation for us, and I'd be paying for it. She wrote something then asked the next question: "Would you like meals?" Again I thought she was making reservations for Anne and me. No problem, we could afford restaurant meals.

"Do you need incidentals?" I looked puzzled, so she said, "Toiletries, clothes, prescriptions, and the like?"

"No thank you," was my puzzled reply.

"Sign here, please." I don't sign anything without understanding what's going on, and I sure didn't understand what was going on!

The lady continued. "Well, in B.C. when you're evacuated in an emergency situation, you're provided up to three nights for a hotel room, three days of meals, and any reasonable incidentals you may need. At no cost."

I got a big smile on my face, signed on the dotted line, picked up an apple and orange, and left. As I left the building, I started to snicker. Approaching Anne and the motorcycle, I was in full-fledged laughter! Annoyed at my attitude,

Anne asked what was going on. I explained and then noted, "Look at me! Less than a week off being a high-powered executive, and I've become a freeloader!" We had never heard of such a provision in Alberta or the oil patch. We both had a hearty laugh as we noted how glad we were to now live in B.C.

The forest fire didn't come close to us, but its smoke sure did! We were evacuated for two days and then returned to our land.

As time went on, both Anne and I became fully trained emergency directors of evacuation personnel reporting to Kelowna. We were evacuated one more time and have been on evacuation alert two more times. We've never been overly concerned, because the emergency evacuation system in British Columbia is so efficient and thorough. We have an excellent certified local fire department fully trained in interface fires, first responders for health emergencies, and residential firefighting. We are proud of our firefighting team out here!

We learned several facts from that experience. Having a fire department as we do in a rural forest interface area is vital. We'd never experienced the need for such protection before moving to B.C. Having an emergency evacuation system is also imperative. We've also learned that B.C. cares. For us ex-pat Albertans, this is so important. It's also one of the many reasons we love where we live and serve today.

It *was* quite a welcoming experience British Columbia gave us for a retirement present!

CHAPTER 67
Recall Credit

People who have accomplished their goals can be justifiably pleased, especially if their efforts benefited others. Most of those people believe it doesn't matter who gets the credit, as long as the work gets done. They are generally appreciated for what they've done and for their humility at the same time. One of my goals is to work like that. Doing so requires burying your ego, and a realization that others can and will probably do more than you.

There are those who are jealous, however. Some have actually done great or good tasks themselves, but they are no longer involved. They try to take credit for what good is going on now by taking "recall credit" for what they've done in the past. When others explain good, current projects, these people speak up and try to make themselves look good, or better, reminding everyone how great they were by their past achievements. At best, this may not be appreciated by those listening; at worst, this could appear pathetic and perhaps laughable. Their past good may even be scorned.

This type of situation can be likened to a china cabinet that displays bright, old china from the past. Each piece could be likened to a great work done—some small, some large. When viewed together and all the pieces are displayed in harmony, each piece or group of pieces enhances the whole display. It can be quite beautiful. If one piece appears better than the rest, it will seem greatly out of place and will probably be removed so the display will remain harmonious.

If what you've done in the past is worthy of praise, it will be remembered. If it's not remembered, it may be out of date and irrelevant today. If what you've been involved with or done is good in the sense that it benefitted others, people will see it and recognize it. There's no need to praise yourself ... unless you believe your contribution wasn't that great. If you're interested in working with people for their benefit, you should definitely not brag about your past. Rejoice that others are building on what you were involved with to improve things even more. Offering constructive input in a cooperative and gentle manner is not bragging as long as your ego stays out of the offering!

One case in point concerns the Westside Road on Okanagan Lake. A group of people worked for fourteen years with the provincial government with great persistence, understanding, and cooperation. Others would have quit, but this group—the Westside Road Improvement Committee—soldiered on, gaining the respect of all levels of government, media, and the people they served. Eventually this cooperation resulted in a major provincial project to assist in improving the road from end to end.

When the funding for this project was announced, those who had nothing to do with the new projects came out of the woodwork to claim credit for being part of the improvement. Actually, they had very little, if any, proof to show they'd done anything substantial. One person took credit because of being in a certain position during the project, even though they'd done nothing. Most of the public and the government viewed this for what it was—laughable.

A different situation elsewhere occurred when older people who had been actively involved in a past infrastructure project came across as though all projects had to have their tacit approval or the work was invalid. They even implied that they weren't aware of anyone else who was doing the current job. They appeared uninformed about who was involved with one of the historical projects, along with the improvements. Finally, they pointed out that "local people" (them) knew a lot about the history (which they did), yet no one had consulted them. This was true ... because of their ongoing behavior. They also noted that some highway historical signs were not where they should be. It became clear that they didn't understand the background requirements for the signs, *even though they had been involved in the naming of one sign.* When it was politely pointed out how and why the signs were placed where they were, they claimed that they didn't see a sign at one of the historical places. When the position of the sign was explained, and it was noted they would drive right by it to reach their destination on a regular basis, they replied with "harrumph," and said they would check it out. The signs had been up for two years and are very difficult to miss!

They bragged about their past good work and stated a "fact" (something they had in their mind), which in reality would have been impossible to accomplish. It was politely noted why this could not happen. This ended the conversation.

Little can be done about these types of people. There are those who feel they are in charge because they believe they know better, even when it can be shown otherwise. They don't want to work with people; they want people to bow to them and their perceived better knowledge. Time and again in my career in both the oil industry and politics these people show up. While they may have done great things, their overbearing attitude, which comes across like everybody is less of an expert than they, leads most people to ridicule them. They not only ride on people's coattails—they want to wear the coat! The pity is, the good work they did is now looked on as being much less than it probably was. The more the "better than thou" attitude is maintained, the less people think of them and the work they did. This is to be pitied.

CHAPTER 68
Seven Pillars

Often after we tell people about another blessing the Lord has poured on us, they ask: "How do you know when God is at work in a situation?" Even for believers in the Lord Jesus, this can be a tough question. Let's look at it and discuss an example.

God's will isn't something we control. We must be obedient to His will. God is always in control. We are taught by God's Word to be discerning. If something is of the Lord, then follow it. If something is not of the Lord, turn and run away! What if you're not sure, or if the circumstance appears trivial to you? If you think the circumstance is not of the enemy and wouldn't take away from the glory of God (a sin), or if it would perhaps give glory to God, prayerfully put it before the Lord (a simple prayer would suffice) and follow the Holy Spirit's lead. If you still have doubts, seek the prayerful advice of a brother or sister in Christ. If the circumstance seems not of the enemy, and you feel prayerfully led of the Lord, follow the leading of the Holy Spirit.

You may not know for quite some time if your decision was of any consequence here on earth. Quite often you may forget the circumstances of the event, but there could come a time when you see how God's glory unfolded, and you'll be blessed. When this happens, give God all the glory, for He was the author of the event.

A seemingly trivial case in point: When planning our house, Anne and I wanted a big wrap-around deck at the front. Our project manager tried to talk us into a deck only across the front prow. Somehow we felt led to insist the prow and the entire front of the house have a deck. We wondered why, considered it, sent a "sky telegram" (constantly take all requests and petitions to the Lord in prayer), and followed the leading we had been given. Why? This decision did not appear significant to the Lord's work; indeed, it might be called extravagant. But it didn't seem to take away from the Lord, so we followed it.

As the project manager worked on our large, difficult deck with us, he asked if we were really happy with the size of the deck. It is an all-weather deck and had to be sloped. It has many angles, and it was a tough deck to build. I didn't know why I'd been led to build it so big, but yes, I was happy.

That night, Anne and I returned to our temporary rental house. Something inside caused me to still puzzle about the deck. Why had our deck been put on my heart? After all, it was just a deck. The Lord heard my questioning heart as a silent prayer, for then a young man we knew asked me how many pillars were in the deck. Thinking about it while again wondering why the deck kept coming up, I noted "seven."

Originally we were going to need eleven log support posts/pillars. If we'd only built it on the prow, we would have had three pillars. But we had seven. Keep in mind the Lord has blessed us with land that is on the highest street up a mountain in our subdivision.

Our young friend read out:

Wisdom has built her house; she has set up its seven pillars. She has prepared her meat and mixed her wine; she has also set her table. She has sent out her servants, and she calls from the highest point of the city... (Proverbs 9:1–3, NIV)

Rest assured that when people come to visit and the opportunity arises, we discuss this. Those who do not know the Lord will hear, gently, what we believe in!

A mundane, insignificant aspect of construction, from my initial perspective, was actually a leading of the Lord, to be used eventually to spread His Word to people who ask about the deck. Did I know God's will was being done when we insisted on a seven-pillar deck? No. What if I'd gone with the project manager's suggestion? The Holy Spirit is powerful and will gently lead those who believe on Him and the Lord Jesus and the Father to do what's right according to His Holy Plan. Pray on it if you're not sure and obey the leading when it comes up. You will be blessed. You may not know how for some time, if ever, but obeying God always is for His glory and your good.

Oh, and by the way—we will be carving Proverbs 9:1–3 on the front pillar!

CHAPTER 69
Shelf Life

Shelf life. The information you see on an item in a grocery store saying the product is "Best Before."

One day as I was contemplating not running for a fourth term as a local politician, I thought perhaps there was a *political* shelf life. As I had experienced various personal shelf lives over the years, there was a strong indication I did indeed have another shelf life!

The term "shelf life" should be taken seriously when dealing with foodstuff. Quite often when "shelf life" is experienced on your job, it could signal a needed change in direction ... one that should be taken advantage of, as employment is concerned.

Relatively early in my employment, I was promoted to Special Services to work with my company's newly introduced pulsed neutron tool. Next I was promoted to station manager in southern Saskatchewan. The job went very well there. I was a province away from headquarters and worked with good, dedicated employees. I was expected to do all the operational and local sales work. It was one of the best times of my life!

Then ambition kicked in. I wanted a "real" manager's job. Normally a field engineer would do a period of time in sales to learn to work with people prior to becoming a district manager. I had done well as a station manager, so promotion to district manager happened without this interim step. I was in over my head almost immediately.

Here was an educationally underqualified employee serving in a district manager's job and not doing well. If there was ever a time for shelf life to come into force, it was now! My company saw something in me, however, as I'd already shown potential in sales, service, and marketing as a station manager. I was eventually demoted to field sales in the company's northern area. This was a huge blow to my ego, even worse than the initial one I'd suffered after one year with the company. My ego had grown since then, and it was being cut down again.

In that northern sales job the company prospered as I also flourished. After a year there were rumblings about having me go back into field management, but some still, little voice inside said "don't go there." A sales position was offered at the same grade as a district manager with one proviso: it was permanent. I would not be promoted any higher.

My ego had a tremendous battle with the rest of me, for I would remain in this job for the rest of my career, which turned out to be another twenty years. I accepted the job, and throughout the years to come younger people would be promoted over me. It hurt at times. Then I noticed something—some of the people being promoted were often not as fortunate as me if and when they were demoted. They were let go. Their shelf life was designated and acted on immediately.

Over the years, my career and reputation grew through working with people and getting the job done to the benefit of my company and the oil industry. I really enjoyed working with our operations people and my clients. I was accepted in a job where I could flourish!

Not all facets of life were that rosy. Deep down there was still resentment that I was stuck in a permanent and level position, even though my career was going so well. This was a manifestation of my ego, and the worst kind—the cancerous, quiet kind. I knew I was good at my job, and my company knew I was good at my job, but my ego said I should be more appreciated.

When I returned home at night frustrated in this manner, Anne and I would go out for walks in the ravines surrounding our house. She didn't talk … I didn't give her an opportunity! For the first half of the walk I'd be yelling—not at her personally, but she could sure hear me! I'd eventually think of a solution and would be pleasant during the last half of the walk. This was hard on Anne, but I didn't recognize it. Life went on. Coming to know the Lord made life much better, both in my career and our marriage.

Three years before actually retiring I was led to comment to Anne that I didn't know what the Lord wanted with me, but it had to be great and His direction would be followed when He indicated. A year later, I experienced the anxiety attack that felt like a stroke. The Lord's direction had arrived; Anne and I were both warned. My shelf life with my company was approaching, and we retired in 1998. We took on a life of volunteering and politics.

Three months into my third political term, the inner voice spoke again—gently but firmly. The job had been done and done well. The enjoyment was fading. After all those years, my old ego was losing the battle. It was finally time to call it a day and accept that for all the education I'd received—formal, experiential, and biblical—I had reached the end of being a servant masquerading as a leader. True, I loved serving people, but there were better qualified people out there to do the leading. These realizations came softly and relatively easy, praise the Lord!

I drafted a letter of resignation in the last six months of my last term to be sent to the media and all those I had worked for as a politician. In the letter, I stated I would not run for a fourth term, believing all politicians have a *shelf life*, and further noting that some just don't recognize it until they are unelected. The letter was finished, but I couldn't bring myself to push the "send" button on the computer. Something inside me was fighting, telling me not to quit. I sent a one-word, silent prayer up to the Lord asking "Why?"

One word came back: "Ego."

I pushed the send button. That horrible word—ego—had been defeated at last!

As an epilogue, several of my media friends talked to me after receiving my resignation letter and asked me to tell other, specific, politicians that they had shelf lives! This I politely declined, yet none of those politicians were re-elected. They just didn't recognize they had shelf lives. Respect for me grew by leaps and bounds in the region, province, and country because I realized I had a shelf life. I now make it very clear that I want to be a servant, not a leader. When people see the personal seriousness of this, respect only grows.

Everyone probably has a shelf life somewhere. Some of us are blessed to have seen it, even after many indications of it occurring in our lives. Some of us are not so blessed, but there is one shelf life date that cannot be stopped in the end. It's called death. It's my sincere hope that all of you readers are blessed by realizing your living shelf lives and react in a manner that is both gracious and practical while you are alive and growing.

Anne's grandfather had a plaque in his house I wish I'd kept after he passed from this earth. It said in fractured German-English: "Howcum Ve Too Soon Ault und Too Late Schmart?" Amen to that, Lord! Thank you for shelf life!

CHAPTER 70
Simple Pleasures in Life

While considering writing this chapter, I had just experienced a simple pleasure in life—a bath in a footed iron bathtub that we bought years before we built our log home. It struck me how easy it is to say to someone "I have this [whatever it is]," yet it's sometimes meaningless to the person being told. While that object may be really nice to have, the experience of it can be very fleeting. A person hearing about that object might just yawn, because it means nothing to them. A desirable, simple pleasure in life should be one that is enduring. If it's not enduring, if it's not worth keeping, why buy it?

We're bombarded constantly with all these so-called nice objects we can buy and experience. Ads in the media or on-line tell us how wonderful these items are. Our sense of wonder, our sense of awe, our sense of want, and our sense of greed sometimes drives us to buy these things. Yet when we get them, we tire of them quickly because they have little, if any, enduring meaning. We spend money only to see the object of our affection resting on a shelf, waiting for us to give it away, sell it, or scrap it. Case in point is getting a new car every three years or so. Anne and I keep our vehicles well maintained and do not "renew" them for twenty or more years. We don't like to give away our good maintenance. Why get rid of them if they're serving their purposes well?

The bath mentioned above took place in a 1923 footed iron bathtub. What is your reaction? Are you impressed? Are you in awe? Are you thinking this author is an old fuddy duddy? Why would anyone go for a bath in a ninety-plus-year-old tub? Why would anybody even think of buying one of them? Modern tubs are miniature saunas and beautiful. Come on, Jim … get with the times!

There's a simple story here about something precious. Let's go back to when Anne and I were young. She remembers her mom pumping cold water in the kitchen with a hand pump. Her baths were definitely low tech! For her first eight years, she bathed in a laundry tub. For eight years when Anne moved to Wainwright, her bathtub was a sloped-back, galvanized steel bathtub in a dugout basement. I only experienced those pressed steel bathtubs of the 1950s through to 1962. They were straight-backed, either too short or too long, shallow, narrow, and lost their heat quickly. The wall tiles came right down to the tub and sometimes mildewed. When we did go camping, the camp showers (if they existed) were something to behold … not something to bathe in. It was great swimming in lakes, especially to avoid those showers! If life had continued that way, Anne and I would really be looking forward to something … anything … modern.

Sitting or lying in those pressed steel tubs for very long was guaranteed to be uncomfortable at best. You got in, had your bath, and got out. In that sense, these tubs fulfilled their designed purpose. Rush in, rush out. Like life in the day.

Then I attended the University of Alberta in 1962. Living out of town, I stayed at a campus residence of the day, Athabasca Hall, which was built in the 1920s. Upon arriving, I immediately checked the bathrooms—one at each end of the hall on every floor. White tiled floors and walls, old ceramic sinks and toilets, and footed iron bath tubs in cubicles! These high, old, footed iron bathtubs were probably installed when the building was being constructed. After the first bath taken in one of those old tubs, I couldn't get out … I just did not want to! You filled those old tubs with hot water, let them sit a few minutes while the cast iron absorbed the heat, got in, and … heaven! Your body was covered with hot to warm water with a warm, cast iron tub holding the heat—a totally relaxing experience!

The desire to someday own one of those tubs stayed with me during my university years. After we were married, we had apartments and houses with the pressed steel tubs with straight backs and shallow reservoirs. We checked around to see if we could order a footed iron tub somewhere. The reaction always was,

"Who on earth would want one of those clunky, heavy, old things anyway?" As noted elsewhere in this book … bad attitudes from salespersons expressing such negativity. I wanted one!

During our travels across rural Alberta and Saskatchewan, I watched for one of these tubs being used as a water trough on a farm. In the meantime, we put up with the pressed steel tubs. A fancy sauna tub was never considered after we tried them in hotels. They were just a toy—an awkward toy, in fact. If we wanted to get something like that, we'd get a real hot tub … which we did when we retired. A hot tub doesn't give you the well-prepared bathing pleasure a cast iron tub does. My search continued.

We went into old hardware stores and antique shops. Nothing. One day we went into the old Fruit Union store in Vernon (since torn down) and saw something hanging from the ceiling—a galvanized sheet steel bath tub! It wasn't a cast iron tub, but it had a nicely sloped back like the Athabasca Hall tubs had, and it was the same size. We needed something on our land to bathe in prior to building our house, so we bought it. We were told it had been hanging in the Fruit Union for years, as no one wanted it. We also bought an electric coil farm water trough heater.

For many years when on vacation on our bare land we would fill that galvanized steel tub, heat the water in it, and bathe in it—in the great outdoors! It lost its heat quickly, but the sloped back gave some comfort at least. We kept that tub for its memories. Someday it will go to a museum. We had part of what we wanted, but obviously it was unsuitable for a house.

One day when returning to Edmonton from Camrose in central-east Alberta, I spotted an old cast iron tub in a farmyard, just sitting there rusting away. A closer check showed the interior of the tub was pure white and not corroded. It had simple cast iron legs and worn out old taps. I bought it for $25, and we carted that tub along as we transferred around for twenty years. It was a heavy old brute, but we looked forward to installing it in our dream home someday. Finally we built our log home. We decided to put the restored tub upstairs in the main bedroom en suite bathroom. The bedroom has a real wood burning fireplace, TV, stereo, and an exterior balcony overlooking our creek. We found some "instant antique" looking taps with a hand-held shower head for the tub, which cost us more than the tub did originally!

To make sure the tub didn't come crashing down into the log bedroom below, we put a huge log beam right under it. This beam, coupled with three other beams, makes the log bedroom below look very homey and rustic.

Our first bath when we moved in was dreamy. The tub was hard to get out of because the warmth of it permeated your body and soul … just like it had when I was in Athabasca Hall. It was a great place to relax and answer emails during my seven years in local politics.

Today they make footed tubs that look like the old cast iron tub we have upstairs. They're made of fibreglass and don't retain the heat like our old tub. They're not heavy nor do they require four burly guys to lift them up the stairs. While they imitate the look of the 1920s, they're not the same. They miss a simple pleasure the old iron tub gives through contained heat that dissipates slowly.

Anne and I don't hesitate to tell others about our tub. People might think we're crazy for going through all we did just for the simple pleasure of lying in that tub and letting it surround us in cozy, comfortable, soothing heat while we relax and soak in all it gives. Anne and I put great effort into getting that tub to its restored shape, designing a home to hold it, and having it placed where it is, just so we could have a simple pleasure in life. This pleasure is enduring—we never tire of it. This pleasure is definitely not fleeting.

Sometimes old things can give simple, enduring pleasures that very few may enjoy. If you can find them and use them, keep them and don't throw them away.

CHAPTER 71
The Cookie Lady

While there are many stories in this book which seem to discuss what Jim Edgson's career was like, the book is not just a chronicle of my life. Far from it. The story of how Anne and I met tells the importance of a relational partnership forming very soon after we met, before we even held hands or kissed. My life as discussed in this book is the result of two factors: God's control in our lives, and the blessing the Lord gave me through the woman He gave me.

Anne and I have had a volatile life. Neither one of us can honestly state it has been all smooth. While we find it amusing a thought can enter one of our brains and show up in the next few seconds or minutes in the other's brain (which goes to prove the Lord made us one), our lives have been the result of seeing circumstances come together for our benefit. Looking back, we honestly hope we're right when we say these results were driven by the Lord not only for our good, but also God's glory.

While Anne sometimes appeared as "the rose in my lapel" during my political days, she was far from it. While she doesn't understand Excel spreadsheets, after the lesson we received from our banker about responsibility and finances, she became very adept at maintaining a chequebook and keeping us on budget. By the time we were forty, we were debt free. When we were forty-four, we came to know the Lord. Since then we haven't had to focus on financial problems because we thankfully became more disciplined in our overall approach to situations.

My oil patch and political careers kept me up front and obvious; Anne worked quietly behind the scenes. One contribution she made after we retired resulted in her becoming well known all over British Columbia—she baked cookies. She didn't sell her cookies; she gave them away. Her gift was very simple and led to her being recognized in a charming way.

When we retired to B.C., she started baking chocolate chip cookies for our local volunteer firefighters for their weekly practices. This was greatly appreciated! She enjoyed doing this for "her boys," who eventually became "her boys and girls." This went on for several years. We made sure we let the firefighters know when we wouldn't be around, and they always cheered when we returned and the cookies showed up again!

About the year 2000, after becoming the Chair of a rural local government commission, I decided to attend the local government board meetings to learn what they did with the commission's advice. This was mainly to communicate back to the commission what the board had done with our recommendations so we could possibly improve our advice. By doing this, the board became very respectful of our commission's advice because they knew it was well considered.

One night at a board meeting, the board members from our major city, five city councillors, and the mayor came in from a late city meeting—so late they hadn't been able to have supper. The mayor in particular was overheard noting this in a joking fashion. I approached the Chair of the board at the end of the meeting and said my wife was an excellent cook and baked cookies for the firefighters in our area. Then, without checking with her first, I volunteered her to bake cookies for the board meetings. The Chair agreed to let her do this and see how it was received.

It went very well! Without me asking, Anne decided she wanted to deliver the cookies to the board and stay and listen to the meeting also. As she noted, she is a constituent and taxpayer too! This was great with me, and we had some very frank discussions about our local government driving home after the meeting, which took about an hour. We both considered and learned facts we had never thought about. Plus, I now had another pair of eyes watching for deer in the dark.

The local government staff noticed this as well. Most of the time there were cookies left over, which went into the staff coffee room. On many occasions

Anne blushed because staff would come up to her and thank her when she came with me to the government office building to do business. She became a bit of a local legend! As time went on, the Edgsons became known as the couple who worked as a team.

Then came the point we decided I should run for the position of the rural local government representative. Papers were filed, and Anne and I continued to attend the government board meetings. Neither of us were elected officials yet, so we couldn't speak from the public gallery unless spoken to or scheduled to speak.

On the last government board meeting prior to the election, as the meeting wrapped up, the Chair of the Board announced: "Just before we dismiss the meeting, I need to speak to some members of the public gallery." Anne and I looked around—we were the only members of the public gallery.

"Mr. Edgson, I understand you are running for Director in the upcoming election." I politely replied "Yes," wondering silently what all this was about.

"If you are not successful, can we keep the Cookie Lady?" This brought laughter from the board members, and Anne and I laughed as I replied, "Yes, but only for one term, when I would run again." The first term was for one year, so this wasn't too big of a promise. Normal terms at the time were three years, but the inaugural term for this rural representative was a shortened one.

Thus the legend of the Cookie Lady began. Anne campaigned with me, which was a great asset, and I won. She decided she would attend every evening board meeting with me when she could for the next seven years and provide her cookies. It got to the point where should I forget to bring in the cookies from the car for a morning board meeting when Anne wasn't around, I would most definitely be reminded!

Of course, elected officials talk to each other about myriad subjects, including "quirks" like things their wives did. Anne's reputation started to spread not only for the cookies, but for the fact that at every convention, she was right there supporting me. She is, and was, a bright- eyed, enthusiastic person, and people are naturally drawn to her. The "Edgson Team" grew in favourable reputation.

Then came the event that cemented Anne's reputation, making her better known in many ways than her husband. It occurred at a local government association convention north of Kamloops, B.C. Part of the convention was held at the resort community of Sun Peaks; the rest was held at Barriere, a newly incorporated municipality on the Yellowhead Highway. As part of the convention, I had registered for some educational sessions to be held at Barriere's municipal building, a recycled school. Anne wanted to come as well, because there were some tours of Barriere and the surrounding areas. We along with many convention delegates jumped on a charter bus to come down from Sun Peaks, about an hour away from Barriere. Some of the delegates were going to golf. Anne and I did our tour and returned to the municipal hall. I was going to attend the session and Anne was just going to wait for me outside the room and knit, which she did when sitting in the "peanut gallery" while attending the local government board meetings.

Suddenly, a provincial official came up to me and asked me to attend his session about escheated (orphaned) water systems. I explained that I had already registered for something else, but he was still anxious for me to attend, as we had some of those systems looming on the horizon in my local rural area. What to do? Seeing the Chair of the association walking by to go golfing, dressed in his golf shorts, I got an idea. Knowing what an excellent note taker Anne was, I approached him and asked if Anne could attend the meeting I registered for while I attended the water session. Not a problem!

After the sessions, Anne and I reunited and boarded the chartered bus to return to Sun Peaks. The Chair of the association sat across the aisle from us. Anne did not recognize him. Anne noted we had a long drive up to Sun Peaks, so she could read her notes to me, which she did. As said before, Anne is an excellent note taker, and what she read to me was clear and concise. Meanwhile, as Anne was reading her notes, the Chair was intensely listening to what she said as well. When Anne was finished, he exclaimed "Wow! Anne, that was great! I thought I was right in the session with you!" Anne blushed, but it was true.

That night there was a huge banquet at Sun Peaks. Anne and I decided we would sit with the Barriere folks on one side of the room, while the folks from our local government in Kelowna were on the opposite side of the room. We wanted to hear how affairs were going in this newly incorporated municipality. Suddenly, the Master of Ceremonies—the Chair of the association—formally dressed this time, bounded onto the stage and started his speech. He noted it was great to see all of us local officials working together to support each other to improve life in southern B.C. He also noted there were many people in the room who, by their everyday efforts, provided valuable help to all of us politicians in our endeavours. "And there is a person in this room who exemplifies this effort— *Anne Edgson*! Stand up, Anne."

Now Anne is short—4'11" She doesn't have very far to go to stand up! She stood up, blushing a bit, and the crowd gave polite applause—nothing spectacular. The Chair added: "And I understand she bakes cookies for the Kelowna crowd!"

Well, the Kelowna table erupted in applause and cheering, followed immediately by the whole room erupting in applause and laughter. Anne turned purple with embarrassment. She didn't view her action as being that important or significant. The applause continued for some time. The legend of "the Cookie Lady" had become known all over southern B.C. Eventually the word got out across the province. Indeed, in some circles it was "the Cookie Lady and Jim Who?" I will readily admit this makes me very proud of Anne, the woman the Lord gave me.

To say Anne was loved across B.C. is an understatement. I couldn't go anywhere on government business after the above incident without hearing, "How's Anne?" or "How's the Cookie Lady?" That so-called rose in my lapel label disappeared—she was well known as an excellent part of the Edgson team!

The time came to retire from politics, with Anne's support. When I retired, she retired as the Cookie Lady of the local government. Frankly, I would wager in some cases she is more missed than me! She continues to bake cookies for the firefighters. One final act illustrates how she was regarded by both the local government board and their staff—the final Christmas party for the previous year's elected officials. Normally a gift is given to the outgoing elected persons. For some reason, I was last on the list. Never had a wife of an elected official been recognized, to my knowledge. They called me up for my gift—a very beautiful picture. Then the surprise—they called Anne up, recognizing her thirteen years of service as the volunteer Cookie Lady and giving her a big bouquet of planted flowers.

The Edgson political team retired; the Edgson team continues!

CHAPTER 72
Cutting Corners

There are many times in our lives when something is doubted. Sometimes the doubt is justified, sometimes it's the result of stubbornness, and sometimes the doubter has seen no evidence of the object or incident he or she doubts. That last "sometimes" can be dangerous.

The Westside Road in British Columbia is a winding, mountainous road. We have often seen people speeding down the road, trying to straighten it out by cutting corners. In B.C. it's legal to pass someone if there's a single line in the middle of the road, as long as it's safe to do so. Passing on a blind curve, one would think, is not safe!

Often on this road as we come around a corner an oncoming vehicle is either partially or completely in our lane. Fortunately, the other driver is the one who has to panic, as he must get back in his lane. We have already plotted our safe exit, as we expect this type of incident to happen. Defensive driving is part of our lives!

Why in the world would someone want to cut corners? First, the opposing driver is "in a hurry" and not paying attention to the consequences of their driving. Secondly, the driver has developed a habit of not staying in their lane on a twisting, windy road. Their attitude is "Why should we? No one will see us anyhow!" They have developed a habit of "cutting corners," which has become so automatic, they do it without thinking. As a result, they cut corners in dangerous places. Such drivers doubt their need to even think about it! They haven't seen the proof enough times to justify them believing in something, and this could destroy them and maybe others.

Another way of "cutting corners" is to speed. Without speeding, it takes us about forty-five minutes in the summer to travel from our home to Kelowna, and forty minutes in summer to travel to Vernon. Those times are with no traffic problems; no four wheeled or four-footed wildlife on the road, and no collisions along the way. Do we plan on taking those exact times to travel? No. We generally add ten to fifteen minutes to every trip. Most of the time we arrive early, but it always seems that for critical appointments, something delays us along the way, so those extra minutes are utilized and we arrive just on time—relaxed, pleasant, and enthusiastic to complete our tasks. In the summer on longer trips we add another ten to fifteen minutes an hour for the same reason. In the winter, we may double that extra time.

Is that a waste of time? Well, try this: Don't do it and see if you feel rushed and agitated when you arrive at your destination. You may also notice the vehicles in the ditch that were in a hurry. Because they cut corners, their vehicle came to rest on its side or roof. Sometimes in winter people will cut a lane going too fast and slide into the opposite ditch. Ask those "victims" how much time they spent getting their vehicles, and perhaps themselves, fixed!

"I'm a good driver," you say. "That will never happen to me!"

Really? Just don't do it around me. I don't want to witness your collision. You see, I plan. I just hope your cutting corners won't waste my time helping take your injured body out of your wrecked car!

CHAPTER 73
Two Forms of "BS"

After graduating from the University of Alberta and getting married in 1966, Anne and I settled into our lives as a married couple, working in an intense and interestingly wonderful career in the Canadian oilfield service industry. While this industry was brand new to both of us, it turned out to be of great benefit to us in that we were imbued with many rare life lessons, which still benefit us today. Some of these lessons were accompanied by relatively crude language—language we avoid in this book. We did, however, use crude and sometimes foul language during our "oil patch" years and are fully aware of its meaning and implications.

One of those terms is "BS." This abbreviation is well known, so we won't dwell on its unabbreviated form, other than to say it's a crude way to tell someone that they have absolutely no idea what they're talking about. In short, "BS" is a crude way of insulting someone; it's a short cut to rant ... an abbreviated rant. Like this paragraph!

There's a second and more insidious form of BS. It's human nature to seek out someone or something else to blame when things turn out poorly and you're likely to blame, or at least share in the blame. It can often be embarrassing, but it happens in everyone's life, both personally and professionally.

We'll illustrate this by first looking at a supposedly inconsequential personal event. Anne and I play cribbage. Statistically, Anne wins far more games than me. Both of us can get emotional about losing, especially when one of us "skunks" the other! Watching Anne when I either get a good hand, win, or—heaven forbid—skunk her, is interesting. Often she blames the dealer of the hand (even though it's sometimes her own dealing). Threatening to burn the cards because they're at fault is another ploy. If she gets too many bad hands, then a Wright brothers playing card effect takes over—the cards go flying! In short, Anne blames someone or something else. We end this by simply playing more crib games so that statistics take over and she wins more games!

Another more serious event occurs when something goes wrong at work and you're held accountable by a customer. Often the blame game commences. Rather than taking responsibility to at least investigate what went wrong and come up with a plan of action to ensure the event is mitigated and hopefully not repeated, you immediately blame someone or something else. Sometimes this blame is aimed at someone else in your own company!

This action may give you about a millisecond of satisfaction. Should a customer be involved, you and your company may lose credibility with them. In your customer's eyes, you are the company and its policies and direction.

In both these cases a second form of "BS" was used: *Blame Shifting*. I've used the term for many years when someone comes forward with the first form of "BS" then loudly blames others for something they should have taken personal responsibility for. I tell the person: "There are two forms of BS. The first kind you're aware of; the second kind is *blame shifting*. You're frankly using both kinds." The conversation generally ends right there.

I only use the above statement when it's obvious the conversation needs to end because the other person isn't willing to listen to reason of any kind because they have a mind like concrete—thoroughly mixed up and permanently set. Sometimes with mental rebar! Caution here …replying with this type of statement will probably slam the door on future conversation. In some cases, this could be desirable!

Use of either form of BS generally leads to some anger. In the worst case, it could lead to a verbal fight. On the other hand, the anger can be silent, leading to the loss of relationship with either a friend or a client. Anne and I have found that rather than using either or both forms of "BS" in public to justify our actions, it is far better to take personal responsibility for your actions, or the actions of those you represent, in a fashion that does no harm to you or those you represent. This requires a high degree of honesty and awareness of the consequences of what you are about to do.

For example, if you as the service provider weren't aware of the incident in question, it's far better to acknowledge that you heard what the customer said, write it down, and commit to look into it and get back to the customer within a specified short time for further discussion. Since you don't know the story from both sides, you shouldn't accept fault before finding out what happened from the other side's perspective.

If you have a strong communication system within your company, you're more likely to be prepared with one side of the story. Then you can go to the customer to hear what he has to say and then sit down to discuss what needs to be done to mitigate the issue going forward. This type of solution is always the far better way, since both you and the customer can look forward to improving situations in the future.

Avoid laying blame. Laying blame is a path to making situations worse. Take responsibility to obtain all the facts and information in a timely manner. Don't even think about accepting blame until all the facts and information have been gathered, examined, and considered. In some cases, the sources of the problem may not be with the company you represent. Look to the future. Manage the procedures within your own company. Work and communicate with your customer. Avoid using any form of BS!

CHAPTER 74
Two Lessons

There are two lessons in this story. One is about cats; the other is about getting involved in a situation in which you aren't competent. Two parts of this story occurred in Flaxcombe, Saskatchewan in the late 1940s.

Young Anne and her Ramsay family were living in Flaxcombe, and Dad Ramsay was the Canadian National Railway station agent. Anne has many fond memories of that time. She unfolds the story by noting she was just old enough to start having memories. In Flaxcombe, Boxer the cat was added to the Ramsay family.

Boxer was born in a shipping case of Kleenex boxes. Anne clearly remembers being old enough to recognize the word *Kleenex* on the outside of the case. Boxer's mommy was all grey, and three other kittens were shades of grey and white. He was the only tabby. Her Jim (the co-author of this book) broke out in tears when he heard the rest of the Flaxcombe story, because he was laughing so hard!

One day in the summer, young Boxer climbed up an abandoned telegraph pole beside the railway station. He sat up there and howled pitifully for three days. Mom and the three kids, including Anne, were very worried about him. Dad Ramsay was cross.

Finally, Anne's dad agreed to do something about it. He borrowed climbing spikes from someone, and after basic instruction from the fellow, climbed up the pole. This was a very old, abandoned telegraph pole that had been climbed by spikes many times. It was not a new, smooth pole!

At the top as Dad reached for Boxer, the cat jumped on top of Dad's head and dug all his claws in. Dad grabbed the pole, straightened up his feet, and the spikes let go. He came down the well splintered-from-climbing-spikes pole way too fast!

When he hit the bottom, Boxer took off running for the house. Anne didn't know if Dad was hurt or not, but there was some awful bad language spouted out from his direction! The kids were hustled away by Mom Ramsay in a big hurry!

Boxer was only down a couple of hours. He had something to eat and drink and went up another pole across the tracks. When Dad Ramsay saw this, he got his 22 rifle and declared he would take care of the problem once and for all! With Mom and the kids pleading for clemency, he put the gun away.

Boxer was up that pole about two days and climbed down by himself. He was the family's treasured pet for eighteen years.

Over the years, Anne and I had cats. Our last cat was a beautiful ginger cat who lived his entire life in British Columbia. He was a little weird, being abandoned by his mother early on and raised by a dog after that. Scooter the cat was his name. Other names were applied at different times—some not too flattering—but he was our treasured pet, as was Boxer the cat to the Ramsay family.

Anne and I learned from Dad Ramsay's incident in Flaxcombe. Young Scooter climbed a big fir tree and, not knowing how to climb down, was stuck up there for some time. As we hoped Scooter would climb down, we waited. Besides, the fire chief we phoned and asked about helping get the cat down gave us some blunt but practical advice. He noted he had never seen a cat skeleton in a tree!

Eventually Anne talked Scooter down. After that, climbing a tree and getting back down wasn't a problem for him. Or us. Valuable lesson number one!

Secondly, Dad Ramsay was not proficient with the use of pole climbing spikes. Climbing spikes point straight down when strapped to your lower legs. When we have seen them used, the user angles his feet inwards to stab the pole, and the person climbing has a safety strap buckled to him and around that pole. If anyone grabbed the pole without that strap and straightened out his feet, there was nothing between the person and the ground to stop him. Not that you would want a nail, splinter, or any other protruding object to halt you while you crashed to the ground!

Valuable lesson two: Get good training before using equipment for any dangerous project. And watch your language around kids!

CHAPTER 75
Understanding the Basics

Since turning sixty-five, Anne and I have re-educated ourselves constantly about driving motorized vehicles. We started this because of the media. When a collision occurred anywhere under any weather conditions, one of the first things mentioned in any media report was often "a senior was involved" or "an elderly person" was noted—even if the collision was caused by someone else! We sat down with each other and frankly appraised our driving habits … not so much our skills, but our habits and attitudes. We noted that if any senior was involved in a collision, their fault or not, there was a pretty good chance the senior would be called upon to retake their driver's test. Now we not only defensively drive, but we do what I learned while training to be a motorcycle driving instructor—practice driving so you're driving for everyone else on the road. We have both avoided collisions that might have occurred had we not avoided another driver who wasn't paying attention to what they were doing and not obeying basic skills.

We have also heard many times of seniors bitterly complaining that they've been requested to take a driving exam and failed. They go to the media and say things like "Unfair," "I've never had an accident," "The examiner didn't know what they were talking about," "I know more than that young guy (the examiner)," and the like. Well, folks, the first mistake they made was going to the media! If anyone thinks they will influence the examining authority in a positive direction by going to the media, they're not thinking sensibly.

Looking deeper at the situation, there are some possibilities that lead to their failure. One possibility is arrogance. Arrogance can be the cause of anger, which may lead to road rage. If observed by an examiner, this would be viewed as a negative trait. There's a bigger possible problem out there, however. The driver may have ignored the basic skills.

Today's new cars and trucks are trending to allow the driver to ignore the basics *if that driver chooses to do so.* It's not the vehicle's problem; it's the responsibility of each and every driver to fully understand those basics. For example, new cars can have side warning devices to alert the driver to something beside them. This can lead to the driver waiting until something is about to suddenly happen instead of being watchful and aware. This device doesn't take the place of the driver monitoring all their mirrors, and shoulder checking to see if something is happening so action can be taken … well ahead of the activation of these warning devices.

Another example concerns backup warning devices. We've been in parking lots where a car rapidly backed out, turned toward us, and nearly hit us while we were driving. Fortunately we observed the driver doing this. In this case, he was peering at his dash in the beginning, but looked up and out his front window while still turning toward us. He was watching his backup camera at the start, and in too much of a rush to even look at either of his mirrors or even out his side windows. Being alert, we saw the vehicle backing up rapidly from a dead stop. We decided to be polite and wait. Amazingly, he stopped about a foot in front of us then drove forward and carried on. The driver in the offending vehicle never appeared to see us!

The basics of all-around observation were ignored by the driver of the other car. The basic of proceeding cautiously was ignored as well. Probably the conveniences offered by the backing up car replaced the basics in the mind of the driver. You cannot ignore the basics of anything. Warning devices are there to help you, not replace you.

Another example comes from the oil patch. When first working in Lloydminster, I helped some of my clients understand that they were interpreting well information correctly, as long as the basics behind these interpretations were understood. They actually didn't understand, so they made mistakes that in some cases were costly to repair … if repair was even possible. Only one information-giving device was run, used, and interpreted to decide how the well production should proceed. Unfortunately, they'd become so attuned to doing this, they forgot the original basic procedure they should have followed. They assumed that everything was always the same, which wasn't always true! True, they saved money by not utilizing more information-giving devices, and in the long run the absence of other basic information could cost far, far more than if those devices had been purchased and run. Not obtaining further information was just not worth it in the long run.

While the reader may not understand oil well interpretation, I'm putting the next bit of simplified information forward to show that not understanding the basics can lead to missed opportunities. To provide those outside the hydrocarbon industry with some very basic knowledge, it can be correctly stated that pure gas is a very poor conductor of electricity. In other words, it is resistive to electrical flow. Pure gas has high resistivity.

Salt water is a good conductor of electricity. Straight salt water has low resistivity. The resistivity of rock varies with its mineral makeup, density, and pore space. Let's propose that we have a reservoir of consistent rock with consistent pore space and with consistent resistivity associated with the rock. There is one more twist to the basics: How much gas is present? We can say gas usually migrates to the top of salt water in a reservoir containing both gas and salt water.

If a reservoir with lots of pore space is saturated with salt water (like very porous sandstone), the reservoir will be relatively conductive (low resistivity). Add a little bit of gas and what happens? One more twist to the basics occurs, and this can be confusing.

When gas enters the salt-water-laden reservoir, it percolates upward through the reservoir. Eventually with enough gas it will displace the movable water. Water clinging in the pore space will get increasingly displaced the more gas under greater pressure builds up. If that gas is at a very low pressure, it does a poor job of water displacement, so lots of salt water clings to the rock, and the resistivity remains low—sometimes very low, only slightly higher than the salt water laden reservoir. As the gas displaces more and more water, which normally means the gas gets aggressive in displacing the water *due to higher gas pressure*, the resistivity of the area containing the gas gets higher and higher. But I digress at bit.

Around Lloydminster there were some very shallow reservoirs that appeared to be water bearing because of their low resistivity. These were judged as being *only* water bearing. When called in to help oil companies understand where some (unknown to them) gas was coming from, I looked at the information obtained through well logs and told them the gas was coming from what they thought was only water bearing reservoirs! They were incredulous until they were informed about the basics. Some skeptics still did not believe, so doing what any purveyor of well information technology would do, I sold them some of my company's surveys … which would provide definite answers and confirm what was known from the basics.

I could have just been a snake oil salesman and sold them the products right away, but my goal was not only to provide products, but to provide understanding and trust in both me and my company. Keep in mind I worked thirty-two years for a company in which many of the people in my position lasted only fifteen years or less! While knowing and utilizing the basics is very important, so is a proper, non-arrogant attitude desirous of helping people.

Point: To survive in today's car traffic, know and always use the basics. To survive in the oil industry evaluation business, know and always use the basics. To survive in life, know and always use the basics—and always respect those around you so you and they can benefit and make the world a better place.

CHAPTER 76
What Do You Gain?

Now that Anne and I are older, we're much more observant of our driving. Quite often this is because we make a point to observe where situations are going and their potential outcomes. Fortunately, most of the factors we observe don't end up in dangerous situations, due to our defensive driving. What is most interesting is watching people who think they know how to drive, or who proceed in a manner they think is more efficient, or who seem to be so blissfully ignorant of the outcomes of their actions.

After my last and most severe collision described earlier in the book in "Grace through Discipline," I continued driving as a much humbler person. Sure, I was a good salesman. Sure, I recognized the difference between an accident and a collision. I no longer had a company car, having wrecked my essentially new car. The company I worked for had disciplined me. They told me to use my personal car for field sales work; they would pay me mileage. As noted previously, I had no personal car. My previous company car I had purchased for my wife. That became "my" personal car.

My first action was to deliberately prove to myself what I had learned during my disciplinary driver's re-training—that speeding is inefficient while driving.

After all, I am a very analytical person! During that re-training we were taught how speeders roar past us, but we meet them at the next traffic lights. We were also taught we would often see those speeders pass us time and time again. I hadn't noticed this, so it was time to open my eyes and observe.

Fresh off a recuperation and re-training period, my first priority was to drive around Calgary. I quit speeding, which was tough. Prior to that violent collision, I "obeyed" the 20 per cent rule—you could go 20 per cent over the speed limit and get away with it. Sometimes. Most of the time. I had speeding tickets to prove that it wasn't a hard and fast rule.

I began to be much more observant while driving around the city. Sure enough, the speeders would whip around me and be waiting at the next traffic light. It rapidly got to the point in my driving where I observed that this was a common occurrence. A side benefit was doing what should have been done for some time—observing what was going on and preparing to handle potentially dangerous situations. Collisions from distracted drivers were even avoided as this was done.

The real test came when we made our first field trip from Calgary, Alberta to Regina, Saskatchewan. It was a very common trip for me before the collision. Once finished in Regina, I would travel around southern Saskatchewan on the way back to Calgary. I knew where to stop for comfort breaks, meals, and fuel. I knew precisely within five minutes how long it took to drive this roughly eight-hundred-kilometre trip from my home to a parking garage in Regina. I also knew what the fuel consumption would be during the trip. Speeding before the collision was common for me—15 to 20 per cent over the speed limit. I never got a ticket on this trip, nor would I after speeding ceased.

Imagine how it felt to set the cruise control to 100 kph for someone who previously set it for 115 kph. At first, painful! Then something became obvious. Cars and pickup trucks would speed by me, but for some reason I'd catch up to them when they were stuck behind a semi-trailer truck and couldn't pass. Sure, they eventually roared around those trucks when the oncoming traffic cleared, but within five to ten kilometres, there they were again—stuck behind another semi-trailer truck. After a while they would disappear and not be observed ahead of me for some time. Then as I was looking in my rearview mirror, they'd come roaring up behind me! They'd zoom by me and disappear on the road ahead. About a half hour later, they'd pass me again. It can only be assumed they had to take frequent comfort or fuel stops.

We left Calgary for Regina exactly at the usual time, taking comfort and meal stops exactly where we did normally, for exactly the normal times. Oddly enough, the fuel stop I took resulted in less fuel being pumped than normal. Even then, vehicles we had seen pass us along the way before taking these stops would speed past us at least once after we got underway.

It was interesting to not get hung up behind semis, like I would previous to my collision. Because my speed was down, I had more time and ability to observe what was ahead in the opposing lanes. It was a more relaxed trip because the time that was previously spent rapidly coming up on "slow moving" vehicles in front of me seemed to mostly go away. I rarely needed to wait to pass a semi, because I could observe where to slightly slow down to allow time for traffic in the opposing lane to clear so these semis could eventually be safely passed—at 100 kph.

I was honestly surprised at the time it took to drive those eight hundred kilometres to Regina. Keeping the 100 kph speed *took fifteen minutes extra!* Fifteen minutes in eight hundred kilometres. It took only 2.5 per cent extra time driving the speed limit compared to driving 15–20 per cent over the speed limit! Notably, the car's fuel economy improved by 10 per cent. Going the speed limit paid off, and it didn't take excessive time. Remember—I was being paid a fixed rate for mileage. The fuel used was personally paid for; less fuel usage meant extra money in my pocket.

Another incident that left Anne and me laughing was the case of the yellow Beetle. As we were driving up to Edmonton from Calgary, we were rapidly passed by a yellow Volkswagen Beetle just outside of Calgary. We'll call it the Yellow. We were surprised, because the Yellow was an older Beetle, and the driver must have had his accelerator pedal pushed far enough forward to be scraping the pavement. We passed him just north of Airdrie, not too far north of Calgary. He was pulled over by the police and receiving a ticket. We smiled as we passed.

South of Red Deer, the Yellow zoomed by us again! All we could think was *that driver has not learned his lesson.* As we drove by Red Deer, about halfway to Edmonton, here was the Yellow pulled over again … getting a ticket! We began to chuckle as we drove on, thinking aloud "Surely he wouldn't be silly enough to tempt this to happen a third time." Wrong!

The Yellow zoomed by us again just south of Edmonton. You guessed it … just inside Edmonton's city limits, the Yellow was pulled over again! This time Anne and I were laughing our heads off. I had to be careful not to get distracted as we roared in laughter.

One final incident we see quite commonly: impatient drivers. Anne and I were driving on a two lane, one-way street in a major city in the rush hour. We were in the right lane moving slowly and patiently toward a traffic light. The left lane was actually moving faster. A yellow car (not a Volkswagen) was observed in my left side mirror—tailgating, accelerating, and decelerating in a jerky fashion. I leave sufficient space in front of me to turn out of the lane in the case of semi-permanent stoppage in front of me, whatever the cause. Sure enough, the yellow car rammed ahead of me without signalling. I just backed off a little.

Then the humorous part started. The cars *behind* Yellow2 in the left lane crept forward past us—five cars in all! Yellow2 snapped back in his old lane to the left. He crept as he tailgated in his left lane slightly ahead of me, with me still in the right lane. Yellow2 got boxed in and actually slipped five cars behind me. I made it through the traffic lights; he was stopped three cars back. Net loss for him of eight cars! I calculated that if he had stayed in place, he would have made it easily through the lights ahead of me.

So what do you gain by speeding, impatience, and general bad behaviour while driving? I personally question if you "gain" anything. The examples above have many repeats from my experience (nothing as severe or hilarious as the Yellow Beetle). One positive note gained by someone behaving this way today— you give me and Anne a moment of laughter! On the negative side, you lose fuel economy. You may gain some time, but in my experience, the time gained, if any, is pitifully insignificant. In heavy traffic, your impatience may actually not only lose you time, but you could get fined or even hurt yourself or others. We haven't even discussed the time you waste if you're in a collision, or your increased insurance fees. It ain't worth it!!

We don't speed anymore. It doesn't make time or economic sense. The ride is far more enjoyable! We haven't had a collision or any tickets since my violent collision. The trips we take are more enjoyable, allowing us to observe everything around us as we drive safely down the road … and observe all those potential Yellow Beetle and Yellow2's out there on their way to continuous risky driving.

CHAPTER 77
Why Are You Hired?

Ever wonder why you were hired for a job? Or why you're still employed? If not, you may be either very sure of yourself, or perhaps you just don't want to consider it!

There are times within our jobs when everything is going very well—so well we assume things either cannot be improved, or we're surely bound for promotion. If people are fortunate, they'll have an employer who gives effective and helpful appraisals leading to improvement or correction. If the appraised employee is smart, those directions will be personally, swiftly applied.

From my experience in both the oil industry and local politics, you shouldn't wait for someone else to do the appraising, especially if those appraisals are a year or more apart. It's far better to constantly examine yourself and all the circumstances of your job.

At the time of my employment, I was the only chemist hired by my company. I'm reasonably sure they have not repeated that mistake! A rather traumatic event occurred a few years after I was hired, when we had a severe downturn throughout the industry. Several of my co-workers, all engineers, were terminated. I was not. I wasn't an engineer; I was a chemist, yet those who seemingly were more qualified were gone. I approached my boss and very nervously asked him why I hadn't been terminated ahead of the engineers.

He put down his pen, leaned back in his chair, and said, "Have you ever bought a battery at a major auto parts store?"

My confused answer was "Yes."

He replied, "Was it charged up ready to go?"

My more confused answer was "No, the battery had to be filled and charged."

His next words set the tone for the rest of my oil industry career. "Exactly. It needed to be filled and charged. All those engineers we let go were like excellent, well qualified batteries on the shelf. They did a good, sometimes great, job. But they had to be constantly filled and charged and given firm direction. You, on the other hand, go out and think situations through, act, and get the job done … sometimes too fast, but you accomplish. We're looking for people who will benefit our company for years and years. In our opinion, you had the potential to be that person. That's why you weren't terminated."

One would think I would say "Thank you" and leave! Not me—I had to ask one more question. "Why was I hired in the first place? I'm not an engineer."

"We hire people we believe can think. Generally within a year, we can determine if we made the right choice. You took a little longer, but we believe we made the right choice, and we hope you'll continue to demonstrate that this is true. Now get back to work!"

From that point on, striving to live up to the above became my goal. If this was the end of the story, it would be a happy one, and Anne and I would have ridden off into the sunset and been happily married for the rest of our life. As in real life, it was not the case! The other side of the story was, and still is to a certain extent, my ego. Ego has the potential to destroy a career and even a marriage.

First, examine why you were "hired." You were hired for a job because you had shown you could think. After sufficiently demonstrating you could do so, you stayed employed—for a time. Now look at why you kept your job. As noted above, you not only did your job, you flourished in your position by being a self-starter, always working to anticipate needs and fulfilling those needs, and probably because you served others well.

You were hired—that's in the past. Why you kept your job is ongoing. This is where self-analysis can be of help. If you don't know something, find out. Learn. Use what you learn and serve clients and customers in a manner that will benefit both them and your company.

What about your marriage? Look at why you were "hired." I could get tongue in cheek here, but let's get practical. An old movie saw the father asking his daughter's suitor, "Do you like her?" The young suitor said, "Well, I love her, sir." To which the father replied something to the effect that love will come, but you need to like her first. If you don't like her, you might want to run when problems arise!

The first time I saw Anne I really, really liked her—her appearance, that is! Then I was fortunate to take the young lady on dates, where her perkiness, zest, and unreserved joy of life were greatly appreciated. I was rather staid; she was not going to allow me to hinder our relationship. Her lifestyle taught me to love camping, biking (first with bicycles, then motorcycles), photography, climbing and hiking, and exploring new places. I liked that girl and all she stood for! I reached the point where I needed that girl. She was clever—I chased her until she caught me. Even when our marriage was rocky, I liked that girl, and fortunately she liked me enough that we worked our trials out. We did not run.

How do you sustain your marriage? Before considering obvious answers, let's get a little practical again. Marriage is a business with equal partners. It's sustained by the love and the likes of the couple. It could come apart if you don't treat this blessed job as a business. Communication is vital. Talk about every aspect and be sure you each know what you want out of the relationship. Work on your relationship. Don't wait for a counsellor (although if you need one, get one). Work together! Recognize this "business" as a serious financial entity. Work on it together. The husband and wife must mutually work to make their business run efficiently. Live within your means as defined and agreed upon by both of you in a manner that can be verified and adjusted to circumstances as the marriage progresses.

Anne and I are approaching our mid-seventies. It's become second nature to efficiently run the business side of this entity we call our marriage. We sit down, review finances, and monitor our future direction regularly. As an aside, I carry only one $20 bill in my wallet—as backup for Anne! We discuss every purchase except food. Anne knows what we need in that category better than I do, by far! Does this sound rather unromantic? Think what a smoothly running marriage does for the romantic side if it's truly effective. Anne and I are more in love than ever!

In whatever you do, work at it diligently. If you and your wife are the sole proprietors of the business called a marriage relationship, work hard to the mutual benefit of the equal partners!

CHAPTER 78
Applying What You Have Learned

Throughout this book we've shared many of our learning experiences, with recommendations for living. We're in our seventies and do our best to constantly apply what we've learned. It's relatively easy to do if you take time to review, plan, and execute events. Emergencies may make planning difficult, leading to poorly executed results.

Early in our lives we had to learn to take personal responsibility for our actions and become fiscally responsible. Following that experience, we went into a "cheap" phase of life, where we swung from living beyond our means to cutting costs wherever possible. We hadn't learned how to responsibly purchase items with thought to the future. This brought its own struggles, which led us to our next fiscal phase.

Learning to plan and purchase wisely for the long term gradually guided our thoughts and actions. We became debt free. We bought sensible homes. Vehicles were purchased and maintained with an eye to keeping them for many years. We bought sufficient retirement land to build our dream home and place it where we wanted it on our property. All this took planning by the Edgson team with an eye to the future.

Anne made it clear when we were building our retirement home that the kitchen, laundry area, and any place she would be working in were her "office," and she would make sure those areas were equipped to her satisfaction. There was no talk about cost only; there was no talk about "getting a good deal." Anne knew what she wanted and shopped diligently. The equipment she purchased and had delivered and installed in 2000 were all the same brand from a major store. She made sure all the appliances would be serviced by that store; thus, when the stove and refrigerator require servicing, it's done the next day. Anne chose her equipment wisely. All this equipment has lasted eighteen years.

In 2018 we had lived in our retirement home longer than any other home both before and after our marriage. We planned our retirement finances to include a healthy emergency fund. Both of us believed very strongly in purchasing vehicles and equipment from places with a good record of service. I worked for an oil industry service company that, in my opinion, was the best. *I did not sell price—I marketed service!* Our collective mindset is to buy quality—quality products with quality service.

One day an emergency hit—the refrigerator quit. When any food storage appliance in a rural area fails, immediate attention is required. Our concern was that the major store we'd bought the equipment from eighteen years earlier had also failed. We were very familiar with the appliance and it had given great service, and we had no experience with any other kitchen appliance store.

We phoned around. Repairing the refrigerator wasn't recommended due to its age. It might have been fixed, but getting someone to service it in fewer than five days seemed improbable. We decided to replace. Anne and I decided to buy both a stove and refrigerator from a major store that promised delivery in two days. That store noted they serviced what they sold, and they had bragged about their low prices.

We couldn't care less about the price—we wanted service, including fast delivery of the new appliances and removal of the old ones. This was promised. At the store, their sales person considered low prices important. I quietly but firmly disagreed, noting this was not my priority—service was. We purchased the appliances and went home.

Unfortunately, they had trouble getting the purchases delivered from their main warehouse in the lower mainland of B.C. I found this strange, as we'd examined floor models in the store. The delivery was delayed one day. I noted this was fine, as long as the delivery was completed before 4:00 p.m. on that day, because we had an event we'd planned for months occurring elsewhere.

The independent contracted delivery company arrived early on the day of delivery to pick up our purchases, which were not available for them. I was informed by the delivery company they would not deliver until late in the day two days later!

I contacted the major store. They offered to bring out the equipment late on that same day with their own delivery service, which required me or Anne to stay home and miss our planned event. At this point I put my foot down and said no. The appliances were delivered late in the day two days later.

Looking back, I admit I was very concerned about the attitude of the store from the beginning. Too much emphasis was placed on "low prices." In hindsight, this should have been a red flag. While we are happy with our new appliances, we have both vowed to look carefully at any future major appliance replacement with more emphasis on overall service and less on promises that are not relevant to us—like low prices.

We have learned another lesson in life: be more discerning about what appliance dealers emphasize when they are attempting to sell you something. If price is the emphasis—especially if there are many big television ads—be cautious. If delivery is part of the promises, ask when and by whom. Use of a contracted delivery service may introduce uncertainty because of intercompany communications issues. If repair service is promised, ask by whom. In-house or contractors? Wherever in-house service is given, one problem may be mitigated: communication.

One other lesson was learned as well. We had known we needed to replace those appliances, as both of them were starting to show operational deficiencies. We could have planned for their replacement a couple of months before the refrigerator failed. In the future, we will heed these forerunners of failure, especially if the appliances are old.

Keeping equipment in good repair so it can be used for a long time is a wise idea and has been discussed. Having sufficient emergency funds is a very good idea. Planning for equipment replacement at an appropriate time is always a wise policy, and it's now one of ours!

CHAPTER 79
Woman Who Scares Eagles

Something I like doing just for fun is being in a group of friends and suggesting they ask Anne what she thinks of bald eagles. I sit back with a big grin on my face as Anne unloads about the subject. Definitely unloads!

In review, Anne is 4'11" "tall." I like teasing her by saying "I like short women! I married a short woman!" Indeed, it still thrills me that I have been blessed so much by this young (er than me) lady. She does have a temper ... mostly under control. And she does have a wicked tongue when the occasion "requires" it!

In further review, we like fishing. The first "big" boat we bought was a used twenty-four-foot cabin cruiser ... and I do mean used! It was fun to be aboard and run, but it leaked like a sieve ... fortunately down, not up! When it rained, it leaked all over. We spent much time sealing all the leaks. The twin alcohol fueled stove didn't work very well; the "head" (a porta potti) wasn't that good, and so on. The main deck was about four feet above the water. When we caught a fish and Anne attempted to net it, there was a strong possibility she could fall overboard because of her height ... or lack of it! But I digress again.

We trained on our first boat and sold it after we bought the boat we have today, which was custom built. Our boat is 19.5 feet long and looks like a ski boat (it would have been, but we had it built as a miniature cabin cruiser). At the stern it is only 2 to 2.5 feet out of the water. Anne can easily use a big net to land our fish without danger of falling in.

When fishing on the Shuswap, we down-rig. We pay out the lure on the fishing line 100 feet at trolling speed, then using a latching plug receptacle placed on the steel down-rigging line between two closely spaced stops, we plug onto the steel line, subsequently lowering that latching plug on the steel line while allowing the fishing line, which is 100 feet back, to pay out down to a depth of 75 to 150 feet below the water surface, depending on the water temperature. We continue at trolling speed until a fish takes the lure and pulls the lure strongly enough to pop the plug out of the plug receptacle on the down-rigging line, or until we see the fishing rod start to bob back and forth when we "pull the plug" with the fishing rod. In either case, we stop the boat and reel in the fishing line.

Then the fun begins, especially if we latch onto a nice, big rainbow trout. They fight! Often they leap out of the water while trying to shake the lure. These lures have single barbless hooks, which can make reeling in fish very interesting! Rather quickly, rainbows are at the surface fighting. Remember that the line had been played out 100 feet and was a least 75 feet down. At least 175 feet is between me with the rod and the fighting fish. It takes time to reel in these fish!

Anne is waiting with a big five-foot-long net. All 4'11" of her. She positions herself at the starboard stern (right backside) and has the net dipped in the lake, dampened and ready to go. During one of these events, the plug on the steel downrigger line was down 120 feet, with the rod's line 100 feet behind it. We were about 100 feet from shore when we caught a fish. The "shore" was a rock cliff with evergreen trees growing about halfway up the 250-foot-tall cliff. We cut the power after the plug was popped but were very close to a steep, rocky cliff that went underwater about 200 feet according to our fish finder. The fish came to service and was fighting about 150 feet back as we had reeled in some line. Suddenly a bald eagle, perched on one of the upper evergreens, decided he wanted "our" rainbow for lunch! The eagle started gliding down to "our" fish! I had my hands full with the big down-rigging rod with a fighting fish attached. I yelled at Anne, "You handle the eagle!" To which she replied "*How?*"

"Yell at it!" I replied.

Pause here for a moment if you will. Anne has a five-foot-long fishing net. She is 4'11" tall. She was as good a cusser as me when we were in our oil patch days. Her voice when angry is a piercing scream—it hurts my ears. The boat has a ledge at the stern, above the engine room of our inboard-outboard setup. The stern of the boat is about two to two and a half feet out of the water. Anne stood on that ledge and began violently waving her net back and forth, swearing at the eagle using language I hadn't heard for years. My ears were hurting, I was fighting a big fish, I was looking as the eagle put out its talons ready to grab the fish, and I was wondering how to land both the fish and the eagle!

Suddenly the eagle realized all the venom coming from the back of our boat was aimed at it, so it broke its flight off and glided back into the trees. We landed the fish—a nice, eight-pound rainbow trout—with great relief!

While the incident was exciting in itself, and the thought of me trying to reel in an eight-pound fighting trout attached to a fighting bald eagle was rather humorous, what happened next was far more laughable. You see, once we settled down, we fired up the boat, proceeding to take up fishing where we'd left off. After setting the plug on the downrigger steel line at 120 feet below, we returned to relaxing, waiting on our next strike. Anne noticed the bald eagle was following us. The Shuswap's shoreline where we were fishing wasn't straight as we followed it, keeping the bottom around 200 feet below us. That silly bird would fly forward to another tree to watch us as we trolled along. Anne's reaction to all this was the funny part. She began describing the eagle in not-too-flattering terms, with such terms as "Oh boy, this majestic symbol of the United States is nothing but a free-loading bum" and "That bird is nothing but a leach!" Other descriptions were uttered by her which in good taste are not printed!

Another fish struck after about an hour, with Mr. Eagle still following us. This time it was obvious we had hooked a Shuswap Lake char (sometimes erroneously called a lake "trout"). These fish are easy to identify, as they dive for the bottom when hooked and may or may not fight until you bring them to surface. The eagle was watching us because we had stopped and were reeling "something" in. This fish dove very deep and took a long time to reel to surface. As the bird saw nothing, it stayed in a tree with its head bobbing up, down, and sideways, watching us. While he was thus occupied, Anne was busy "commenting" about the bird, using not too soft a voice!

Finally, the big char got close to surface, all tuckered out. Anne netted and landed it; the eagle was obviously upset because he missed an opportunity, flapping furiously in the tree to show his displeasure! Then we saw something unique about this bird—it was missing a feather on its right wing. We noted that and kept on fishing. The eagle flew off.

That was the way we left the lake that year. The next year we were out fishing and decided to try the same area. Lo and behold, our bird buddy, complete with right wing missing a feather, showed up again and followed us. Those birds aren't dumb—they appear to be able to recognize our boat! Anne's attitude toward bald eagles hasn't changed a bit, nor is she shy about telling others what she thinks of them.

Oh … and the title of this story being "Woman Who Scares Eagles"? I got the bright idea to approach some First Nations friends of mine and ask them what the title would translate to in their language. They politely declined to tell me!

Thoughts and Gleanings

That's our story, entitled *Rocks Don't Move*. The experiences in our lives have truly been more that what they seem from the outside looking in. Anne and I hope many of you will relate to our stories. Although similar stories have been written by others, we wanted to print stories that happened in our lives to illustrate circumstances for the benefit of others. As noted in the beginning, we cannot vouch for the absolute accuracy of these stories, but they are accurate as we remember or heard them. We applied the lessons to ourselves and have lived a very interesting and blessed life together. We're not the average set of senior citizens, and we have never been the average couple! While we are elders in age, we are constantly striving to become elders in wisdom. Both Anne and I will finish learning when we part this earth to change addresses to be with our Lord.

We'd like to share one last set of cautionary thoughts with you concerning presenting yourself to others. While we address sales and political representatives, keep in mind every time you're in a discussion or are trying to convince somebody of some point, you are in fact being representative of something you believe in. You're hopefully presenting a case for a better side. Some people are just plain nice people, and they have naturally presented their case for that perception. Whether "presenting a case" or using a "business case," you're representing something of yourself.

After serving three political terms, the inaugural term being one year, I realized all I wanted to accomplish had either been done, was being done, was being planned, or—by the wisdom of the local government board I served on—was not going to get done! I realized some people I served were very insular, only concerned about local issues that directly affected them. All they wanted was to keep their taxes low and not to be bothered. They weren't happy I was working with people in the provincial and federal government to ensure the local government benefitted as much as possible from the senior governments. I realized my desire to ensure the local people could be served by all three levels of government to the maximum extent made little sense to those insular persons. They had little sense of any community other than their own, and little sense of the wider communities of British Columbia and Canada.

I enjoyed working with the vast majority of people as a local politician. Times of reflection led me to some very serious observations and conclusions, both from a political point of view and from the perspective of my former position as an oil patch service company representative. Major point: you cannot please everyone all the time. This is obvious. There are people you can never please at all because your beliefs and goals to boost the community/client may mean some short term monetary expense for future benefit. To improve the image of any community requires the buy-in of that community. There were pockets of some communities that embraced improvements quite well. Those pockets of people were served relatively rapidly with improved services and infrastructure. While one cannot state that funds to improve something always go where the support is, it certainly seems true! While it cannot be stated as a proven fact that forward-thinking people tend to benefit from improved services and lifestyles, past events seem to point to that conclusion. It can be stated everyone in the community eventually benefits from those improvements. It certainly seemed some people were kicking and screaming as improvements were implemented.

Some people I met during my political career beyond their mid-sixties had a very self-centred view of their community. One person was quite adamant the water system improvement costs were not going to benefit him because he was old. There was no sense of community from that person if it meant no direct, immediate benefit to him. There was no sense of gratitude to those before him who had paid to get the services he enjoyed now. There was no sense that younger people would benefit in the longer term, no sense that more and younger people would be attracted to the community to help bear the tax costs, and no sense that the person wanted anyone to be served but them alone … and served now. Never mind the future.

This attitude was not limited to people being served by local government. It was pervasive in parts of the oil industry as well. Sometimes encouragement for a service representative to improve business components that were proven in the short and long term to provide a future benefit was lacking in the industry.

That's life and the way it is. Letting the negative attitudes of others drag you down is never productive. For those of you who are blessed by the knowledge of the Lord, we have found taking *your* attitude, concerns, and problems to Him and seeking His guidance and control leads to a fulfilling life. A successful and happy service representative or politician is one who looks beyond the "now" and is pleasantly helpful while working with people and representing them in the present.

This approach requires a strong and sometimes very firm stance on the part of a local politician or service representative. The politician or representative must realize there is a strong need to work with people, sometimes over a long time, to reach goals in spite of all the grousing and seemingly inappropriate attitudes of those being served. That politician or representative must patiently look for all avenues to legally and morally obtain whatever will benefit the community/ client. This is accomplished best by working with people to determine how a goal can be reached in the most expedient manner to benefit those he serves now, as well as those to be served in the future. The whiners and complainers will not be remembered in the future … unless they were the ones who dragged their community down. While it may not seem to matter presently, twenty or so years out, costs avoided early on multiply. And those multiplied costs will hit harder twenty or so years later.

It has been often stated in this book that working with people is paramount. Working with people includes gathering facts and information about a desired subject or goal to determine how, and if, that subject or goal can be attained. It requires a tremendously broad mind to discern if the goal is not only attainable, but morally so. Patience, persistence, and understanding are required. Dictating is not the way to go—that is not working with people.

No secret is made of the desire for my current and future life to be directed by the Lord. This fact made it much easier for me to discern if proposed subjects or goals were realistic and attainable, or if they should be discarded. At times subjects or goals had to be abandoned because there was no business case that showed they were feasible or attainable now or in the future. This is difficult for a representative to handle, because activists want decisions their way no matter what. In most cases, better long term subjects or goals that became priorities more than balanced the disappointment of abandoned ones. Interestingly enough, it seemed this became obvious to certain considered people who used to complain! Those types eventually saw the beneficial reason and heard the bells ringing.

At times there were almost violent objections to either the abandonment or proceeding of a project by some people. In the abandonment decisions, where there was no business case showing long term benefit, it was often sad to see media stories of others who had tried what was abandoned and suffered greatly through taxes and time spent futilely. Similarly, projects with strong business cases that should have been approved for their long term benefits were cancelled due to self-centred people who only looked at today or their own narrow viewpoint. The circumstances of these future-needed projects became very expensive over time, to the point where they had to be done … at greater cost than originally expected. In both cases, less attention paid to self-centred people and closer examination of goals should have been done. Whether people like it or not, the greater good should take priority—as long as that greater good is well thought out and can be justified with good business cases.

Politicians or service representatives benefit from their relationship with the Lord when they allow themselves to be directed by that relationship. Any politician or representative has a choice: take the easy way out and personally benefit in the short term, only to be possibly reviled and ridiculed in the long term because of the increased costs, or work with and for people in a manner that brings all government entities into agreement to serve the communities with what may seem high costs at present, but in the long term will be relatively low. The service representative working with people in the industry he represents must diligently examine whatever long term benefits will outweigh short term costs. Well thought out and professionally presented business cases should be made and paid attention to in both cases.

In the short term, there is a possibility action taken by a political or service representative may not be appreciated. In the long term, if done correctly, their completed actions may benefit people far more than even you or they realize. Anne and I prefer to be remembered as persons and representatives who believed in what they were doing, showing what we did was best for those served and represented rather than persons blown about by the winds of loud mouths.

Anne and I are always learning and are blessed by memories of events in our life together. Lessons learned helped us grow when the events occurred. Memories further that growth. We understand all of us are different and have different challenges as we walk this earth. We hope your strengths and knowledge of your limitations will lead you to work with others possessing different strengths and limitations to the benefit of many others!

Have a blessed life!

—Jim and Anne Edgson

About the Authors

Jim Edgson was born in Edmonton, Alberta on July 6, 1944. He spent his youth in that city and in Edson, Alberta, then his teenage years in Grande Prairie, Alberta prior to enrolling in a BSc program at the University of Alberta. There he met Anne Ramsay. After graduating in May of 1966, he began a thirty-two-year long career with a large oilfield service company. He could not live without his fiancée, Anne, for very long, so they married on July 15, 1966. Upon retiring in 1998 and moving to the Okanagan in British Columbia, Jim became extensively involved in volunteering in local committees and on a regional government commission. From there he successfully ran for three terms as an elected rural local politician. He was the de facto spokesperson for the Westside Road Improvement Committee, working with people in the provincial Ministry of Transportation and Infrastructure to improve a scenic paved route on the Westside of Okanagan Lake.

Anne Edgson was born in Smithers, British Columbia on July 31, 1944. Her father worked first on the Canadian National then the Northern Alberta Railways. Her dad transferred around within Saskatchewan and Alberta, providing Anne with a love of the outdoors and a zest for life, which would be very attractive to the fellow she met on the Ides of March, 1963, at the University of Alberta! After getting her Nurse's Aide Certificate, she eventually married Jim and became part of a successful and dedicated married team. After Jim retired and they moved to the Okanagan Valley, Anne dove into local volunteer work. She became part of the vital campaign team for Jim's political life, resulting in her being gratefully recognized locally and provincially.

Jim and Anne have two children, Gail and Peter, four grandchildren, and two great-grandchildren.